UNSPOKEN

Unspoken

A. M. HARRIS

ISBN (print) 978-2-9573666-0-6
ISBN (ebook) 978-2-9573666-1-3

For Seamus, David, Patrick and Alexis

'But surely you will come back one day to me and I shall still be waiting.'

Edvard Grieg, Solveig's Song

'You never did ask each other anything, did you? And you never told each other anything. You just sat and watched each other, and guessed at what was going on underneath.'

Edith Wharton, The Age of Innocence

Chapter One

Sinéad's funeral service was held just outside Bordeaux, in a pretty village surrounded by vineyards a few miles from the city. Although Sinéad had not been religious, she had insisted on having a proper service in a proper church. She had donated her organs for transplant 'to make sure I'm really dead when they put me in the coffin', a typical Sinéad remark. It was quite unlike any funeral Jack had ever been to before; it looked more like a wedding. Everyone was well-dressed, and he was surprised to see that nobody wore black – in fact everyone seemed to have donned their most colourful outfit. Some of the women, including Sinéad's mother, wore extravagant hats, and there were white lilies and blue hydrangeas – Sinéad's favourites – everywhere.

The service was in French and English and the speeches were simple and for the most part funny. He wondered if Sinéad had dictated them. The music was – he searched for the right word – challenging. One of her sons, clearly a talented musician, played excerpts from Schnittke's Requiem on the cello.

'Everyone knows the Fauré, the Mozart and the Verdi,' she'd told her son only days before. 'Let's annoy the hell out of everyone and educate them as well.'

And of course there was Grieg, a nod to events best forgotten as far as Jack was concerned. A friend played a Bob Dylan song, *See That My Grave is Kept Clean*, which made everyone smile. Afterwards, at the graveside, a rabbi friend of Sinéad's husband's family sang a lament in Hebrew which had everyone in tears.

Jack was in Dublin when he got the news that she had died. It was quite a shock, as they had met again recently and were planning to have lunch next time she came to the city. He went through the file of emails on his laptop before taking her letters from the safe in his office and reading through them the night before leaving for the funeral. He remembered that she had once sent him her obituary. With a successful career already behind her, she enrolled in a leadership course and was highly amused when the students were asked to write their obituary as they would like it to appear in the *Washington Post*. And naturally hers had been read out as an example to the class. She'd sent him a copy, and at the time it had left a bitter taste in his mouth.

He rummaged through the papers and finally found it, hidden away in a file marked *Miscellaneous*. Sitting there, re-reading it in his darkened office, he realized that what had irritated him at the time was that there was no reference to him, and only an oblique reference to the events that had shaped her whole life.

Sinéad Murray died last month, at the age of ninety-five, it began. *In the company of her devoted husband, four* children and countless grandchildren and great grandchildren, in the tiny village near Montpellier in France where she had made her home for some forty years.

Well, she'd certainly got that wrong, he thought. She was only sixty-five. And she had gone to live near Bordeaux, not Montpellier. Grief and anger welled up as he read on.

In accordance with her wishes, her ashes were scattered on the vineyard she and her husband had recreated with passion. 'It will add a little je ne sais quoi to next year's vintage,' she had joked.

From her early childhood, Sinéad was a contradiction. She always wanted to do good, yet didn't want to be associated with the 'do-gooders' she claimed to despise. In school she disconcerted her teachers by getting excellent marks while being punished for such misdemeanours as letting her pet mouse run wild in class and smoking in the toilets.

University in the late sixties proved to be a liberating experience and she threw herself with relish into student politics, being the first woman in her male-dominated faculty ever to be elected to the students' representative council.

A painful crisis in her personal life led her to leave Ireland, resolving never to return, and she took up a position with an international organization at the age of twenty-two. She was the youngest, and one of the very few, women to be promoted to the organization's senior ranks. While most of the officials around her aspired to a quiet life, she embraced challenge, pestering her superiors to let her take on new assignments. Her colleagues recall her persistence, and her dogged pursuit of goals. 'Sinéad always got what she wanted in the end', one of them told me later, 'although she said herself that often when she got it, she wasn't sure she still wanted it'.

Jack put the paper on his desk, stood and walked to the window. Had she got what she wanted in the end? Had he? He stayed there a while, thinking back to the times they'd spent together, then sat down again and continued reading.

The golden period of her career began when she joined the private office of the head of the organization, Gudrun Moller, a highly respected politician and the toughest woman she had ever met. 'She taught me about power and how to make your mark,' she said. Her work with Gudrun Moller took her around the world to meet heads of state, and she often regaled her grandchildren with scurrilous stories about some of the famous people she met.

By the late 1980s, however, the glamour was wearing off and her fascination with powerful figures was beginning to wane, so when an opportunity arose to return to Ireland to be part of a think tank on reform in the health sector, she jumped at it. 'I knew absolutely nothing about such issues,' she said later. 'My expertise, if you could call it that, was elsewhere entirely. That was the challenge!' The transition to her new role was not smooth, and she soon missed the buzz of her former job and the multicultural milieu she loved. She became even more disillusioned with politics and politicians. 'I want to run my own show,' she said. 'I'm tired of doing the politician's job and letting them always take the credit.'

Nobody was surprised when she announced out of the blue that she was leaving Ireland again to go and live in France, to run a vineyard and maybe write a book or two.

The rest is in the public domain. The move to France, where she wrote her first book. The success of the book and its film adaptation enabled her to set up a fund to help people who had had similar experiences to hers. In order to raise money for her fund she drew on the extensive network of political contacts she had built up over the years, never hesitating to 'call in a favour' when one of her protégés was in need of help.

The vineyard – a rubble-strewn piece of ground in the Languedoc-Roussillon – was bought on a whim after a leisurely lunch. A Californian wine supremo tried to buy some land in the area but was voted down by the local council. Sinéad's mixture of Irish blarney and fluent French won them over, and she never stopped delighting in her acceptance there. With her husband's business acumen and the goodwill she built up among the locals, the vineyard became profitable and most of the money went to her fund.

She referred to these latter years, spent mainly writing and managing the fund and the vineyard, as the most productive and satisfying of her life. She was finally 'doing good without being a do-gooder'. I think the many parents and children she reunited would agree.

It was quite uncanny that she appeared to have achieved so much of what she had set out to do, although she had never actually written the book, and there had been no film. In better days, they used to joke that their story would look good on the big screen, but she always said that she would only agree to sell the rights if Robert de Niro could play the male lead, so she could meet him.

He folded the paper and put it back in the file, with all the letters, photos and post-it notes he had so carefully kept. It was unlike him to be sentimental, and he had to get ready for the flight the next morning.

Chapter Two

'THERE'S SOMETHING I NEED to tell you.' The words hung limply in the air, and Sinéad saw surprise and then growing apprehension, on her parents' faces. What was it they said about reactions – first shock, then denial, then grief and finally acceptance? But that was for bereavements and this most certainly was not bereavement. If anything it was quite the opposite.

Sinéad began to suspect she might be pregnant in early April 1970. It took her a fortnight to pluck up the courage to see a doctor – a random doctor, whose plate she had spotted from the bus on her way to college, too terrified to go to the family GP. It took another week for the test result to come through. The doctor was kind, but said there was nothing he could do and that she needed to tell her parents. Yet another week passed before she felt able to tell them. Her father sat motionless as she spoke.

'Pregnant?' Her mother went pale.

Sinéad began to shake, and her father went to her. He made her sit down and put a blanket around her shoulders.

'Oh Sinéad, how could you?' Her mother almost shouted. 'And you a medical student? How could you be so stupid?'

Sinéad shook her head, unable to speak, tears streaming down her cheeks.

'And who is the father?'

'Michael,' said Sinéad. 'Michael Daly.' She wiped away the tears and blew her nose. 'You don't know him. He's in the class ahead of me and we just went out for a few weeks. We're not even seeing each other anymore.'

'A few weeks! Oh Sinéad.' her mother said. 'And your exams coming up.' She turned to her husband. 'God, Noel, what are we going to do?'

'We'll need to meet this Michael,' her father said. He turned to Sinéad. 'I take it you've told him?'

'Yes Daddy. We've talked about it. I don't want to marry him and I'm pretty sure he doesn't want to marry me either. And his father has just had a major heart operation so he can't tell his parents. They'd be devastated.'

'Would they now,' said her mother, the colour coming back into her cheeks. 'And what about us? Are we not devastated? Why should he get away with it and leave you to take the consequences? Oh, Sinéad, how could you be so… Why didn't you use one of those…you know…?'

'Hush, Jane love,' her father said. 'Let's stay calm and think about how we're going to deal with this.'

'You're not thinking of keeping it?' said her mother, looking at her husband who just shook his head. She thought for a moment and then said, 'But if you did want to, I suppose I could give up work and look after it…'

'We need to decide what's best for Sinéad and the child,' said her father.

They reassured her that they would stand by her no matter what decision she took – which was all very well, but she hadn't the faintest clue herself as to what it was exactly she wanted. It wasn't something she had ever dwelled upon or discussed with anyone – why would she? And in her nice middle-class surroundings, her expensive convent school and her university frequented by well brought up young women like herself, she had never heard of this happening to anyone she knew.

★

Michael came over the next day and he and her father talked at length in the living room while Sinéad and her mother made tea in the kitchen. When he left, they all sat around the kitchen table.

'He seems like a nice enough young man,' said Sinéad's father, 'and he's willing to do whatever is necessary, but I can see that he's in a difficult situation too, what with not being able to tell his parents. I suppose if neither of you wants to get married, we can't force you.'

Sinéad's mother looked as if she was about to say something, but he stopped her with a raised palm. 'In any case, I don't think that would be right,' he finished. 'But you're going to have to decide what you're going to do, and we need to act quickly.' He leaned across and patted her shoulder. 'I'll talk to Father Brophy tomorrow. He'll know what to do.'

Once the initial shock had subsided, things happened really fast. Father Brophy, the parish priest, came to the house. There were more cups of tea and whispered discussions in which Sinéad had little or no input. She would go to a mother and baby home, have the baby, have it adopted and then get back to college as quickly as possible before anyone noticed. The question her mother raised about keeping the baby was never mentioned again. Then it was the social workers at the adoption agency, with its funereal atmosphere, tut-tutting, frowning and averted eyes. There were two of them. An older woman, Miss Brennan, who seemed to be in charge, and another, younger one.

As Sinéad waited in the ante room while her parents talked to Miss Brennan, the younger woman, who had been silent up to that point, said, 'You're lucky, you know. Your timing is perfect. Your body shape will only begin to change after college breaks up for the summer holidays, and the baby will be born just after classes begin in the autumn so nobody will notice anything.'

Sinéad wanted to slap her. Lucky? How could she be so unfeeling? All they seemed to care about was that no-one should know.

An abortion was completely out of the question, especially now that her parents were involved. Her aunt Catherine, the only other person in the family who knew about her pregnancy, had been surprisingly supportive, even taking her aside one day.

'Look, I know it's supposed to be wrong,' Catherine said, 'and I probably shouldn't be even talking about this, but if you want to have an abortion I'll pay for it. I suppose in a few years' time it'll have become common practice, and that'll certainly solve a lot of problems for lots of young girls like you.'

Looking back, Sinéad thought it was an extraordinary position for her aunt to take, but it wasn't an option that they explored any further, as neither Sinéad nor her aunt had the faintest idea how to actually go about doing such a thing. Despite her brief show of liberal thinking, Aunt Catherine made it quite clear that Sinéad should on no account keep the baby, as it would be totally unfair on her mother. She wasn't the only one to stress this point. In fact any suggestion that she should keep the child was greeted with shock and horror by everyone involved.

'It would be selfish to do such a thing. It would destroy the lives of your child and your parents,' said Miss Brennan on one of the rare occasions she was alone with her. 'Think of the child,' she said, 'who'll be sneered at in school for having an unmarried mother. Think of your poor mother, the shame of it, shunned by the neighbours. Think of yourself, too, Sinéad, having to give up all hopes of a proper career, never mind the fact that nobody would ever want to marry the mother of an illegitimate child.'

Illegitimate, *unmarried*, all these words thrown at her made her feel dirty and shameful. But she didn't know how to react. She was sure of only one thing – she didn't want to be locked up with disapproving nuns in some gloomy convent in the back of beyond.

She'd read or heard somewhere that unmarried mothers in the UK fared better, and that there was some sort of arrangement in place where you could work as an au pair with a family during the pregnancy until the baby was born. What would happen after that wasn't clear, but it sounded a lot better than anything on offer in Ireland. 'England?' her mother had said when she broached the subject. 'But you don't know anyone there.'

'I don't know anyone in the mother and baby homes here either,' she said. 'But at least in England I could live a fairly normal life. Can we at least try and see how it works?' What she didn't tell them was that it would also give her the space to think about other options – keeping the child, for example. She needed to be able to think this whole thing through without all the pressure, and she knew that if she stayed in Ireland she would never be allowed that luxury.

It took a while, but after much pleading and tearful discussion, her parents agreed. Her father knew someone who knew a priest in the south of England, who in turn put them in touch with an agency in London. This was all much to the annoyance of the Dublin agency, who undoubtedly saw a potential adoptee slipping from their grasp, but to Sinéad's surprise her parents stood up to them, and the next thing she knew they were on the boat to England.

Her aunt Catherine made her two 'good' outfits in case she had a day off from whatever work she would be doing. When she heard Sinéad was going to London, she immediately began to pore over her smartest patterns.

'We can't have you wandering around London looking like an unmarried mother,' Catherine said with a wink.

One was very smart – a navy blue sleeveless tunic and a matching navy and white check skirt with an elasticated waist for the cooler days. The other was an empire style dress in a pale yellow paisley print, quite summery and light.

Her aunt also gave her an old wedding ring which had belonged to her long-deceased mother-in-law to wear in public.

★

'Hello, Mr and Mrs Murray. And you must be Sinéad. Do come in and sit down. You'll be tired after your journey. Can I get you some tea or coffee?'

The woman at the London agency had a warm smile and introduced herself as Janet, speaking directly and kindly to Sinéad, who felt she could trust her. The office was cheerful and nicely decorated, and the whole experience was a complete contrast to the funeral parlour atmosphere in Dublin and the dour Miss Brennan. Janet explained the deal. Sinéad would stay with a carefully-chosen, caring and experienced family until the baby was born. She would work as an au pair, for which she would receive a small stipend. She would attend the local hospital for check-ups and the birth, and the agency would look after the adoption, if – Janet stressed the word – that was what she wanted.

Janet took out a sheaf of files. There were three families on offer for Sinéad to stay with. One was a middle-aged Jewish couple with no children, the second a fairly boring-sounding English family with one child and a dog. The third was an Irish doctor, with a wife and two children living in the East End of the city.

Sinéad had a brief romantic notion of being cared for in a rose-covered cottage in the country by the nice Jewish couple (someone had once told her that Jewish people were very kind to unmarried mothers), but the look on her father's face convinced her to stay silent. There had been enough arguments about her wanting to go to work in a kibbutz the year before. Needless to say, the Irish doctor won. Anyway, doctors tended to be kind and cultured, Sinéad thought, so it wouldn't be all that bad. And he was Irish. And Catholic.

A couple of phone calls later the interview was set up.

*

'Are you sure this is right address, Noel?'

Sinéad's mother sounded worried, and it was hard to believe that anyone actually lived there. It was the first in a row of quite large houses, three stories over a basement. It may once have been an elegant street, but it was now pretty run down. Some of the houses looked uninhabited, others looked as if they had been turned into flats, with mismatching, dirty, torn curtains spoiling the once-grand facades. Across the road there was a patch of waste land that looked like it hadn't been touched since the Blitz.

'There, look.' Sinéad's father pointed to a gleaming brass plaque, that looked out of place on the shabby facade. 'Doctor's surgery, it says. Has to be the right place.' They rang the bell. The door – grandiose, wooden, its dark blue paint peeling off – was ajar, so they pushed it open and entered the house. A tall, dark-haired man appeared and introduced himself as Doctor Malone, ushering them into his surgery on the ground floor to the left. Sinéad noticed that the staircase leading to the rest of the house where the family presumably lived was blocked off by locked wrought iron gates. She had a gnawing sense of foreboding about the house and took an instinctive dislike to the doctor, but she hadn't the heart to say anything to her parents. They had been so good to her and so anxious to do the right thing that she didn't want to worry them any further.

It was decided she would move in straight away. After her parents left, she was shown to her room – a bare, drab single room with a linoleum floor and one thin mat by the bed. It was on the second floor of the house (all those flights of stairs – perhaps they hoped that the exercise would make her miscarry!). The room was soulless, like a cheap hotel room, and there was no sign that anyone had ever lived there before, although according to the doctor the previous girl had only just left to have her baby.

Romantic notion number two about doctors being kind and cultured was quickly dispelled. Dr Malone was a large, gruff man who clearly did not approve of unmarried mothers. He was a man of few words who liked his eggs perfectly cooked. It was one of the first things his wife, Gloria, said to Sinéad, when they were introduced.

'You can call me Mrs Malone,' she said, while showing Sinéad around the house, trying to make herself heard above the racket made by the screaming toddler in her arms and the whining older child that tugged at her sleeve.

'I've made a list of your duties.' Gloria handed her two badly-typed sheets of paper, one with a daily routine and the other with a list of household tasks on it. 'I find it easier than explaining everything each time we get a new girl,' she said. 'They change so often. You can have a look at it later, but the most important thing is to get the breakfast right. Dr Malone doesn't like his eggs overcooked. We can't have him starting the day in a bad mood, can we Maria?' She laughed and tickled the toddler's chin. Mrs Malone had been very attractive when she was younger. There were photos of her on the grand piano in the living room in which she looked like a model, but now to Sinéad she just looked worn out and harassed.

Emily, the older child, had long straggly mousy hair and was quite plain. She slipped her hand into Sinéad's and offered her a shy smile. Maria was quite the opposite – very pretty, with golden curls and a chubby face, clearly the favourite and totally spoiled. Sinéad took an instant dislike to her, and the feeling appeared mutual.

Romantic notion number three was that she would be 'one of the family', that she would look after (which meant play with) their delightful children, do a bit of washing up and generally help, and that in return they would give her advice, support and some pocket money. This too proved to be an illusion.

Mrs Malone was totally obsessed with a new house they were building somewhere out in the suburbs, and was constantly talking about the very specific taps she had ordered for her whirlpool bath and her new kitchen which to Sinéad's ear – untrained as it was to such domestic niceties – sounded something like 'hygienic'. Sinéad had no idea what she was talking about half the time.

HOUSEHOLD TASKS for MALONE FAMILY HELP

MONDAY
Clean stairs. Hoover and wash but do NOT polish as someone could slip. Clean own room (Change bed, dust and polish all furniture, clean Windows and hoover and wash floor)

TUESDAY
This is your Day Off. All medical appointments should be made for your day off. NB If you go out, please come back at a Reasonable Hour.

WEDNESDAY
Clean living room and dust and polish all furniture but do NOT put polish on the Piano.

Hoover carpets and sofas. Clean windows. Polish ALL brasses and silver.

THURSDAY
Hoover stairs and parents room, clean bathroom and children's room.

FRIDAY
Clean Dining Room and dust and polish all Furniture. Hoover floor. Polish ALL silver.

SATURDAY
Clean all kitchen surfaces thoroughly. Sweep, hoover and wash floor. Clean oven and fridge BEFORE you wash the floor.

SUNDAY
Accompany family to new house and help Mrs Malone.

Sinéad was surprised at the amount of housework she had to do. It wasn't that she had any objection to it, but she couldn't understand why they didn't simply employ a daily cleaner to do it. Why employ a young and inexperienced pregnant girl to do that kind of work? Changing home help every few months was surely a disruption for everyone, and the fact that Gloria had had to write down everything that needed to be done spoke volumes.

She assumed at first that the family took in girls like her for philanthropic reasons and that they would want to help her, talk to her, guide her in her future decisions. But any time she attempted to talk to Gloria she found her distracted, too busy and generally unable or unwilling to engage. Her answer to most questions was to tell Sinéad that the other girls did this, the other girls did that, but she never offered an opinion. As for Dr Malone, she couldn't imagine asking his advice about anything personal, and it set her wondering about medical vocations in general.

But she persevered. There was so much Sinéad wanted to know and eventually, wearied by her constant questions, Gloria suggested she visit Debbie, the girl she had replaced.

Sinéad gave Debbie a call and arranged to see her on her next day off. Debbie proved to be a large, cheerful young woman from London who wore lots of bright blue eye shadow. When Sinéad arrived at her flat she found her surrounded by friends, all cooing over the baby. They were all very friendly, but Sinéad felt out of place and awkward. When she asked how the birth had gone, she was greeted by shrieks of laughter. In her broad cockney accent Debbie told her she would soon forget about the pain and that once she held her baby in her arms, she would never want to let him go. When Sinéad asked her how she was going to cope bringing up the baby on her own, she just laughed.

'I've got me mates. And I'll try to get a live-in job with a family like the Malones, where they let me bring the kid along. That's what most girls do.'

When Sinéad finally left, she felt more confused than ever and spent the rest of the evening in her room sobbing into her pillow.

The days passed slowly, but she gradually settled into a sort of routine. It soon became clear that when Gloria went to the new house *en famille*, she didn't want Sinéad trailing along as well, so Sundays generally became days spent alone in the old house. She asked Dr Malone about possibly going out on Sundays, but he told her in no uncertain terms that Tuesday was her day off, and that he wanted someone in the house at all times in case someone thought about breaking in. She noticed that the piano was always locked, and she once asked Dr Malone if she could play it from time to time, but he replied that it was a very valuable instrument and that nobody was to touch it.

As an only child, Sinéad was used to her own company and could always find solace in books, but apart from a few dog-eared romantic novels, there were none to be found in the house apart from the shelves of medical tomes in Dr Malone's office. She couldn't face the discussion that would inevitably ensue if she asked to read some, so she began to write her thoughts down just to pass the time.

Her pregnancy was advancing, and she had no-one to confide in or help her make the crucial decision about what to do after the baby was born. She had attended one appointment at an ante-natal clinic at the local hospital, but the experience had been grim and unfriendly, and everyone seemed to be rushing around, too busy to sit and talk things over. She had read and re-read the book on pregnancy that her aunt had given her, which taught her all about the Lamaze method. The book was full of strange diagrams and breathing exercises and promised a painless childbirth, but at the clinic they talked about injections and gas and air. She wished she could talk it all over with someone kind. She missed her family.

★

'Karen? It's Sinéad.'

There was a pause at the other end and Sinéad could hear voices in the background. Sinéad and Karen had known each other since primary school, but had drifted apart when Karen took up with Tom, who fancied himself as some sort of intellectual. Karen and her boyfriend Tom were spending the summer working in London and had a flat near Stoke Newington.

'Sinéad? Hi – how are you doing?' Karen put her hand over the mouthpiece and Sinéad heard her shouting at someone.

'I'm fine. I'm here in London and was wondering if I could come over and see you sometime. I only have Tuesdays off.'

'Oh yeah, no problem – whenever you like.' Karen sounded strange, a little offhand. She told Sinéad that Tom was doing some work in a surveyors' office and she had a part-time job as a waitress in a cafe in the evenings, but that she was free during the day. Sinéad scribbled down the address and made plans for her next day off. The journey was long and complicated, and when she got there, she knew she had made a mistake. The flat was chaotic, with sleeping bags on the floor and overflowing ashtrays everywhere. The curtains were drawn in the living room, creating a gloomy atmosphere not helped by the lugubrious music playing in the background. There was a couple lying on a couch smoking something that smelled sweet and herbal. They ignored her completely and seemed to be stoned. Karen made her a cup of tea and cleared some space for them to sit down.

'So, what are you doing in London?' she asked Sinéad. She clearly hadn't noticed Sinéad's bump, which was beginning to show, but kept well-hidden by Aunt Catherine's dressmaking skills.

'Well, actually...' Sinéad began, thinking maybe she would confide in Karen, then, aware of the couple who were within hearing, changed her mind and said, 'I'm working in a doctor's surgery. Down in the East End. It's work experience for my degree.'

'That's nice,' said Karen.

'It's OK,' Sinéad said, 'but I don't get out much. It's a bit far from everything. And you, what about your job?'

They chatted for a bit, but their exchanges were awkward. Sinéad could sense Karen was ill at ease, and when Tom came in later, he seemed irritated by her presence. She had never liked him much anyway, so she made some excuse about having to get back early and left, feeling frustrated. To cap it all, she got into trouble with the Malones as when she came back, the door was locked from the inside and she had to ring the bell, disturbing the whole household according to Dr M.

So she decided not to repeat the experience and to be more sensible. Determined not to waste any more of her days off, she resolved to use them to discover the city and learn something. Each Tuesday morning she set off early, having planned her day meticulously with the help of a little guidebook she had bought at Euston station when she arrived. She was earning only £2 a week with the Malones, so she had to budget carefully for her outings.

Sinéad developed a routine for her Tuesdays. She would generally visit an art gallery or a museum in the morning, perhaps have a bite to eat there if it wasn't too expensive, and then in the afternoon she would just stroll around, discovering different parts of the city and perhaps doing some window-shopping. She tried to collect as many free brochures as possible, just to have something to read when she got back to the house. On one of these outings it rained all day so she went to the cinema in the afternoon and watched *Brief Encounter*, which she loved but which made her depressed. Another day, she decided to treat herself and had a cream tea in a lovely café in Knightsbridge. She found a wonderful but expensive maternity shop close to Sloane Square and sometimes she would just go to look at the window display, promising herself that one day, when she would be legitimately pregnant (she laughed inwardly at the concept) she would come back here and buy something frivolous.

Chapter Three

One Tuesday in late June, Sinéad had taken the tube to Aldgate and was waiting for the bus to take her back to the house. She had been to a lunchtime concert at Saint Martin-in-the-Fields Church and was reading the programme for the third time when she became aware of a young man standing close by.

'Excuse me,' he said, startling her, 'don't you live in Commercial Road?'

She turned around and looked at him. His face was vaguely familiar, but she had no idea who he was.

'I'm Sam,' he said. 'I live quite close to the bus stop there. My parents own the jewellers.'

That's where she had seen him before, she realised, waiting for the bus at the same time as her on a Tuesday. She knew the jewellers' shop too, and had often looked in the window while waiting for her bus. The shop stood out, and she thought it was a bit too up-market for such a rundown area. There were some pretty things in the window, and the displays were changed regularly to keep everything looking fresh and clean. She remembered the name – Bloom's – because she thought it would have been more appropriate for a flower shop.

Sam Bloom – probably Samuel, very possibly Jewish.

He looked nice, she thought. Understated, nicely dressed but not too flash, longish hair but not too long, lovely brown eyes. Just a little bit overweight.

'I see you've been to the concert at Saint Martin-in-the-Fields,' he said, nodding towards the programme she was holding. 'I really wanted to go to that, but I couldn't get there on time. I study piano at the Academy, and have lessons every Tuesday.'

They chatted easily about the concert, and when the bus arrived he asked if she minded if he sat beside her for the short journey. He told her he was hoping to be a concert pianist and was currently preparing for his final examination. Sinéad confided in him that she had taken piano lessons until the age of thirteen, even winning a scholarship to the Dublin College of Music, and that she now regretted not continuing. When they arrived at their stop, he told her to be careful walking back and she was aware of him waiting until he saw her entering the house before going into the shop.

Sinéad felt light-headed – happy for the first time she could remember – as she walked back. Later, lying in bed going over the events of the day, she put it down to the fact that she'd enjoyed what was perhaps the first normal human interaction since she started working for the Malones. Someone – a complete stranger – had spoken to her in a perfectly friendly, kind way, and despite her now visible bump had not mentioned her pregnancy or anything connected with it.

The rest of the week was uneventful. The children were reasonably well-behaved and she was beginning to find the housework routine useful, as it kept her focused on things other than her advancing pregnancy. She still wished she had someone to talk to about what to expect over the next few months, and wondered if she shouldn't try to contact the agency. In the end she decided to give it another week or two.

The following Tuesday morning Sinéad was waiting for the bus as usual, poring over her guidebook and wondering what she was going to do that day. She had originally planned to go to the British Museum, but the weather was so good that she was thinking about going sightseeing instead. Or maybe she would splurge on a guided tour. As the bus drew up, she saw Sam running towards the bus stop. He just managed to jump on as the bus pulled away and plonked himself down beside her, out of breath.

'Well, hello again! Do you go into London every Tuesday too?' he asked.

'Yes,' she said, 'it's my day off.'

'Your day off? You mean you work?' he said, looking at her bump. 'Sorry, it's your accent. I thought you must be here on holiday. So what sort of work do you do, if you get a Tuesday off?'

Sinéad hesitated. 'I really can't say,' she said. 'It's top secret.'

'MI5 or CIA?' he asked, visibly amused.

'Neither – if I told you I'd have to kill you.'

'And what about your husband – does he also work for the secret service?'

'I'm not…' Sinéad stopped and took a breath, trying to look suitably chagrined. 'Unfortunately, my husband was captured by the Russians when his spy plane crashed near Minsk. He is currently in a Siberian gulag.'

'What an exciting life you lead,' Sam said, looking at her in mock awe.

As they alighted from the bus near the Underground, Sam took her by the elbow, guiding her towards a newsagents. 'Don't say anything,' he said, hiding behind the newspaper stand outside. 'I think we're being followed. I didn't like to say it on the bus, in case I was overheard, but I am actually a Mossad agent.'

Sinéad found herself giggling and suddenly realised that she hadn't laughed like this for a long time. She asked him how come he was studying the piano if he was working for Mossad, and he explained quite plausibly that being a pianist travelling around the world giving concerts would provide the perfect cover for his future activities. 'Plus it exercises my trigger finger,' he said, making her laugh again as they walked down the steps to the Tube station.

He made her promise to meet him for the return journey at Baker Street station at five. 'I'll be carrying a rolled-up newspaper,' he whispered as he left.

Sinéad spent the rest of the day walking around London and was tired when she arrived back at Baker Street. She was early, but Sam was already there. She saw him immediately as she walked into the station, leaning against the wall, wearing dark glasses, a rolled-up copy of the *Guardian* under his arm. He looked…comfortable…that was the word she was looking for. Not at all like a spy.

As she approached, he stood up straight and beamed. 'Do you have time for a cup of tea? What time are you expected back?'

'No specific time, but they do like me to be in before dark.'

'Lucky the nights are so short at this time of year,' he quipped. They left the station and walked a little, stopping in front of a tea shop. It was very pretty, very English, and there was one of those three-tier cake stands in the window filled with delicious looking scones and an assortment of cream buns.

'Just the place for someone in your condition,' he said gaily. 'Shall we?'

He pushed the door open and a bell tinkled as they entered.

Everything was fresh and cool and she sank into a comfortable chair. Her ankles were beginning to swell from the heat and the pregnancy and her feet were sore from the day's walking. A middle-aged waitress came out from the back and took their order. She smiled at them and asked when the baby was due. They answered in unison.

'November,' Sinéad said.

'October,' Sam said.

'It'll be your first, then?' the waitress asked.

'Oh yes,' Sam replied, 'and we intend to have at least five more.'

When the waitress had left, he turned to her and said, 'Look, I'm sorry. I didn't mean to say that – I got a bit carried away and just couldn't resist seeing the look on her face.'

'It's OK,' said Sinéad. She tried to smile, but to her horror tears welled up in her eyes.

They sat in silence as the waitress came back, arranging the plates and knives, scones, butter, clotted cream and strawberry jam.

Sinéad took a deep breath.

'Sam, I need to set something straight. I'm not married and I don't really work here in London. That is, I don't work in the normal sense of the word – I mean…'

He held his hand up and stopped her. 'I haven't been completely honest with you either, Sinéad. I know about the Malones. Once I'd seen you go into their house, I had a fair idea. They have a regular intake of unmarried pregnant girls. My father knows Dr Malone.'

'You knew?' she said in astonishment 'And you don't mind being seen with me?'

He looked genuinely puzzled. 'Why should I mind?' he said. 'Actually, the reason I asked you to meet me was that I was wondering if you would like to go to an informal concert next Tuesday – it's just a few of my fellow students at the Academy. They're all pretty good, and they occasionally play for each other to get used to playing in public. It will be at 4 pm.'

'I'd love to,' she said.

The week felt particularly long and the days dragged by. Before coming to London, Sinéad's pregnancy was hardly noticeable, even to her. Now it was as if everything had gone up by a few degrees, and she was alarmed by the changes in her body. Her breasts were heavy and sometimes painful, and her bump got in the way and made the household chores more difficult. The children had both been unusually cranky all week, and the weather had been hot, and if she hadn't had the concert to look forward to, she didn't know how she would have coped.

Sam wasn't at the bus stop the following Tuesday morning, and she felt a twinge of regret. She thought of waiting for the next bus just in case he was late, but then told herself to stop being silly and set off as usual.

After a morning of intense cultural activity and a frugal lunch at the Tate, she decided she deserved some respite and took a stroll along Oxford Street. Dawdling along, looking in the shop windows, she stopped in front of Selfridge's, where a very fashionable longish raincoat in a lovely dark green caught her eye. It looked to be made of vinyl or PVC, and it was totally impractical in her current state, but Sinéad couldn't resist going in and trying it on. It fitted perfectly at the back – although obviously she couldn't fasten the buttons – and the material was soft to the touch, not unpleasant at all. The colour really suited her too. The sales assistant was *oohing* and *aahing* and telling her how it would be perfect for after the baby's birth, but Sinéad was looking at the price and realising that while £5 might not seem like a lot of money, it was more than two weeks' wages and represented a huge extravagance. Reluctantly, she put it back on the rail and told the assistant she would think about it.

She made it to the Academy just in time, and to her relief Sam was waiting for her on the steps. The concert was a very relaxed affair, with lots of laughter and banter between the players and the other students. Sam introduced her to some of them; they were all very confident and well-mannered and talented and interesting, and nobody asked her anything about the baby. Afterwards, they went back to 'their' tea shop near the Tube station and chatted about their day.

Without quite knowing how they got onto the subject, she found herself telling him the whole story – how she hadn't even realised she could be pregnant, how marriage to the baby's father was out of the question and how she could bring disgrace on her family if anyone found out. Dublin was like a different world, she explained, and told him how she had thought she was being clever coming to London but now found she was desperately lonely and realised she had made a huge mistake. She admitted that he was the only person she knew in London apart from the Malones and Karen.

'I'm really worried about what's going to happen when the baby is born, Sam. I had this idea that the family would be kind and want to help but all I am to them is some kind of cheap cleaning woman. As soon as I give birth, I'll be out the door and some other poor cow will be shuffled in to take over.' She paused and smiled ruefully. 'Do you know, the other day I was cleaning in the doctor's office and I found a piece of paper on the floor. It was a salary slip with my name on it. £10 a week, he's declaring, then he's deducting board and lodging so that I end up with £2. He's obviously getting tax relief. God, I can't believe I really thought these people were doing this because they wanted to help.'

She took a sip of her tea.

'I've even been thinking about going home and going into one of those mother and baby homes. At least I'd have company, and I'd be closer to my family. I mean, they're very nice at the hospital, but it's huge and impersonal and everyone is really busy. They don't have time for people like me.'

Sam buttered a scone and handed it to her. She toyed with it for a few moments, then sighed. 'Thanks. The only day I feel normal is a Tuesday!'

'Sinéad, I don't know what to say. But maybe you could talk to my mother? She would probably be better qualified than me to give you advice.'

Normally she would never dream of confiding in another stranger, but she found herself nodding wordlessly to Sam, as her eyes welled up with tears once more.

★

'Tea or coffee?'

Sinéad was sitting in the living room of the Blooms' house. Sam had introduced her to his mother, Ruth, before rushing off to attend his courses. Sinéad had been reluctant at first to meet her, half embarrassed and half not wishing to impose, but Sam had insisted, and now she knew he had been right. As soon as she arrived, she was made welcome. Ruth ushered her into the most comfortable living room she had ever seen, quite unlike the Malones'. A beautiful baby grand piano stood in the corner by the window and a vase of lilies sat on a mahogany table, filling the room with a heady scent. Every object in the room was elegant, probably expensive but not ostentatious. She sank into a small sofa and wanted to stay there forever.

'Tea, please,' she said. 'My pregnancy book says I shouldn't drink too much coffee.'

Ruth laughed. 'If you only knew the things people drink when they are pregnant,' she said. 'And yet somehow the babies manage to survive. But you are right – it's better to be careful'.

Sinéad took an instant liking to her and they chatted easily. Ruth told her how her family had come to London from

Germany just before the war, but had almost gone to Dublin instead. She wanted to know all about Ireland, and Sinéad told her about her grandfather who had been a tailor in the Jewish area of Dublin, an area called Little Jerusalem off the South Circular Road.

The morning flew by, and apart from the coffee/tea choice her pregnancy had still not been mentioned. Sinéad asked if she could look at the piano and Ruth encouraged her to try it out, pulling out some of Sam's old music books. She leafed through them and some loose pages fell to the floor. Ruth picked them up.

'Sam studied this Impromptu last year,' she said. 'I think it's one of Schubert's most beautiful pieces.' Sinéad tried the first few bars, but it was far too difficult for her so she rummaged among the sheet music until she found some simple pieces, surprised to find that many of them were familiar.

'You really should take it up again,' said Ruth. 'I've always regretted not having taken lessons – it's such a gift to be able to play, even if it's only for yourself.'

Changing the subject, she said briskly, 'Now, why don't I take you out for lunch? Sam told me you only have one day off a week and it seems a shame to spend it indoors on such a beautiful day.'

They quickly tidied away the tea things and set off in Ruth's Mini towards the city. Ruth took her to a delightful café by the river where she took a table under a parasol. It was like being on holiday in a foreign country, Sinéad thought.

It was only when they had finished their lunch that Ruth brought up the subject.

'Sinéad, Sam has told me about your dilemma. I'm not sure if I can help, but give me a try anyway.'

Sinéad spilled out her story again, adding how confused she had been when she had met Debbie and realised that she was keeping her child. She hadn't realised that such a thing was possible.

'It is possible, Sinéad, but it's a very difficult choice unless you have a good support structure. If you were to stay here in London, you would have to find a place to live and get a job to support yourself. Without friends and family you'd have to find someone to look after the baby while you were at work. It's a vicious circle, dear, I'm afraid. And even if you did find a job, I think you will find that attitudes haven't changed that much here and many landlords won't rent to an unmarried mother.'

'It's even worse in Ireland,' Sinéad said. 'Everyone tells me it's completely out of the question to keep a child if you are unmarried – not just because of the stigma for me, but for the child and the rest of my family. My mother offered to give up her job and help me mind the baby – she's just gone back to work after years of being at home – but everybody says I can't do that to her, that none of the neighbours would speak to her and they'd make fun of my baby. I've been thinking, though, If I could just get through the next year I'd have enough qualifications to get a decent job. Maybe then I could move over here and afford to keep the baby.'

'You need to think it through carefully, Sinéad – you don't have to take a decision right away,' said Ruth. 'I don't know if Sam's told you, but we are going away tomorrow for a few weeks on holiday. Make sure you come and see me again when we come back.'

Chapter Four

IT WAS THE INCIDENT with the rat that brought things to a head.

The weather had been getting warmer for several weeks and Gloria and the children were tense and irritable. Because it was so hot in the city, the Malones decided to spend the whole weekend at their new house where they could enjoy the garden, leaving on Friday afternoon and returning on Sunday night. Sinéad was not asked to accompany them.

After they left, Sinéad read the newspaper in her room before going down to the kitchen to make some supper. The kitchen and dining room were in the basement, the small barred windows letting in little in the way of natural light. She loathed that kitchen. Not only was it gloomy but it was incredibly difficult to keep clean, with its cracked linoleum floor and ancient appliances. There were tiny gaps between each cupboard, making it pretty much impossible to retrieve anything that fell.

As she entered the room, she thought she heard something – a sort of scuffling noise. She froze, thinking it might be an intruder, but then listened again and realised it was coming from a cupboard near the sink. Assuming it was a mouse, she moved forward, trying to make as little noise as possible, then threw the door open and found herself staring at a very large rat. Sinéad had no fear of mice, but had never encountered a rat before and was pretty sure she shouldn't go near it. She slammed the cupboard door shut, retreated quickly, closed the kitchen door and went back upstairs shaking with fear.

She sat in her room for a long while, wondering what to do. She had no phone number for the Malones, as the phone had not yet been installed in the new house, and anyway even if she had, she didn't think Dr Malone would be amused if she made him come back in the middle of his weekend.

In the end, she decided there was nothing she could do. She couldn't ask Sam because he was away on holiday, and she wasn't going to call the pest control people, because for a start she didn't know how to find the right service, and anyway she knew Dr Malone would be furious if anyone suspected there was a rat in his house.

The next day was Saturday, her day to clean the kitchen, but she was too frightened to go there. Instead, she slipped out to the local shop and bought some food to tide her over. She spent the rest of the day and all of Sunday in her room, occasionally making a foray to the living room to look at the piano and sit on the lumpy sofa. The room was indescribably dreary and depressing, with heavy, dark and unattractive furniture. The sofas were uncomfortable and covered in drab fabric, and the curtains were heavy brown velvet drapes which looked as if they had been there for years without ever being drawn. It wasn't surprising that the family never spent any time there. She wondered why nobody ever played the piano.

On Sunday afternoon she heard the car draw up outside at about five o'clock. The front door was opened and she heard the children running up the stairs, shouting and screaming, followed by Gloria, trying desperately to calm them down.

Dr Malone followed them slowly. 'Everything alright here?' he asked.

'Well, actually...' she began.

Her mouth was dry and her hands started to shake as she told him about the rat and how she hadn't been able to go to the kitchen all weekend.

He stared at her for a few seconds without saying anything, then abruptly turned and ran down the stairs to the basement.

She followed him down because she didn't know what else to do, and stood outside the kitchen listening to him banging about. When he finally emerged, he brushed past her, avoiding eye contact.

'There's nothing there now,' he said, 'and I've blocked the hole it must have come in through. You'd better start setting the table – the children need to eat.'

She ate her evening meal in the kitchen as usual while the family had theirs in the dining room. She was on edge still, listening out for any scuffling noise that could be the rat coming back. Emily came in a few times, asking for random things and hanging about, clinging to her arm as if she sensed something was wrong.

The following morning Sinéad was back in the kitchen, listening for Dr Malone's footsteps on the stairs so that she could start cooking his egg. As soon as she heard him, she heated the frying pan and cracked the egg into a cup before sliding it into the pan. She'd learned from bitter experience that this was the best way to avoid breaking it.

She was totally unprepared for the tirade she received when he walked in the door.

'You know why there was a rat here, don't you?' he said. She shook her head. 'This kitchen is filthy. Look, look here at the dirt.' He pointed at a patch of cracked lino that had been like that since before she arrived. 'You never clean between the cupboards. Oh, your own room is perfect. You could eat off the floor there. But cleaning other people's kitchens is a bit beneath you, isn't it?'

As the tone of his voice became louder, his Irish accent, which she had never really noticed before, became more apparent, his carefully modulated vowels becoming broader and coarser. 'Being a student doesn't make you better than my wife. You think you're too good for us, with your university education and your concerts on a Tuesday.' He was almost shouting now. 'We took you in and put a roof over your head after you'd got yourself in trouble. We even pay you. But you show no sign of being grateful. You're selfish and spoiled and I feel sorry for your poor parents.'

She stared at him, stunned, fighting back the tears and desperately trying to work out what had provoked this outpouring of vitriol. Finally, he stopped and walked into the dining room. Robot-like, she prepared his breakfast as usual and placed it in front of him as if nothing had happened.

Later she cleaned the stairs but not her room. Gloria made no mention of the incident, behaving as if everything was normal, and Sinéad wondered just how exactly she had given her the impression that she felt superior. Emily was particularly clingy all afternoon, demanding stories while Maria glared at them, throwing toys around the room. That night, she couldn't sleep and by morning she had made her decision.

Sinéad left the house with a sense of purpose. After weeks of uncertainty and worry she finally had a plan, and she felt relieved and almost happy. She walked to the Blooms' house and rang the bell. Ruth answered the door – she had returned from holiday earlier that day and looked relaxed. She smiled warmly and Sinéad wanted to throw herself into her arms and tell her the whole story, begging her to take her in and let her live there forever. Instead, she asked politely if she could come in and make a phone call. 'I'll pay for the call, obviously,' she said.

'You look tired,' said Ruth. 'Come in and sit down and tell me what's going on.'

Sinéad burst into tears and Ruth sat her down on the sofa and made her tell her everything that had happened, shaking her head as Sinéad told her about the abuse she had received from Dr Malone.

'I don't know why they dislike me so much,' she sobbed. 'I try to do everything the way they want, but I've always had the feeling that I didn't fit in.' She wiped her eyes with a tissue Ruth held out to her. 'I've been thinking about going back to Ireland, even if that means going into a mother and baby home. It can't be much worse than this, and at least I'd have company. There'd be other girls like me.' She sighed. 'I need to call my parents to ask them if they could contact the right people to set it up, and I can't do that with the Malones breathing down my neck'.

'Are you sure this is what you really want, Sinéad?' Ruth asked her gently.

'I've thought about nothing else for the past couple of weeks. But I really need to do something now before I'm too far gone to travel.'

Sinéad called her parents, and although they were surprised, she sensed that they were also relieved. She had never told them how unhappy she was in London and she didn't tell them the full story of what had happened as she knew they would feel guilty. She simply said that she had been thinking a lot about things and that she had come to the conclusion this was a better solution as she would be closer to home. They promised to call back as soon as possible, and by the early afternoon it was settled. There was a place for her in a home in Blackrock, just outside Cork. It was far enough from Dublin to ensure that nobody would see her, although Sinéad had a pretty good idea that outings were unlikely to be on the agenda.

Ruth took her to a travel agent she knew, and they spent the rest of the afternoon looking at train and boat timetables. Flying was out of the question as it was far too expensive, so Sinéad's journey would be quite complicated. She would have to take a train from London to Fishguard in Wales, then a boat from Fishguard to Rosslare and then another train to Cork. Ruth worried about how she would manage.

By the time she left the Blooms' house that evening, everything was in place. She would tell the Malones, giving them a week's notice so that they could find another girl. If there was any problem, or if they asked her to leave before that, she could stay with the Blooms. The tickets were booked for the following Tuesday, when Ruth and Sam would be free to take her to the station.

The next morning, Sinéad served Dr Malone's breakfast as usual and when he had finished eating, she went into the dining room. He looked up in surprise. She wasn't supposed to come in unless he called her.

'Dr Malone, I've been thinking a lot about what you said,' she began. 'And I think it would be better for everyone if I left. I called my parents yesterday and I'm going back to Ireland.'

He looked at her, then turned his gaze to his empty plate and sat for what seemed like an age. 'Well, that just confirms my opinion,' he said finally. 'Selfish and spoiled, with no concern for other people's welfare.' He stood up. 'How exactly do you think my wife is going to cope, having to deal with another new girl? Have you even thought about the effect this will have on the children?'

She stood there in silence, her cheeks burning. She almost asked him why, if he was so worried about his family, he didn't employ someone permanent to do the work, as she would have been leaving in a couple of months in any case, but she didn't, because she knew the answer.

He told her to go upstairs and look after the children, then called his wife and took her through to his office to talk. Emily tugged at her sleeve and asked her with pleading eyes if she was leaving. Sinéad, genuinely sad at the thought of leaving her, gave her a big hug, telling her that she wasn't to worry and that there would be someone even nicer coming to look after her soon.

Things were tense for the rest of the week, with everyone skirting around the subject, although at one point Gloria asked her how she was going to travel, adding that on the following Tuesday she would be taking the children to their grandparents' house and that she would not be able to drive her to the station.

On Friday, a girl who may or may not have been pregnant called to see the Malones. She was ushered into the office and Sinéad understood from the snatches of conversations she overheard afterwards that she would replace her.

★

At seven in the morning on the first Tuesday in August the doorbell rang and Dr Malone called Sinéad. He stood by the door as she struggled to carry her suitcase down the stairs. Ruth was standing outside, with Sam behind her. As soon as he saw Sinéad with the suitcase Sam rushed to help, while Dr Malone looked at Ruth strangely

'I wasn't aware that you knew Sinéad, Mrs Bloom,' he said, and as Sinéad walked past, she heard him mutter something about interfering busybodies. She turned to say goodbye but he had already gone back into his office. She had said her goodbyes to Gloria and the children the previous evening so as not to disturb them so early, but as she looked back at the house from the car she saw Emily waving madly from a second floor window and she blew her a kiss.

When she was finally in the car and driving away, Sinéad felt light-headed and giddy with relief and expectation, like a child setting off on a school trip. She said as much, realising how paradoxical that must sound to the Blooms. Here she was, exchanging what some would consider a fairly normal existence for being locked up in an institution, and yet in some ways she was looking forward to it.

'You'll see, it'll be just like boarding school,' Ruth patted her knee. 'I'm sure it won't be that bad. And hopefully you won't have to deal with rats – human or otherwise.'

When they arrived at Paddington station, Ruth parked the car and she and Sam walked in with her. There was plenty of time before the train left, so they went to the café next to the waiting room. As they walked in, Sinéad was reminded of the café in the film she had seen – *Brief Encounter* – and then told herself she was being absurd and hoped she wouldn't cry when she had to get on the train.

Ruth was fishing in her handbag for Sinéad's ticket. 'We have a little surprise for you, and I hope you will like it,' she said, showing an envelope to Sinéad and handing it to Sam. 'Sam is going with you to Rosslare.'

Sinéad looked at them both in amazement.

'He won't be able to go all the way to Cork with you, though, as he has to be back in London by Wednesday evening,' Ruth continued, smiling at Sam. 'He has an important meeting on Thursday morning. He'll tell you all about it on the train.'

She stood up. 'I must be off,' she said. She hugged Sinéad warmly and turned to go. 'Take care of yourself and make sure you stay in touch.'

The journey to Fishguard flew by. Sinéad wondered how she would have survived it without Sam. He carried her luggage on and off the train and fielded questions from fellow passengers, making up all kinds of ludicrous stories about the baby and their life together. He talked incessantly to Sinéad about the book he was reading, the piano pieces he was working on and his holiday.

When they got onto the boat they went up onto the top deck. Sam was quieter and Sinéad seized the opportunity. 'This meeting on Thursday,' she said. 'Tell me more.'

He shifted awkwardly in his seat and shrugged his shoulders. 'It's nothing really,' he said. 'One of my teachers wants me to apply to the Juilliard School and we need to talk through the audition procedure.'

'The Juilliard School? In New York?'

'The one and only.'

'That's fantastic!' she said.

He shrugged again. 'There's no guarantee I'll get in.'

'Don't be ridiculous,' she said, 'of course you'll get in. And you'll become a world-famous pianist.' She stopped. 'Damn – and I've only heard you play once. Give me your autograph, quick!'

'I'll do better than that,' he said. 'Here, I have something for you.'

He rummaged in his backpack and pulled out a folder. It was the sheet music for the Schubert Impromptu she had attempted to play at his house.

'My mother said you could probably manage this with a bit of work, so here it is. If you promise me you'll take up the piano again and learn this piece, then I'll give you my autograph.'

Without waiting for her to reply he scribbled a message on the back of the music and signed it with a flourish. Then he reached back into his bag and pulled out a small package, clumsily wrapped in brown paper.

'This is a little something to cheer you up,' he said. 'But you have to promise not to open it until you get to Cork.' Then, before she could react, he said, 'Sinéad, I've been thinking. We hardly know each other, but if it would help you to keep the baby, I'd be happy to marry you. I mean, it could be just a formality and you wouldn't even have to live with me if you didn't want to.'

This was the last thing she expected. She sat there, stunned, then shook her head slowly. 'I don't know what to say, Sam – that is so kind of you. But you have your career to think about. You'll never get this opportunity again. And suppose you meet someone and fall in love with her and *really* want to get married…' she trailed off, confused.

Sam took her hand. 'The offer is there – think about it, and if you change your mind you know where to find me.'

Sinéad slid the music and the package into her shoulder bag.

She had never seen the sea or the sky so blue. With not a cloud in sight it could have been too hot but a light breeze made it pleasantly warm on the deck. As they approached the Irish coast, the sight of the harbour and the familiar green landscape behind it with its rolling hills made Sinéad feel strangely excited and nostalgic at the thought of going home.

The boat took forever to dock in Rosslare and the train guard was blowing his whistle repeatedly as they reached the platform. Sam just had time to put her luggage on the train and give her a quick peck on the cheek. She leaned out of the window, waving until she could no longer see him and then settled back into her seat, suddenly alone again.

There was hardly anyone on the train apart from a serious looking middle-aged couple at one end of the carriage, both engrossed in their newspaper. He was reading the sports section and she was leafing through the rest. At the other end two teenage girls read comics and giggled and Sinéad envied them their innocence. Ruth had given her a small bag with some sandwiches for the journey, guessing correctly that there would be no dining car on the train. Sinéad folded her cardigan and placed it between her head and the window so that she could sleep. It was going to be a long five hours.

It was almost dark when the train arrived in Cork. All the other passengers had disappeared and she was alone in the carriage. She managed to attract the attention of a porter who took her case to the taxi rank. There was only one taxi waiting – a dented and rusting Ford Cortina, its driver seated at the wheel reading the *Evening Press* and smoking a cigarette. When he saw her, he jumped out to help, throwing the butt on the ground and stubbing it out with his shoe.

'Lovely evening,' he said, as he sat back into the driver's seat. 'Where are we off to?'

'Blackrock,' she began.

He turned around sharply and looked at her. 'The convent is it?' he asked. She nodded and he started the engine. For a while he said nothing but she could see his eyes in the rear-view mirror and saw him glancing at her every now and then.

'So, where have you come from today?' he asked, finally breaking the silence. He seemed surprised to hear that she had travelled from London, but Sinéad supposed that most girls heading for Blackrock came from other parts of Ireland. He told her that he had worked in London for a long time but in the end he'd missed Cork, so he decided to come back. Then when he came back he couldn't find a job, so he ended up driving a taxi. He chatted away easily until they arrived at the entrance to what seemed like a large country estate. He drove in between two imposing stone pillars and wound his way up the long drive, stopping in front of a grey and forbidding building. It didn't look very welcoming. There was a statue of the Sacred Heart to the right, arms outspread, looking in towards the convent and turning its back on the city, barely visible below and grey, like the sky.

'Here we are,' said the driver, jumping out to get her case. He carried it to the door and rang the bell. The door opened almost immediately and he began to walk back to the taxi, shouting back at Sinéad, 'You take care of yourself now.' Sinéad was rummaging in her bag for change. 'Hang on, I haven't paid you,' she said.

'That's alright love,' he said. 'You keep your money – you'll need it for when you get out of this place.'

Before she had time to answer he was driving off and she was being ushered into the convent by a young woman wearing a postulant's robe. She found herself in a wide hall with dark tiled floors and several large, heavy wooden doors leading off. There was a strong smell of furniture polish and the air was chilly.

The postulant showed her into the visitors' room and, avoiding eye contact, told her to wait until the Mother Superior arrived. Sinéad remained standing by the large mahogany table and looked around. Everything was spotless and the furniture gleamed. There were two large bookcases filled with leather-bound books. There was no key visible and Sinéad wondered if they were locked. She was about to look at the titles when she heard footsteps echoing down the corridor and the door opened abruptly.

'You must be Sinéad Murray,' said the nun who had just entered the room, her long black robes swishing. She smiled at Sinéad and waved her to a chair, but her eyes remained cold. Unlike the postulant, she looked straight at her with a piercing gaze.

'I am Sister Mary Theresa, the Mother Superior here. I have been speaking to your mother,' she said. 'She's given me all your details. You'll be tired after your journey, so I'll have some tea and sandwiches brought and then you will be shown to your room. Breakfast is at 7.30 am in the refectory and you'll meet the other girls there. But the first thing we need to do is to give you a name – nobody uses their own here. Do you have a name you would like to use?'

Sinéad hadn't expected this, and her mind went blank for a few seconds. Finally, she blurted out the first name she could think of.

'Emily – it's the name of one of the little girls I was looking after in London,' she added, noting the flicker of surprise on the nun's face, the slightly raised eyebrows. It was an expression she was to see a lot of over the next weeks. She supposed most girls took a saint's name, and wondered if there was a Saint Emily.

There was a knock on the door and a girl about her own age came in carrying a large tray. She placed it near Sinéad, never once raising her eyes. Sister Mary Theresa stood up. 'When you have finished, ring this bell and Bridget will show you to your room. I hope you have a good sleep.'

Left alone once more, Sinéad looked at the tray. The sandwiches looked appetising and freshly made. There was even a plate of biscuits – Mikado and Kimberly, her favourites – and a steaming mug of cocoa. Maybe it wasn't going to be so bad after all.

Chapter Five

Sinéad woke to the sound of a bell ringing. It was 6.30 a.m. and the daylight was already filtering through the thin curtains. She had somehow assumed she would be in a dormitory, and was surprised not even to be sharing. The room was small, but it had a cosy feel to it and was far nicer than the room she'd had at the Malones. A crucifix hung above her bed, which was a good-sized single with plenty of blankets and fresh sheets, and there was a wardrobe and chair by the window, from which she could just catch a distant glimpse of the city, not grey anymore, but now bathed in the morning sun.

The previous night she had tried to encourage Bridget to talk, but the girl had been silent and uncommunicative, so she had no idea what to expect for her first day at Blackrock.

Hearing sounds in the corridor outside, she pulled on her dressing gown and poked her head out the door. There were several girls in dressing gowns and various stages of pregnancy heading towards the washroom and one of them stopped and smiled.

'You look lost,' she said. 'Are you the girl who arrived last night?'

Sinéad nodded, and the girl introduced herself as Paula, stumbling a little over her name. 'It takes a few days to get used to it,' she said and laughed. 'I've been here for two months already and I still have to stop and think when someone asks me my name. I've no idea why I chose it – it was the first name that came into my head.'

'Me too,' Sinéad said, 'I never expected to have to change my name!'

After finding her a towel and showing her the washroom, Paula explained the routine to her. 'Mass is at seven. You don't have to go, but they'll frown on it if you haven't got a good excuse. Breakfast is immediately afterwards in the refectory. Then you'll have to go to see Sister Gerald – she's the midwife – and have your checkup.'

The Mass was quite unlike the Masses Sinéad used to attend with her family in their local parish church. There was no sermon for a start, and no interminable queues for communion. The chapel was light and airy, very different from the rest of the building, and the atmosphere was serene and soothing. She was surprised at how few pregnant girls there were, given the size of the building. There were a few nuns, some very elderly, others postulants. They sat at the front, and the inmates – patients, Sinéad reminded herself – were at the back, presumably so that their sinful presence did not disturb the nuns' prayers. One of the elderly nuns turned around and smiled and nodded at her, and Sinéad could have sworn she winked. The postulants, however, looked pale and serious. At one point in her childhood – like most little Catholic girls, she supposed – she had wanted to be a nun. The thought of spending her life singing Gregorian chants in incense-filled chapels was intoxicating. She felt that desire again, listening to the nuns' ethereal voices, and wished she could stay in the chapel and hide away from the world forever.

After Mass she followed the line of girls to the refectory, where the contrast could not have been more striking. The room was large and plain with white walls, spotlessly clean and soulless.

The girls filed in, their footsteps clattering on the tiled floor and their voices resounding off the bare walls. They sat around the rectangular wooden tables. Each girl appeared to have her own place, so Sinéad waited until they were all seated before taking an empty place close to Paula. Paula smiled at her, then got up and walked over to a woman who appeared to be in charge. Sinéad watched as Paula said something to her. The woman disappeared into the kitchen and came back a few moments later with a linen napkin in a napkin ring with 'Emily' handwritten on it.

'Everyone has their own napkin,' Paula said, 'and you leave it on the table in your napkin ring. They are washed once a week, but if you need a clean one – if you spill something on it – just ask Mrs Murphy and she will look after it for you.' She stopped suddenly as a tall, stern-faced nun appeared at the door. The chatter died down, the room went deathly quiet and everyone stood up and made the sign of the cross. They all recited grace and then sat down while the food was brought to the table. Paula elbowed Sinéad in the ribs and whispered, 'That's Sister Ignatius. She's in charge of doling out chores and you definitely don't want to get on the wrong side of her.'

Paula whispered a few introductions. To her left was a girl called Antoinette, who told Sinéad she was hoping to 'drop' any day. Another girl, Dolores, also in the advanced stages of pregnancy, looked as if she had been crying and kept her eyes down throughout the meal.

Ruth was right so far – it was exactly like Sinéad had always imagined boarding school to be, except for the prominent bellies of course. There was a lot of whispering and giggling going on, and she spotted one girl slipping a piece of bread into her pocket. She wondered if they had midnight feasts or if that was just something invented by English authors of books for schoolgirls.

At exactly eight o'clock another bell rang and all the girls jumped to their feet. Everyone tidied up their dishes and placed them on trolleys. Sinéad was vaguely aware of a small group of young women standing about in the kitchens and who seemed to be waiting for the trolleys to be wheeled in, but none of the girls who had been eating breakfast seemed to pay any attention to them and left the refectory without a backward glance. She felt uneasy, as if she had seen something she wasn't supposed to have seen.

Paula took her by the arm and guided her to Sister Gerald's office. She knocked, but there was no response. There was a row of chairs in the corridor outside, so they sat down to wait. Sinéad asked Paula if there was a daily routine, or timetable.

'For us? Not really.' Paula shrugged. 'Apart from the three Ms – Mass, mealtimes, and medicals. Some of the girls have tasks. I think it depends on whether or not your parents pay. Of course, if you misbehave you might get a chore, but up to now I've managed to avoid that.'

52

Sinéad asked about the girls in the kitchen and Paula shook her head.

'Emily, there are things about this place I really don't understand. There are a lot of girls working here – in the laundry, on the farm, in the kitchens and it's not clear where they come from. I'm told there are girls who have their babies and then stay here to work. Why, I have no idea, I have every intention of leaving this dump as quickly as possible, but you can sometimes hear children's voices coming from that direction.' She waved vaguely to the left of the entrance area. 'We have no contact with them. I've heard rumours, but it's not the sort of subject you want to bring up with the nuns – not that you'd ever have a conversation with them about anything. Look, I just want to have this baby and get out of here, so I keep my head down and get on with things.'

Sinéad was about to ask more questions, but Paula jumped to her feet and smiled at a nun who was approaching. 'Good morning Sister Gerald,' she said. 'I've brought you the new girl. See you later, Emily.'

Sinéad followed Sister Gerald into her office, which wasn't actually an office at all. It was more like a small alcove next to what was clearly the delivery room, with a desk, a filing cabinet and some bookshelves taking up most of the space. Sister Gerald sat down and invited Sinéad to do the same. She was in her forties, Sinéad guessed. She was not very tall, and quite slim, but there was something about her that exuded strength. Her face was handsome and slightly suntanned, setting off the remarkable blue of her eyes.

'So, it's Emily, is it? You arrived last night?' The nun smiled at Sinéad, then looked down at a file in front of her.

'I see you came from London. That must have been a long journey for you. How are you feeling today? And more generally? Have you had any problems during your pregnancy?'

'No, Sister. I've actually had no problems at all, not even morning sickness.'

'Good, good. I'll take some samples anyway, so that when you see the doctor he'll have all the information he needs. Let's have a look then, shall we?'

Sister Gerald led her into the delivery room. The examination was quick and efficient, and she made Sinéad feel quite at ease, not embarrassed or uncomfortable as she had been at the hospital in London. Everything was fine, Sister Gerald told her, and she estimated her baby would be born in about six weeks' time.

'Six weeks?' Sinéad was puzzled. 'But I calculated November.'

Sister Gerald shrugged her shoulders. 'Maybe you made a mistake in your dates. It sometimes happens.'

The next few days flew by. Sinéad spent them getting to know the other girls and going for long walks in the convent grounds. The girls were a motley bunch, from all over the country and from all kinds of different backgrounds, but Sinéad found most of them friendly and good company, and she quickly fitted in. Most of them were in their teens, like her, although some of the girls she saw working looked older. There were two separate groups in Sinéad's part of the building – the ones who were pregnant and the ones who had recently had their babies – and there was very little contact between them. The girls who had just had their babies slept on the ground floor in a large room that looked like a cross between a hospital ward and a dormitory, with the cots by the beds. Sinéad hardly ever saw them. The others were on the first floor, and again Ruth was right when she said it would be like boarding school. There was lots of sneaking into each other's bedrooms at night to chat and share treats and gossip. Although it was a fairly rare occurrence, some of the girls had visitors, and when that happened they usually asked them to bring in something to eat. It wasn't that the food from the convent's kitchens was bad, it was just bland and uninteresting, like the school lunches remembered from her younger days.

The day after she arrived, Mother Superior called Sinéad in to take a phone call from her mother, who had decided to come down to see her and wanted to know if she needed anything. She seemed a bit surprised when Sinéad reeled off a list of foodstuffs – roast chicken, fancy biscuits, walnut whips. She said she wasn't sure if she could carry all that on the train, but in the end she arrived with a bulging shopping bag with everything Sinéad had asked for, plus some home-made castle puddings, a family favourite.

Meeting her mother in the parlour was a strange experience. It was a bit like a prison visit, she thought, except there was no barrier and they were the only people there. When they embraced, they both pulled back and laughed awkwardly as Sinéad's bump got in the way. Her mother seemed different, a bit nervous, and the conversation was stilted at first.

'You look well.'

'So do you. How's Daddy?'

'He's fine. Sends his love.' For a moment, Sinéad thought her mother was going to cry, and it struck her that the only time she had ever seen her crying was at granny's funeral.

'Don't worry, Mammy. It's OK here, not as bad as I expected.' Sinéad tried to convince her mother she was fine. 'I'm really glad I came back from London. I was lonely there, and at least here there are other girls to talk to.'

'Have you thought any more about...' she nodded towards Sinéad's bump.

'I haven't changed my mind,' she said. 'All the girls here are having their babies adopted.'

'Yes, I know, love, but...' Her mother took her hand. 'You know Daddy and I will support you if you decide to keep the baby.'

Sinéad thought back to the discussions with the social workers and the parish priest. Even her own aunt. Even Ruth.

'I can't do that, Mammy, you know I can't. You'd have to give up your job and stay at home again.' She shook her head. 'No, I've thought about it and it's not just what you or me or Daddy want. We have to think about the baby. It's much better if it grows up in a proper family.' Something in her mother's expression made her stop. 'Oh, Mammy I don't mean our family isn't a proper family...' Sinéad stammered. 'It's just...you know what I mean.'

'I know, love,' she said, patting her knee. 'So, tell me what you get up to all day here.'

'You're going to be popular,' said Paula later, looking through the bag before they crept down the corridor to Antoinette's room. It was a bigger room then theirs, with four beds, one of which was unoccupied after one of the girls had her baby. Dolores and Marie, the other two occupants, made space for Sinéad to sit down and they spread out the food on the spare bed.

'Roast chicken,' said Marie, inhaling deeply as she opened the carefully wrapped parcel. 'I haven't had proper roast chicken since I came to this place. Emily, you're my friend forever.'

'Hands off,' said Antoinette. 'Let Emily dish it out. And keep the noise down, girls or we'll all be on sluice room duty tomorrow.'

'What's the sluice room?' asked Sinéad.

'It's where they wash all the dirty nappies. Down the corridor, near the delivery room – just follow your nose,' said Dolores, laughing.

They divided up the food and there was silence for a while, broken only by the rustling of greaseproof paper and some muffled groans of pleasure as they began to eat.

'God, we're just like that Famous Five or whatever they're called,' said Dolores, trying to find a comfortable position.

Antoinette looked at her, eyebrows raised. 'More like the Infamous Five,' she said. 'Can you imagine any of those nice kids getting knocked up?'

'Especially George,' Paula laughed.

'Wasn't there one book called *Five Get into Trouble*?' said Dolores and they all sniggered, except for Marie, who sat looking puzzled.

'What are you all talking about?'

'Enid Blyton books. Adventures. Midnight feasts. Did you never read them?' Dolores asked. 'Oh, I forgot, they don't have books in Cork.' She dodged as Marie rolled up a sweet wrapper and threw it at her.

'Wasn't there one called *Five Run Away Together*?' Dolores mused. 'Maybe we should do that. We could set up a hippie commune in West Cork and Marie could grow vegetables and feed us all. Marie lives on a farm in Cork,' she added, for Sinéad's benefit.

'Not anymore she doesn't,' said Antoinette.

There was another silence and Antoinette turned to Sinéad.

'OK Emily, what's your story?'

Sinéad shrugged. 'Same as you all, I suppose.'

'Tell us about the father. Was he good-looking?'

'I suppose he was…is…he's not really in the picture.' Sinéad said.

'Were you crazy about him? Did he dump you when you got pregnant?' Antoinette asked.

'Shut up Antoinette,' said Dolores. 'Let her tell us herself.'

Sinéad told them briefly what had happened, and about her time in London.

'That was brave, going off to London like that,' said Marie. 'I bet the adoption people didn't like it when you stood up to them. My parents would never have let me do a thing like that.'

'How did they react, your parents?' Sinéad looked around the room.

Dolores wiped her mouth with her sleeve and said, 'Mine wanted me to get married straight away, but the father did a runner. I don't know where he went. England probably.' She looked down at the floor. 'He hasn't been in touch, and anyway my Da says he'll kill him if he ever comes back. We live in a small village near Athlone so there's no way I could keep the baby there. I'm hoping to go to Dublin afterwards.'

'You're going to keep the baby?'

'Well, I don't know yet. My boyfriend has friends in Dublin so maybe I'll get back in touch with him through them. I'm sure once he sees a picture of the baby, he'll change his mind.'

'I wouldn't bet on it,' said Antoinette. 'They're all the same, men. When I found out I was pregnant, my "boyfriend" told me he was already engaged to somebody else. Can you believe it? We had been going out for six months and all the time he was engaged to somebody else, some snooty miss from the next town. Deirdre, she was called. I was going to choose that name when I arrived here, just to spite her, but...' She looked around the room defiantly and Marie raised her eyes to heaven.

'Would you have married him if he hadn't been engaged?' Sinéad asked.

Antoinette shook her head vigorously. 'Lucky escape, that's how I see it now.'

'What about you, Marie?' Sinéad asked.

'My sister's husband.'

Sinéad looked at her, shocked, but a sharp look from Dolores made her change the subject.

Antoinette stood up and opened the window. She took a battered packet of Woodbines from a box in the wardrobe and took a cigarette out. 'Smoke, anyone?' she said.

Dolores wriggled herself off the bed with difficulty 'I'll keep a lookout, in case one of the nuns is on night patrol. Sister Ignatius'll kill you if she sees you smoking.'

'You shouldn't really be smoking, anyway. It's bad for the baby,' said Sinéad.

'Thank you, Doctor Emily, I'll bear that in mind. In the meantime, when I want your opinion I'll ask for it.' She took a few drags on the cigarette, then put it out. 'Ah, you're right, I shouldn't be doing this. Sorry girls, just talking about that bastard puts me in a bad mood.'

Chapter Six

ABOUT TWO WEEKS HAD gone by, and Sinéad woke up hoping the events of the night before had been a bad dream. The previous day Sister Ignatius had called her and told her she would have to change rooms as they needed hers for a new arrival. She said she would put her in a room with someone called Majella, and that if she had any problems to come and see her. Sinéad had no idea who Majella was, and when she asked the other girls if they thought she was being punished for something, Antoinette burst out laughing and said that she would certainly have lots of entertainment. They all seemed to think it was really funny, except Paula, who told them to shut up.

Sinéad didn't meet Majella until bedtime that night, when she realised who she was. She wasn't part of their group, but she had seen her around the convent, usually cleaning floors or windows. According to the others she had been there for years. She looked quite a lot older than any of the other girls, and seemed a little strange. Rumour had it that she came in pregnant some years previously and stayed on after her child was adopted and had then had several more babies in quick succession. Antoinette said she went down to the farm and slept with the farmhands whenever she got the chance. She added that the nuns tried to keep her in, but that she always managed to find a way out. Sinéad found it hard to believe but all the others seemed quite convinced.

On the first night, Majella got into bed without saying a word and turned to the wall. About half an hour later, Sinéad heard her getting up and the door opening. She disappeared down the corridor and when Sinéad woke the next morning there was no sign of her. She wondered if she should tell one of the nuns. She asked herself if that was why she had been put into the room with her, to keep an eye on her, but she decided to wait. There was no point in being a tell-tale. After breakfast, she saw her in the corridor with a bucket and a mop, cleaning the floor as usual, so she supposed she must have got up before her. Or maybe she had gone down to the farm.

But on the second night she didn't go out. Sinéad wished she had. She had just drifted off to sleep when she woke suddenly, hearing the sound of moaning from Majella's bed. At first, she wasn't sure if Majella was in pain, but she soon realised what the other girl was doing. The moans got louder and louder and the bed was creaking faster and faster. She looked to see if someone else was in the room with her, but she was alone. She tried to block out the sound but she couldn't. When the noise finally stopped, Sinéad was wide-awake and hardly slept at all for the rest of the night.

At breakfast next morning, Marie looked at her and asked if she had slept well. Paula told her to shut up and changed the subject. As they walked down the corridor after breakfast, Paula took her aside said, 'Don't mind Marie. We've all had to share a room with Majella at one point or another. It's like a rite of passage.' She looked behind her to make sure no-one was listening. 'Talk to Sister Gerald. She likes you and I'm sure she'll get you another room.'

After two more sleepless nights, Sinéad had a chat with Sister Gerald. She felt her cheeks reddening as she tried to explain to the nun exactly why she couldn't sleep, but Sister Gerald just patted her hand and seemed to know exactly what she was trying to say, reassuring her that she would have her moved as soon as possible.

Three days later they moved her to Paula's room. As she began unpack and put her things away, she found the package Sam had given to her on the way over, hidden and still unopened in her suitcase. She opened it slowly, deeply ashamed that she'd forgotten about it. Under the brown paper she found another, more delicately wrapped parcel. She peeled the paper back and discovered the dark green raincoat she had tried on in Selfridge's. She sat back, overcome with emotion. How kind of him to have thought of that – but how could he have known? She must have told him about it that day she was feeling so miserable in the tea shop. She pulled it out and a postcard fell to the floor – a cartoon image of a spy and a message wishing her luck.

Paula came in just then and Sinéad showed the parcel to her, her eyes still bright with tears.

'I like the coat,' Paula said, but seemed distinctly unimpressed when Sinéad told her about Sam and how he had travelled with her to Rosslare.

'You need to hide that away. The nuns often search our rooms and sometimes take things if they think they came from outside.'

Sinéad held out the postcard to her and she turned it over.

'Nice message,' she said, 'but I wouldn't reply if I were you. You have to leave letters unsealed so the nuns can read them and he'd probably never get it if they thought there was anything in it that would make this place look bad.'

Sinéad removed the tag, folded the coat and placed it back in her suitcase – for all the nuns knew, she could have had it already. She hid the postcard under the mattress.

The next sleepless night was entirely her own fault as she and Paula stayed chatting until the early hours.

'He asked me to marry him. On the boat.' Sinéad said. 'Can you imagine that? He's so nice and funny and kind. His mother is too. She was lovely. But that would be a mad thing to do.'

'Completely,' said Paula. 'And anyway, he's Jewish. There's no way you could marry somebody Jewish. You'd have to convert and learn Hebrew and stuff.' She twisted in the bed, rubbing her belly. 'Tell me more about the family you were staying with. Was the doctor Irish?'

Sinéad told her about the house, the routine, the eggs and finally, the incident with the rat.

'That's hilarious!' Paula said. 'I'd love to have seen his face. And I would have shoved his eggs up his you know where.' She winced and moved slightly. 'Damn. This baby always starts kicking when I get comfortable. He's going to be a rugby player like his father.'

'Are you still in touch with him? The father?'

'Oh yes. We've been going out for ages. We'll probably get married next year, once all this is over.'

'I thought you were going to have the baby adopted.' Sinéad looked puzzled.

Paula looked uncomfortable for a second, 'Yes, my mother and the social workers thought it was better like that,' she said. 'I was too far gone when I found out I was pregnant and if we had got married everyone would have known it was a shotgun wedding.'

Sinéad hid her surprise and said nothing. As if sensing her reaction, Paula carried on.

'His family are very well known in Dublin. They're always in the papers and so on, so it was just out of the question. They don't even know. My own father doesn't know. My mother organised everything so they think I'm in England for the summer holidays with my cousin in Oxford. I send letters to the family via my cousin — she's the only one in on all this — and she posts them back to Dublin.'

'Did you ever think about keeping it?'

'The baby? You mean, like running away with Mark or something?' She stopped and put her hand over her mouth. 'Oh God, Emily, forget I said that, I'm not supposed to tell anyone his name. But no, keeping it is just not an option — especially as he didn't think it was a good idea either. We've decided to just do what everyone wants and get on with our lives.'

'Don't worry, I won't tell anyone,' said Sinéad.

Although it was strictly forbidden, that night they exchanged real names, addresses and telephone numbers and made a pact to meet up again afterwards, come what may.

Chapter Seven

TIME PASSED SLOWLY FOR Sinéad, but not because she was
busy; in fact, she had been doing remarkably little – daily
Mass, meals, long walks around the grounds, the usual gos-
siping. She wrote very little in the diary she had started to
keep when she was in London because she was worried that
the nuns might find it. What little she wrote was usually in
code and on scraps of paper which she then hid carefully in
unlikely places.

Dolores had her baby during the night, and when they
came down for breakfast the next morning it was all over.
The ward was off limits so nobody had spoken to her and they
didn't even know if it was a boy or a girl. A couple of girls
had left and some new ones arrived, but in their little group
absolutely nothing else had happened. Sinéad was bored.

Most of the girls spent their spare time knitting, and
Sinéad reluctantly agreed to join them. Her worst subject at
school was domestic science, but she had some memories of
turning a heel on a sock, wondering what the point was, as
they never actually made a whole sock.

In the recreation room where they spent most of their
time during the day there was a large box with bits of wool

and various needles in it. One of the girls, Jacintha, guided her towards some bright yellow wool.

'There's no point choosing pink or blue, because you don't know if it's a boy or a girl, and once it's born you won't have any time for knitting,' she said, laughing.

Jacintha sat beside Sinéad and showed her how to follow a simple pattern. She was a quiet girl from Sligo who was about a week away from having her baby, and she had made the most beautiful outfits, all in white, each one in two different sizes. She had made two bonnets, two matinee coats and two sets of bootees, decorated with lace and ribbons. She showed off a crocheted blanket, embroidered with baby rabbits.

'I want my baby to have one really beautiful outfit to wear when she leaves the convent and a bigger one for later – perhaps for the proper christening,' she told Sinéad.

Sinéad looked at her, surprised. 'But I thought they were christened here, in the convent, before they leave?'

'Yes, but the people who adopt always re-christen them and sometimes they give them a new name. So it feels more like their baby.'

'You're wasting your time,' said Antoinette, who had been sitting in the corner, watching but not taking part. 'The people who adopt babies don't keep the clothes or the names. They don't want to be reminded of where they came from. They probably throw the clothes away or give them to the poor. Maybe they'll even end up back here.' She stood up, rubbing her back. 'Now that would be ironic, wouldn't it?'

Jacintha reddened and turned on Antoinette. 'I have neighbours who adopted a baby and they kept everything that came with him, even information about his real mother, in a special box to give him when he got older.'

Antoinette shrugged. 'If that's what you want to believe,' she said.

Jacintha looked around the room for support but the other girls just looked down at their knitting, or shook their heads.

'Let's hope that's what they do,' Sinéad said to Jacintha, throwing a warning look at Antoinette, who pretended not to notice.

★

It had rained all day, so there were no walks. Sinéad spent most of the day knitting. She had really begun to enjoy it, especially because she'd never thought she could be good at something like that. It helped to have some quiet time to concentrate really hard on something and not think too much about anything else. She now had a set of bootees and a bonnet made and was starting on a matinee jacket – all in bright yellow.

Paula, who had resisted joining in, finally asked Sinéad if she would knit something for her, offering to sew the pieces together. They made a good team as Sinéad's sewing was terrible and Paula couldn't knit at all.

That evening, just before they went to bed, Antoinette came to their room in a panic to say that Jacintha was in labour and seemed to be in a lot of pain. Between them, Sinéad and Antoinette helped her down to Sister Gerald's office. Sister Gerald seemed quite surprised when Sinéad asked if there was anything she could do, and said no, but she would think about it. Sinéad had re-read the book her aunt had given her several times, but it all seemed quite unreal and she wanted to have a clearer idea of what was going to happen. A year of medicine and all she knew about obstetrics was what she had learned from the Lamaze book!

The next morning Sister Gerald called Sinéad over after breakfast and told her that she wouldn't need her help as Jacintha had been taken to the local hospital with complications.

'I've been looking at your file,' she said. 'You should have told me from the start that you were a medical student. I was wondering...' she paused. 'Would you like to help me with the next birth?' Sinéad nodded eagerly. 'Here – this is a textbook on obstetrics. You can start reading right away.'

Several days passed and there was still no news of Jacintha. Someone said she'd had to have an operation and had almost died – others said the baby was stillborn and that it was probably just as well. Sinéad wondered how she would cope in the hospital with no visitors, in a ward with all the other legitimate mothers peering at her and whispering.

The speculation went on all morning, and at about two that afternoon, they saw an ambulance pulling up outside the main door. The driver and his helper jumped out, looking up briefly at the facade, and then went around the back and opened the doors. They saw Jacintha being taken out in a wheelchair, clutching a small bundle. She looked pale, but she smiled and waved when she saw the girls, who immediately hid behind the curtains for fear of being spotted by the staff.

Sinéad ran to the front door, but Mother Superior appeared from nowhere and told her to go back to where she had come from. On her way back to the recreation room, she passed Sister Gerald, who was walking quickly down the corridor, looking agitated. She went out to meet Jacintha, wheeling her and her baby into the delivery room and then in a few moments she re-appeared with the empty wheelchair which she gave back to the ambulance men. She went straight back to the delivery room and another nun Sinéad had never seen before went in and stayed for about twenty minutes. After she left, they heard the baby crying for a while, then Sister Gerald emerged and called for Sinéad and Antoinette to come and help Jacintha walk to the dormitory. They took an arm each and held Jacintha as she walked gingerly down the corridor. Sister Gerald followed with the baby, and once Jacintha was settled on her bed, she told the girls to go back to their knitting and that they could come back later to see their friend. Sinéad tried to catch a glimpse of the baby but Sister Gerald held him towards her and she just managed to see a tiny waving fist.

The next day at breakfast, gossip was flying about.

'I heard the baby stopped breathing during the birth and he has brain damage,' said Antoinette.

'I heard he's deformed,' said Marie.

'Have any of you actually seen him?' asked Sinéad. She looked around the table defying them.

'Nobody? Well, let's wait and see, until one of us has spoken to Jacintha.'

As soon as the meal was finished, Sinéad slipped away to go to the ward where the new mothers and babies were. She tiptoed past Sister Gerald's office and gently pushed open the door of the room.

Jacintha was sitting by her bed giving her baby a bottle and looked up as Sinéad approached.

'Come and meet baby Fintan,' she whispered, pulling the blanket away. The baby stopped feeding and turned his head towards Sinéad, showing an angry purplish birthmark that completely covered one side of his face. Sinéad stroked his face and he gripped her finger. 'He's perfect except for the birthmark,' said Jacintha, 'but Sister Mary Theresa says nobody will want to adopt him because of that.' Tears slid down her face. 'Oh God, Emily, what am I going to do?'

As Sinéad struggled to take all this in, Sister Gerald appeared at the door. 'Emily, come here. I have a job for you.' Sinéad followed her to her office, bracing herself for a telling-off, but the nun pulled a stool over to the bookshelves, climbed on to it and passed down a number of large books. 'I want you to look through these books and see if you can find anything about birthmarks and their evolution.' Her face reddened as she continued, her voice rising slightly, 'I think it's completely wrong that people don't want to adopt a child simply because it has some flaw. That poor child – we have to do whatever we can to help.'

Sinéad had never seen the nun like this before. She was usually so calm, but now seemed agitated – angry, even. She took the books away and trawled through them diligently, but found very little to satisfy Sister Gerald. As she suspected, there were no easy answers. The birthmark might fade, it might even disappear, but then again it might not. The best thing would be to show the baby to a skin specialist, but somehow Sinéad didn't think that would be on the agenda.

When she reported back to Sister Gerald, the nun had calmed down and seemed sad, even vulnerable.

'What's going to happen with Fintan?' Sinéad asked her, but she just shook her head. She put the books back on the shelf and, changing the subject, began to tell Sinéad about her work in Africa with the missions. Their discussion was cut short when Antoinette arrived at the door of the office, clutching her stomach.

'My waters broke,' she said, bent almost double and very distressed. 'And the contractions are coming every five minutes. Marie timed them.'

'It never rains but it pours,' said Sister Gerald, rolling up her sleeves and returning to her normal self. 'Right, Emily are you ready to help?'

Sinéad helped Antoinette undress and get into a comfortable position on the delivery bed.

'I hope that's not going to grow back all spiky,' said Antoinette, trying to stay still as Sister Gerald shaved her.

Antoinette moaned as another contraction began.

'Breathe. Breathe like I showed you in the book,' said Sinéad.

Antoinette turned her face to the wall.

'Look at me, Antoinette,' said Sinéad, pulling at her shoulder. 'Watch me. Breathe.'

'Fuck off, you and your bloody book,' Antoinette shouted.

Sinéad turned and looked at Sister Gerald, expecting her to be shocked at the language she had just heard, but the nun just smiled and said that was normal and not to pay attention to anything a woman said in childbirth.

As the contractions became faster and more painful, Sister Gerald asked Antoinette if she would like some pain relief. Without waiting for an answer, the nun took out the longest syringe Sinéad had ever seen and filled it with a clear fluid.

'Pethidine,' she said to Sinéad.

'Get away from me with that needle, you bitch!' Antoinette screamed as the nun approached her. Four injections were necessary and Sinéad had to hold her down until they were done. The injections seemed a lot more painful than the contractions, but once the drug had taken effect, Antoinette calmed down, and Sinéad was reminded of the stoned people she'd seen in the flat in London. It was only a few weeks ago, but it seemed like another world.

'Is my baby here yet?' she asked Sinéad. 'Is he a lovely little boy? I'm going to call him after his Daddy. He's going to come and pick me up here tomorrow and we're going to get married and go and live in America.'

Sinéad held her hand for what seemed like hours, until gradually the effect of the pethidine began to wear off. Antoinette seemed to wake up and said she had to push. Sister Gerald took over, trying to tell her when to push and when to just relax and breathe. But Antoinette wouldn't listen and just kept pushing and shouting. Sinéad could see the top of the baby's head beginning to show, but the surrounding tissue was stretched to the limit and she wondered how on earth the baby was going to come out. Sister Gerald went quickly to the steriliser and came back with a pair of scissors. When Antoinette had her next contraction and was almost delirious with pain, she deftly made a snip just where the baby's head was and with a gush of fluid, the baby shot out onto the bed. Sinéad just managed to catch her.

Everything went silent for a few seconds. Antoinette looked as if she was in shock. Then the baby took a gulp of air and began to scream. Sinéad held her in wonder as Sister Gerald dealt with the delivery of the placenta and asked Sinéad to cut the cord. She didn't remember much about what happened after that – the baby being taken away to be weighed, Sister Gerald stitching the cut she had made, the baby being brought back and given to Antoinette. She was mesmerised by the change in Antoinette, who was now singing softly to her baby, tears running down her cheeks. She looked at Sinéad.

'She's so beautiful,' she said, 'but I wanted her to be a boy. Boys can look after themselves much better than girls and I don't want her to end up like me.'

Once Sister Gerald was satisfied everything was in order, Antoinette and her baby girl were taken down to the ward. Sinéad noticed that the bed in the corner where Dolores had been was empty and asked where she had gone. Jacintha told her that her parents had come to take her home.

'And the baby?' she asked.

'A social worker came and took him away,' she said. 'They can't be put up for adoption until they're six weeks old, so he'll be placed with a foster family until then. She could have stayed here until he was old enough to be adopted, but her parents thought it would be better if she spent as little time with him as possible.'

That night Sinéad couldn't sleep and lay on her bed talking to Paula about the events of the past few days, asking her how she thought she might feel after the birth. Up to now, she had managed to avoid thinking about what would happen. The whole situation had always seemed surreal, and somehow she had managed to bury any doubts she had and convinced herself that once the birth was over she would hand her baby over to his or her brand new happy life and then go back to hers as if nothing had happened. But seeing Jacintha and Antoinette with their babies had turned her carefully constructed scenario on its head.

Paula was clearly not interested in pursuing the discussion. 'Look,' she said, 'I know it'll probably be difficult, but I'm trying not to think about it because it's the only way. That's what everybody says. We just have to get through it and walk away. You can't have an illegitimate child in this country, and that's that, so unless you're prepared to go off to England and live in a cheap bedsit or a hostel, or work as a live-in maid somewhere, there's no way you could support yourself and a baby. And people will take advantage of you – look at what happened to you in London. And then even if you could get a job, who would mind the child while you were out at work? Plus nobody would marry us, knowing we already had a child. No, in the end it's better for the child to have a nice family who will give him everything he needs. And we can marry and have more children later.'

Paula said goodnight and turned to go to sleep, but Sinéad lay awake for a long time, her thoughts racing.

Chapter Eight

SINÉAD SPENT A LOT of time talking to Jacintha and playing with Fintan. She managed to get Jacintha to open up and talk about her family and learned that she had an older sister, Geraldine, who was married and lived in Manchester. Geraldine didn't even know that Jacintha was pregnant, so Sinéad helped her draft a letter. One of the other girls had a cousin coming to visit and she gave the letter to her to post to avoid the prying eyes of Mother Superior. To Jacintha's surprise and delight Geraldine responded immediately and phoned her at the convent. She was very supportive and offered to look after Fintan while Jacintha found herself a job and sorted herself out.

The next step was to work on getting out of the home. Jacintha's parents had paid for her stay, so in theory there was no problem about leaving, but when she finally plucked up the courage to tell Mother Superior, the nun wasn't too happy about it. By now Jacintha had become stronger and more determined, and in any case everyone at the convent knew that finding a family to adopt Fintan would be difficult if not impossible, so in the end the nun gave in. Jacintha never said very much about her parents, but reading between the lines, Sinéad gathered that they would be relieved if she took the problem elsewhere.

The day Jacintha and Fintan left was a difficult one for all of them and they watched with mixed emotions as she dressed her baby lovingly in the clothes she had made for his christening, never thinking she would get to see him in them. She hugged Sinéad and told her she would never forget her. As she drove away in her sister's car they all waved from the window of the day room, but by evening the subject had somehow become taboo, and nobody was prepared to discuss the possibilities that Jacintha's departure had opened up.

The days dragged by, and the only break in the monotony of their routine was the day the doctor arrived to examine them. All the girls whose due date was within the next month were summoned to Sister Gerald's office, and a special room was set aside for the examinations. As Sinéad sat outside in the corridor waiting her turn, she watched the girls ahead of her coming out, one after one, pulling faces. The doctor was a taciturn middle-aged man who never looked her in the eye and only asked her the briefest of questions relating to her condition, examining her under a blanket as if he might be offended by what he saw or infected by her sin. He reminded her of Dr Malone, and not for the first time she wondered how a person who had qualified as a doctor could show so little humanity.

Life continued as if nothing had happened and nobody mentioned Jacintha. Sinéad began to feel anxious. What if the same thing happened to her – what if the delivery went wrong and she too had to go outside to the hospital?

What if there was something wrong with her baby and no-body wanted to adopt him? She had no sister in England to turn to, and if she didn't return to college fairly soon people would notice and start asking questions.

There was a rumour going around that if the baby showed signs of being late, a good dose of castor oil would speed things up. She knew that some of the girls had resorted to this, but had no idea if it worked. She talked to Sister Gerald about it but she just laughed, saying the worst it could do would be to give the girl a bad dose of stomach cramps.

'And if, as you insist, your baby is not due for another month, it won't make the slightest difference.' But in the end Sister Gerald caved in to Sinéad's insistence, taking the bottle from her medicine cupboard and giving her a large spoonful.

Her contractions began at about two o'clock the fol-lowing morning. Sinéad woke up in intense pain and crept downstairs to the delivery room, not sure whether she re-ally was in labour. She waited there for a while before des-perately needing to use the bathroom. She began to walk down the corridor towards the toilets but was stopped in her tracks at the sight of a large spider in the middle of the floor. She leaned against the wall, petrified and moaning in pain, unable to move. She heard a door open, and saw the ghostly figure of Majella in a nightdress walking towards her. She brushed past Sinéad, averting her eyes, but Sinéad was desperate. She grabbed her by the arm and pointed at the spider. Majella seemed not to understand at first, then turned abruptly and disappeared wordlessly into a store-room, re-emerging with a large brush and dispatching the spider with one well-aimed blow.

She looked at Sinéad triumphantly and said loudly, 'It was the devil come to take your baby.' She scuttled back into the storeroom, replaced the brush and disappeared up the corridor. Sinéad stood watching her in amazement – it was the first time she had ever heard Majella speak. Her legs shaking, she picked her way carefully past the scrunched up body of the spider and made her way to the washroom, just as Sister Gerald, woken by the noise, arrived to help.

★

Sinéad's baby – a perfect little boy – was born eight hours later. She remembered little of the actual labour, except that despite her best attempts to follow the advice in her book she too had pethidine – four injections, just like Antoinette – and that at one point she almost kicked Sister Gerald as she saw her approaching through a fog of pain and drugs with what she thought were scissors. She remembered the birth vividly though, and Sister Gerald's skill in delivering her baby, shouting at her to push, then stop, breathe then push again with the next contraction. Sister Gerald smiled at her as she delivered the baby. 'No stitches?' Sinéad asked in amazement.

'No stitches,' Sister Gerald confirmed, nodding in approval. 'And a most beautiful baby boy. And he looks full term to me.'

The baby was weighed and checked over and the placenta was delivered. With calm restored to the room, the nun came to her side. 'Just one more thing. I have to give you an injection of Anti-D, as your blood group is O negative.' In later years, Sinéad was to realise how important that injection had been for her future children and often thanked the nun silently for her professionalism.

Sister Gerald pottered about, leaving Sinéad to rest as she tidied up before coming to ask her what name she wanted to give him.

'It doesn't matter what I call him, they'll change it anyway. I'll call him after you.'

'That's what most of the girls say – the whole of Cork will be populated with Geralds if we go on like that.' She thought for a moment. 'Why don't you call him Lorcan? That's my father's name.'

The next few days passed by in a haze. She remembered having her breasts bound so that the milk supply would dry up. She remembered the pain and discomfort that followed, the binding so tight she could hardly breathe. Girls who were not staying on in the home after the birth were not allowed to breastfeed.

She remembered Mother Superior coming in to see her, oohing and aahing and saying what a beautiful baby he was, and that she was very lucky as they would have no trouble having him adopted. There were lots of good, nice families waiting for babies like hers.

Antoinette called him the little canary. 'He doesn't cry, he sings,' she said, laughing as Sinéad struggled to put on the bright yellow jacket she had knitted for him.

She lived from moment to moment, trying not to think about going home, trying in vain not to feel any emotion as she held Lorcan for his feeds, bathed and dressed him, soothed him when he cried and then watched him sleep peacefully in his cot.

When Lorcan was five days old Mother Superior came to see her again.

'I have good news for you, Emily,' she said and Sinéad felt a knot in her stomach. 'Miss Brennan has found a wonderful family for baby Lorcan and they will send someone down to collect him the day after tomorrow. He will stay with a foster family until he is six weeks old and then his new family will take him.' For some reason she never understood, it was arranged that she would take her baby to Dublin herself; a social worker from the adoption agency in Dublin would come down to meet her and travel back up on the train with her and the baby.

'Lucky you,' said Antoinette as she hugged her and kissed Lorcan goodbye. 'I don't know when I'll get out of this place. And, you know, in a way I don't care, not now that I've got her.' She pointed to her daughter, sleeping peacefully in the cot.

'Good luck,' Sinéad whispered to Marie, tapping her bump. 'I hope everything goes well for you.'

Paula came hurrying down the corridor as she was about to leave and they embraced. 'I didn't realise you were leaving so soon. Take care, Emily,' she said, out of breath. 'And let's meet up again in Dublin when I get out.'

The social worker was waiting for her in the parlour, a youngish woman with a distant, closed expression that didn't invite conversation. They took a taxi to the station and boarded the Dublin train.

The journey was a nightmare. Sinéad was tense and Lorcan seemed to sense it as he was very unsettled and cried a lot. His cries were a lot more strident than in the convent.

The social worker did nothing to help and looked out the window most of the time, almost as if she was pretending that she wasn't travelling with them. Sister Gerald had prepared two bottles for the journey, and at one point Sinéad had to ask the woman to go to the dining car to have one heated, which she did with a great show of reluctance. When she came back, the milk was far too hot and Sinéad waited for what seemed like forever for it to cool, trying desperately to soothe a frantic Lorcan. In the end, she went to the dining car herself to get some cold water to try to cool it down more quickly, leaving Lorcan with the social worker who held him awkwardly, as if she might catch something from him.

There was an elderly couple sitting across the aisle from them and when Sinéad came back and finally had him settled and feeding they smiled at her.

'What a lovely baby,' said the woman. 'Is it your first?' Sinéad nodded, trying to keep the tears at bay. She wondered if they had any inkling what was going on. If they had, would they have been so friendly?

Lorcan fell asleep just as the train pulled into Kingsbridge station, and Sinéad saw her mother and aunt waiting on the platform. The social worker sprang into action and gathered her things, leaving Sinéad to struggle with Lorcan in his Moses basket as well as her suitcase.

Her mother came to the door of the carriage and helped her out as the social worker stood back and watched. She would never forget the look on her mother's face as she first saw her grandchild, taking the Moses basket gently from Sinéad.

'Your aunt and I have decided that I'll take him over to the adoption agency, love. It'll be easier for you that way. You go for a walk with Aunt Catherine and we'll see each other later at home.'

Too weak to argue, Sinéad let go of the basket, and suddenly her mother was hustled into a waiting taxi with the social worker. Lorcan was gone, and she hadn't even kissed him goodbye.

*

Sinéad went back to college the following week as if nothing had happened. If anyone had asked, she would have told them she'd been in London for the summer, working as an au pair and getting work experience in a doctor's surgery. But nobody did ask. She had changed university from UCD to Trinity, and had changed her course from medicine to business administration, obliging her to make new friends. In the circumstances it was probably for the best.

At home nobody mentioned her pregnancy or the baby, and she slowly began to blot out the memories of the last few months, throwing herself into debating societies and student politics. She was elected to the Students' Representative Council and studied hard, filling her days as much as possible, determined to finish this new degree quickly and get herself a job.

One day she tried to phone Paula – or Louise as she was known outside the convent. She went to a public telephone box, which in retrospect was probably a mistake as the woman who answered the phone immediately sounded suspicious.

'What did you say your name was?' she asked.

'Emily,' said Sinéad.

'I don't know any of Louise's friends called Emily,' the woman said. 'Where do you know her from?'

'We were at school together,' Sinéad said, beginning to realize her mistake.

'Oh yes? What school was that?' asked the woman. Sinéad couldn't remember which school Louise had been to. Some posh southside school or other. She heard Louise's voice in the background. 'Who's that, Mummy?'

'Nobody,' said the woman. 'Somebody called Emily. I think it's a wrong number,' and she hung up.

The next day, Louise called Sinéad at home and begged her not to call again. She sounded frightened and was whispering. Her mother was determined she should put everything behind her too, and any contact with anybody from the home was forbidden.

'What did you have?' asked Sinéad.

'What?'

The baby – was it a boy or a girl?'

There was a silence. 'A boy. But I don't want to think about it.'

Chapter Nine

JACK MCDONAGH WAS ATTENDING the annual conference of the Union of Students in Ireland in Killarney, representing his university, UCD. His main role at the conference was simple – to make sure UCD resolutions were adopted. He had something of a reputation as a hatchet man and his team had given him the task of eliminating the opposition and making sure no other university managed to have more resolutions passed or got credit for any of their own work. It was all fairly good-humoured, but also good practice for the career in politics to which many of the students aspired.

Part of Jack's strategy involved keeping people up late and making them drink too much, which was why at one o'clock in the morning he was embroiled in a poker game with two of the Galway delegation, Michael Leahy and Gerry Mulcahy. Just as he was about to deal a hand, he became aware of someone standing behind him. It was Ian Hollis, President of Trinity SRC, along with a girl he had glimpsed during the plenary sessions.

'Can we join in?' Hollis asked amiably.

Before Jack could reply, Leahy, who had had far too much to drink, muttered, 'This is a man's game, Hollis – no women allowed.'

'That's fine, Leahy,' Hollis said, 'Sinéad here is one of the lads.' Jack could almost hear the cogs in Leahy's brain churning as he searched for a suitable reply, but instead he just shrugged and moved slightly on the couch to make room.

'Sixpence to be in and you can only raise sixpence at a time.' They were students after all, and by January their grants had been seriously depleted.

Sinéad took a bright red purse out of her bag and put a small pile of coins on the table. Jack dealt the cards and the game began again.

Hollis was a good player, but he seemed distracted that night, and after a few rounds he muttered something about having to see someone. He gathered up his winnings and left. They were down to four, including Sinéad, and it was Jack's turn to deal. The game started normally, with everyone in.

Leahy, to his left, took one card, placing the other carefully in front of him. Mulcahy stared at his hand for a few seconds and then asked for one card as well. Sinéad smiled cheerfully and said, 'Three please.' Jack had a pair of fives, so he also took three cards. Leahy opened the bidding, placing two sixpences in the pot. Mulcahy folded and Sinéad, after a moment's hesitation, pushed three sixpences forward.

'I'll see that, and raise you another sixpence,' she said.

Jack had drawn another five and two threes, so he felt pretty confident and added his three sixpences to the rapidly increasing pot.

Mulcahy sat with his pint of Guinness half-way to his mouth, gaping.

Leahy looked at the others. Then, after what seemed like an age, he said, 'OK, if that's the way you want to play it, I'll see your sixpence…and raise you two shillings.' Jack knew he couldn't back out, but couldn't believe it when Sinéad rummaged in her purse and took four sixpences out, placing them in the pot with a defiant look. He followed, cursing under his breath and hoping Leahy was bluffing. Leahy placed his cards on the table, slowly, one by one. 'Four tens,' he said triumphantly.

'Beats me,' said Jack, forgetting it wasn't up to him anyway. Leahy was about to reach for the pot.

Sinéad said calmly, 'I think that's mine, actually.' She laid four queens on the table.

'Bloody hell!' said Leahy. 'That was a stroke of luck.' Sinéad smiled at him innocently. For the next few rounds Leahy won steadily and built up quite a pile of coins. Then Sinéad won again, this time with a full house. This pattern repeated itself for about an hour.

It was Jack's turn to deal again and Leahy was ahead, with quite a nice stack of coins in front of him. He had relaxed considerably and was smiling for the first time in the evening.

He opened the bidding with sixpence, and everyone followed. Sinéad hesitated, then took a deep breath and raised the stakes to one shilling. Leahy looked at her intently and slowly pushed another sixpence into the pot. Jack only had a pair of sevens in his hand but he followed and asked her how many cards she wanted.

'I'll stick with these,' she said quietly. Leahy shot her another glance.

'One card,' he said. Jack dealt him his card and took his three. Leahy seemed pleased with himself and sat back in his chair. 'It's up to you, Sinéad,' he said, grinning.

She looked intently at her cards, frowning, then counted her money slowly. She pushed a shilling piece out and looked calmly at Leahy.

'I'm out,' said Mulcahy and threw his cards on the table, then sat back, obviously glad to see Leahy being challenged.

'I'll see that,' said Leahy, and then, after a pause, added, 'and I'll raise you half a crown.' Jack hesitated. He knew he had no chance of winning the hand, but somehow felt it would be unfair to leave Sinéad to play on her own against Leahy. But then again three and sixpence was a lot of money and he had been hoping to invite her for a drink afterwards, so...

'I'm out too,' he said finally and Sinéad looked at him with mild amusement.

She looked down at her pile of coins. 'I'll see your half a crown and raise you five shillings,' she said to Leahy.

Leahy looked at her, and then at Mulcahy and Jack, and started to laugh. 'If you think you're going to take all my money tonight, young lady, you're very much mistaken. I've been watching you, and I'm on to you. You only ever bet when you have a really good hand, so you're not going to catch me out this time. If you want to be a good poker player you need to know when to bluff, and not let everyone know what's in your hand.' He laid his cards on the table and stood up. 'Time for bed, said Zebedee,' he said, gathering up what was left of his winnings.

Leahy walked off, followed shortly later by Mulcahy, leaving Sinéad and Jack sitting in the corner of the bar. He looked at her curiously. 'Were you bluffing then?'

'Maybe,' she said. He leaned across and tried to look at her cards, but she slapped his hand and said, 'You know you can't do that.'

'How long have you been playing poker?' he asked her, his curiosity aroused now.

'All my life,' she said, laughing. 'I was practically reared with four male cousins, so I had to learn to stand up for myself.'

Jack looked at her more closely. She was attractive enough, but not turn-around-in-the-street material, and she wasn't the type of girl he would normally notice. She looked like she might be studying architecture or history of art. He knew the type – long hair, duffel coat, desert boots and cord Levis. Except she didn't have a duffel coat. She had an unusual dark green raincoat in some shiny fabric. She looked cool – not cool in the current slang sense, more aloof and self-contained. She returned his gaze with that faintly amused air.

'Would you like a drink?' he asked, trying to sound casual.

'Not really,' she said, 'but I could do with some fresh air and a cigarette.'

'Do you mind if I come with you? It's quite mild outside for this time of year. We could go for a walk around the lake,' he said, probably a bit too eagerly. A walk around the lake! *Listen to yourself, McDonagh,* he thought – *suppose she says no.* But she didn't. She stood up and grabbed her bag and coat.

'Come on then.' On their way out of the hotel they bumped into Hollis.

'Where are you two off to at this hour?' he said, slurring his words a little.

'Just getting some air,' said Sinéad.

As they walked past, he grabbed Jack's sleeve. 'Mc-Donagh,' he said, 'Come here – just a quick word.' He took him by the elbow and whispered. 'You lay so much as a finger on her, McDonagh, and I swear I will have both your legs broken.'

'She seems quite capable of looking after herself, Hollis.'

'I'm warning you, McDonagh – I'm deadly serious here.'

'Fine, fine,' he said, shaking off his grip, 'I'll be a perfect gentleman'.

Sinéad was standing outside and had already lit a cigarette. 'What was all that about?' she asked.

'Your friend Hollis is being over-protective.'

'He's a sweetie pie,' she said, smiling.

'A sweetie pie?' he echoed. 'You can't be serious. That guy is a cold, calculating psychopath. He'd walk all over his grandmother to get what he wants.'

'I think I know him better than you,' she said. 'Anyway, that's what they say about you too, but watching you playing poker you all seem quite harmless. It's an act, isn't it?'

She took a packet of Majors out of her pocket and offered him one. 'No thanks,' he said, 'I prefer these.'

She watched as he took one of his cigarettes. 'Rothman's,' she said, 'why is it that all you southside boys smoke those?'

He began to think they might be getting off on the wrong foot and wondered why he had invited her to go for a walk in the first place, when she put out her cigarette and said, 'Right then? Shall we go for that walk?'

She pulled on her coat and he helped her awkwardly. 'Won't you be cold? Isn't that a bit light for this time of year?' he said, touching the fabric, which felt a bit rubbery and thin. 'Nice coat, though. It really suits you.'

'Thank you,' Sinéad replied. 'It was a gift from a special person and it keeps me warm in more ways than one, if that makes sense.'

It didn't, but he left the subject, not sure he really wanted to know who the special person was.

They set off down the path from the hotel towards the lake. Looking back, he would like to have been able to say it was a moonlit night, but it wasn't. It was quite mild and a bit misty. They hadn't heard about energy efficiency back then and there were lights all down the path and even half-way around the lake, as far as he could see. They walked in silence for a while until they reached the edge of the lake. Sinéad stopped and looked across the still black expanse of water.

'It looks a bit eerie on the other side, doesn't it? I hope you're not afraid of the dark, Mr McDonagh.' Again, he felt irritated at the way she always seemed to be mocking him. He wasn't used to girls talking to him that way. In fact if he were to be truthful he would say that as a pure product of Catholic single-sex education, he wasn't really used to girls talking to him much at all, and most of the conversations he'd had with them were fairly stilted and uninteresting.

He lit another cigarette, pointedly not offering her one, and asked, trying not to sound too interested, 'So, what part of Dublin do you come from?' *Good God, what kind of banal question is that, McDonagh,* he thought. He knew he'd have to do better if he wanted to impress her.

'The wrong part,' she said. 'The northside. You know, that place on the other side of the Liffey where the pearls are fake and the...' She stopped and laughed at his expression. 'You know the rest of it, don't you?'

Of course he did, but he pretended he didn't. 'There's nothing wrong with the northside,' he lied. 'I have cousins who live in Howth and a friend in Malahide.' He didn't tell her he had only been to his cousins' place once, or that his friend lived in a large Georgian house in the old, posher part of Malahide.

'You know that James Joyce was very fond of the north-side, don't you?' she continued, ignoring his attempt to please.

> '*O, it was out by Donnycarney,*
> *When the bat flew from tree to tree,*
> *My love and I did walk together,*
> *And sweet were the words she said to me.*'

He looked at her blankly.

'Poem thirty one from *Chamber Music*. Never heard of it? You're not the only one. My father recites it at family gatherings.' Jack couldn't for the life of him imagine anyone, least of all James Joyce, writing a poem about Donnycarney. In fact, he didn't even know that James Joyce had written poetry. He changed the subject quickly.

'So, tell me, why are you studying at Trinity?'

'Because it's closer to Clontarf than UCD now that the campus is moving to Belfield. And because Business Administration sounds so much better than Commerce.' Again that mocking tone. But he was relieved that she said Clontarf and not Donnycarney or, worse, Artane, with its industrial school. Mind you, his only experience of Clontarf was driving through it on his way to Howth, but it seemed quite leafy, the sort of place where you wouldn't need to lock the car doors when you stopped at a traffic light.

'I thought Catholics weren't allowed to go to Trinity.'

'Who said I was a Catholic?'

He was really putting his foot in it here, he thought.

'Of course I'm a Catholic…aren't we all in this great little country? Catholic, but rarely Christian, that is.'

He decided to ignore the last remark.

'Did you get a dispensation from the Archbishop?' he asked.

'No…' she said slowly.

'But…'

'But I could be excommunicated? Is that what you were going to say?'

'Yes, I was always told that you could only go to Trinity if you received a special dispensation from the Archbishop, and you would only get that for very serious reasons.'

'Well, times have changed. I've been there for several months now and no Spanish inquisition has turned up on my doorstep,' she said. 'I presume the Archbishop has other things to worry about anyway. I mean, I doubt if the fact that I'm studying Business Administration in a university with a Protestant work ethic will bring the institutions of the Catholic church crashing down around our ears. If it was theology, that would be another matter.'

'Or medicine,' he added.

'Medicine?' She looked at him sharply.

'Yes, you know, different attitudes on moral issues. Contraception.'

'I did actually study medicine for a year in UCD,' she said. 'Pre-med.' He looked at her in disbelief.

'But I never saw you.'

'That's because us northside girls are invisible to you lot, plus I'm younger than you and you spent all your time playing rugby and drinking yourself senseless in the bar,' she said.

So she had noticed him, he thought. That must mean something.

'And if it's not indiscreet, why did you leave?' he asked. 'A woman of your shining intellect can't possibly have failed her exams.'

'Well, I did, actually.' She looked at him defiantly and pulled another cigarette out of her bag. 'But I did something much worse too, and it just wasn't possible to go back after the summer'.

'I'm all ears,' he said, but she wouldn't be drawn.

They walked a bit further until they reached a bench. Sinéad sat down and looked at him. 'Tell me about yourself, Jack McDonagh,' she said. 'Am I right in thinking that you're not quite as dangerous as your reputation makes you out to be?'

'You might be,' he said. 'But there's only one way to find out.'

'And what's that?' she asked.

'Meet me in Dublin when we get back. We could go to the pictures or have a drink.'

'Under the clock at Clery's? It's not too far into the northside so you should be safe enough.'

'Why not? Monday week? Eight o'clock?'

Chapter Ten

JACK WOKE FEELING UNCHARACTERISTICALLY nervous. He lay in bed looking forward to the evening ahead, wondering what he was going to wear, what film they would go to see, whether he would take her home afterwards, whether she would let him kiss her goodnight.

He heard the telephone ringing downstairs, and shortly afterwards his reverie was interrupted by his mother knocking on the bedroom door.

'Jack? Time to get up. We have a lot to do today.'

When he finally trudged down for breakfast, Mrs Murphy, the daily, was polishing the big square hall and his sister Sarah was sitting in the kitchen with all the silver spread out on the table, checking for tarnish. His mother was on the phone, speaking excitedly to someone.

Jack was halfway through his cereal when his mother came into the kitchen and sat down at the table opposite him, looking very pleased with herself.

'I had a phone call from Mrs Stewart this morning,' she said, looking down and straightening the tablecloth as she spoke. She always did that when she wanted to avoid a discussion. 'Your father and I have been talking to the Stewarts a lot recently, and we were saying that since you and Lorna have been going out for quite a while now, we could start thinking about you getting engaged. We've invited them over here this evening to discuss the plans.'

Jack knew Lorna from his holidays in Ballybunion. They'd pretty much grown up together, as their families spent all their summer holidays in the same seaside town, renting two neighbouring houses every year in August. Her family represented everything his parents were not, but constantly aspired to be. There were six children: four boys and two girls, with Lorna being the youngest. Her father was a leading academic in medical science who they hoped would be a great help to Jack in his career. Her mother was descended from some landed gentry and the rambling house they lived in in Ranelagh was full of inherited antiques and paintings of sour-faced ancestors. Everything seemed to come easily to them – their wealth, their manners, their friends, their brilliance.

It had seemed normal that when he needed a partner for a school dance, he would ask her and that she would accept – which she did, perhaps a little too eagerly in retrospect. From then on, she seemed to assume that they were a couple, and he was proud enough to be accepted by her family that he brushed any misgivings aside. Besides, it seemed to him that the relationship had given him new standing within his own family and among his friends.

Jack put down his spoon, feeling mild panic rising. 'But I'm going out this evening,' he said.

'Not anymore, you're not. Where were you thinking of going anyway?' she asked sharply. He floundered, trying to think of a credible excuse, but clearly there was no discussion possible. 'You can see your friends anytime. You'll just have to tell them you can't make it,' she said as she walked off to give further orders to Mrs M.

He quickly reviewed the options open to him. He didn't have Sinéad's telephone number – he didn't even know where she lived – all he knew was that it was on the northside somewhere – had she mentioned Clontarf? He stood up and walked to the hall where the phone book was kept in a mahogany telephone table. He started to trawl through the Murrays but there were hundreds in the Dublin area, and he didn't know her father's name. And anyway, they could be ex-directory, like his own parents. His mother thought that was the height of class.

No matter which way he looked at it, there was no way he could get into the city to meet her and back again in time for the evening his mother was setting up.

'I have to see someone,' he muttered as he brushed past his sister Sarah, who looked at him coldly.

'I hope it's not a girl,' she said. 'You don't know what side your bread is buttered on, Jack McDonagh.' Not for the first time he wished she would evaporate – she had a knack of getting inside your head in a way that was profoundly irritating.

He pulled on his jacket and left the house, slamming the door behind him, then went up to the local shops where he smoked two cigarettes as he stood outside the public telephone box. The woman in there was clearly recounting her life story, and the person at the other end could well have died of boredom, judging by the one-sided nature of the call. During that time, several of his mother's friends passed by, looking at him with interest and probably wondering why he wasn't using his own phone at home. He had no doubt that this interesting fact would be reported back to his mother.

When he finally got into the booth he phoned Hollis, but it was a flatmate who answered, and he said Hollis was out and didn't know when he would be back – perhaps not until the next day. In desperation, Jack leafed through the telephone directory to find the number for Trinity and phoned the SRC office, but the girl who answered said she couldn't give out private phone numbers without the student's consent.

He leaned back against the glass and cursed his luck. Of all the days his mother had to choose... By now there were three people waiting to use the phone, so he left, bought some more cigarettes and went down to the seafront to think.

The solution was obvious. He would have to send someone to meet her. He trudged back to the phone box and began phoning all his friends, one after another. The only one to pick up was Paul Fitzpatrick, a former schoolmate, who didn't need much persuading.

'So can I take her to the cinema in your place?' he asked. 'She must be a fine thing if you're so anxious not to stand her up. But, seriously, Jack, under the clock at Clery's? What a cliché! You disappoint me.'

'Shut up, Fitzer,' Jack said. 'I just want you to meet her, tell her something has come up and that I can't make it tonight. I honestly don't think she's your type anyway. Oh, and get her phone number, would you, so I can call her.'

His mother's evening went off as planned. His parents and the Stewarts agreed that they should marry after graduating and Jack abandoned all thoughts of resistance. It seemed like the right thing to do, and all his friends were getting married. Mr Stewart suggested that the honeymoon should be in Italy, as he had a friend who was doing archaeological research there who could organize things. The following day, Jack went into the city with his mother to buy an engagement ring; a sapphire. 'Mrs Stewart told me that blue is Lorna's favourite colour,' she said. That evening, he presented her with the little box and she feigned surprise as she opened it. She looked very pretty and happy and he asked himself why he was even thinking about another woman when he had everything he had ever wanted right here. As far as love was concerned, he wasn't even sure what it meant. He admired her, she was bright and attractive and everyone said they made a lovely couple. He was lucky, he thought. He owed a great deal to his own family, and now he would be part of another one, even more successful. He felt validated.

A few days later, the engagement announcement with a very flattering photo of the two of them appeared in a prominent place in the *Irish Times* for all to see, and his fate was sealed.

He phoned Fitzpatrick, who took great pleasure in telling him that he had waited for almost half an hour before some girl called Karen had turned up with a dodgy-looking boyfriend in tow to tell him Sinéad couldn't make it either. Jack was annoyed and relieved at the same time, and over the next few days he walked through the grounds of Trinity College a few times, and even made totally unnecessary appointments to meet with Hollis and his crew, trying to convince himself that it wasn't because he secretly hoped he would bump into her. Once or twice he thought he saw that green raincoat, but after a few rebuffs from startled students he put it down to his overactive imagination.

Chapter Eleven

March 1971

SINÉAD'S NIGHTMARES BEGAN ABOUT two months later. It was always the same scenario – she was in the train station, on the platform, holding a baby in her arms and screaming as her mother dragged the baby away from her. She would wake up drenched in perspiration and the images would haunt her throughout the day.

She felt a desperate need to talk to someone, but decided she couldn't talk to her parents – especially her mother – about the dreams. After much hesitation, she made an appointment to see the college psychiatrist. Ironically, she knew him quite well through her role as student welfare officer within the SRC. She was supposed to help other students and never imagined she might actually need help herself.

If he was surprised to hear her story, he hid it well. Sinéad, who had worried that it would be awkward talking to someone she knew, found herself gradually relaxing in his presence, responding to his gentle questioning. It definitely helped, being able to unburden herself, and the nightmares began to recede. She saw him three times before the incident. She was sitting on the bus on her way to college. The bus was stopped in traffic and she was watching a woman pushing a pram in the street. Then as the bus moved off something caught her eye. She looked back and she saw a flash of yellow – a jacket? – in the pram. Convinced it was Lorcan, she jumped off at the next stop and ran back towards the woman. As she approached, she realised that the child was almost a year old and quite obviously a girl. The woman looked at her in terror.

'I thought you were someone else...' Sinéad mumbled an apology and turned around, her cheeks burning. She walked the rest of the way to college and went straight to the doctor, once again feeling she was no longer in control of her life. He called her parents and between them they decided that she should go into a private clinic for what he called a 'sleep cure'.

When she looked back, all she could remember from her week in the clinic was the blissful sensation of slipping in and out of consciousness and of being far away from everything and everybody she knew. Somebody – probably one of the nurses – had suggested she start to write everything down. It would help her come to terms with things and it would also be something she could give to her child later, to help him understand. And once she had finished writing she could lock her journal away, both literally and symbolically. The idea that she might one day meet her child again gave her hope.

The sleep cure calmed her down and the nightmares eventually stopped. Sinéad went back to college and began to prepare in earnest for her exams. Some of her friends were planning to spend the following summer in the States, working as waitresses, so she decided to apply for a job there too.

In May, she got a phone call.

'Emily? It's Jacintha.'

'Jacintha! Hi, how are you? *Where* are you? It's great to hear from you!'

'I'm doing really well. I've been meaning to call you for ages. I just wanted to thank you for everything – the advice and all that. I don't think I would have had the guts to go through with this if you hadn't encouraged me. Fintan is fine, too and – you'll never believe this – his birthmark is beginning to fade. It's much less noticeable now. When I think that I almost let him go… But anyway, how are you? Are you back at college? Are you still studying medicine?'

'Yes, I'm back studying, but I've changed courses. I want to finish up as quickly as possible and get out of this place.'

'I know what you mean. It's a lot easier here in England, you know. People aren't so judgmental. And I've been so lucky to have my sister. I've managed to find a job in an office, and she minds Fintan while I'm working.'

They talked for about an hour and when Sinéad finally put the phone down, a plan was already beginning to form in her head. She was supposed to sign the adoption papers in July, but she would put the agency off and try to gain a bit more time. Then she would earn as much money as possible when she went to the States – some students she knew came back with enough money to get them through a whole year of college. She would take her baby back and go to England

and find a job. She had cousins living quite near Jacintha, and she knew she could manage. She could always go back to college later.

Sinéad finished the term and felt she had done well in her exams. She was beginning to feel excited about her upcoming trip to the States. She had heard nothing from the agency and crossed her fingers, hoping they had forgotten about her.

The day before she was due to fly out, her parents went out for a walk, leaving her to finish her packing, so she was alone when the phone rang.

'Sinéad? Miss Brennan here.'

Sinéad froze.

'We need to discuss you signing the papers – the final consent order. It's been over six months now.'

'I'm so sorry, Miss Brennan,' said Sinéad, trying to keep the panic out of her voice, 'but I'm leaving for the States tomorrow morning, so I can't do it just now. I'll sign them when I get back.'

Without missing a beat, Miss Brennan replied that she had plenty of time to come in to sign the papers that afternoon. Clutching at a straw, Sinéad pointed out that there was a bus strike on in Dublin and there was no way she could get into the city. Even if her parents had been there, they hadn't got a car. She repeated that she would sign the papers when she got back.

There was a long silence at the other end before Miss Brennan spoke again.

'That's not possible, Sinéad. You knew very well that you had to sign these papers. You're putting me in a very difficult position.' Her tone had changed and her voice was harder.

'You know what will happen, don't you? You're an intel-ligent girl and all this was explained to you before. If the papers are not signed in the next week, the adoptive family may not wish to keep him any longer, running the risk of having him taken away from them. That means we will have to place him in an orphanage.'

Sinéad tried desperately to think of an answer, but Miss Brennan continued.

'Is that what you want for your child?' she asked. 'To be taken from a secure and loving family and put in an insti-tution? To destroy not only his life but also the adoptive family's, just because you won't sign a paper?'

'No,' Sinéad whispered, feeling trapped. 'My parents aren't here. I can't...'

'I'll tell you what. Stay where you are and I'll drive out to your house. I can be there in twenty minutes and we can talk about it.'

Sinéad paced up and down in the house. She didn't know what to do and had nobody to talk to. She prayed her par-ents wouldn't come back before Miss Brennan arrived, as she dreaded placing them in this dilemma. She could just see her mother's face crumpling and offering again to take care of Lorcan. But the woman's threats rang in her head. What if she really did destroy his life as well as her mother's? Precisely twenty minutes later, a car pulled up in front of the house and Miss Brennan rang the bell.

When Sinéad finally answered the door she found that Miss Brennan's tone had changed. 'Sinéad,' she said, almost gently. 'Come with me. We can talk in the car. I'm sure you don't want to worry your parents.'

Sinéad grabbed her bag and followed her to her car. They drove for a while in silence and then Miss Brennan pulled over and switched off the engine.

'I know this is very difficult for you, Sinéad, but we've talked about this before and you know this is the best solution, especially for Lorcan. They're lovely people, and they'll give him the best in life.' She tapped the steering wheel for a moment, then turned to face Sinéad. 'You'll break their hearts if you don't sign the papers, and it wouldn't be good for Lorcan either to be taken away from that lovely home and put in an orphanage. He's settled in really well, and he's such a happy little baby. You really need to think about your child and put his interests first.'

Sinéad nodded. She knew all this.

Miss Brennan switched on the engine and began to drive again. She talked about all the babies she had placed and the wonderful lives they had. She talked about all the mothers who had gone on to get married and have other children, happy that they had done the right thing.

'You're young, Sinéad. You have your whole life in front of you and you'll meet a nice boy and settle down. You can have other children. These people can't have children – that's why they want to adopt Lorcan. You are giving them a great gift.'

By the time they arrived at the registrar's office, Sinéad was wracked with guilt at the thought of signing her child away, but at the same time unable to respond to the arguments Miss Brennan put so forcefully to her. She signed the papers in silence in front of a stony-faced official, and Miss Brennan told her she had done the right thing. Their business done, she called a taxi and sent her home, paying the fare in advance.

Sinéad got the taxi driver to drop her at Dollymount strand and went for a long walk, the cold sea air blowing her hair and biting against her face. She walked to the edge of the water and looked out across Dublin Bay, the grey expanse drawing her in. She had read about people who just walked into the sea and drowned themselves, and wondered how it would feel. She imagined the people on the beach watching in horror, the lifeguard being called, her limp body lying dead on the sand. She imagined her parents' grief, the questions they would face, and their guilt.

'Sinéad!' A familiar voice shocked her out of her musings.

She turned around and with a sinking feeling saw two former classmates from her school waving at her

'Hi,' she said, waving back,

'Haven't seen you for ages,' said one. 'You look terrific. How's college?'

'Oh it's great, yeah. But listen, I can't stop. I'm off to New York tomorrow, going to the States to work for the summer. I was just getting some fresh air before I head off. Catch up when I get back?'

'New York? It's well for you, Sinead Murray. You students have a great life.'

She left the two girls looking after her enviously.

She flew to New York the following day and travelled on to New Hampshire by bus. She arrived at the hotel where she was to spend the rest of the summer working and trying to blank out the previous year. Most of the seasonal staff were just like her, young students trying to earn enough money to get through the next year of college, and they made their own entertainment, sitting around a campfire in the evenings, listening to one of the girls doing a fair impression of Carole King. The hotel owners' son, who was about sixteen, fell in love with them all and took them to see drive-in movies in his father's enormous car. She earned far more money that she ever imagined possible – the Americans were very generous with tips, especially when being served by a genuine Irish colleen with a cute accent – and she went back to college at the end of the summer to finish her degree.

As soon as she graduated, she took the first job she was offered, in a large international organisation, and left the country, determined to put it all behind her.

Chapter Twelve

Dublin, 1984

IT WAS A RAINY Friday afternoon in November, and Jack McDonagh was sitting in his office in the Department of Health, where he worked as a senior adviser to Jim Dempsey, the Minister. They got on well, despite their different backgrounds and the age difference. Jim's people were farmers in Tipperary, the same area where Jack's mother had grown up. Unlike Jack, he'd been educated by the Christian Brothers, and while he shone academically at school, he remained a bit naive and gauche socially.

Reforming the health sector was a top priority for the government at the time, and one of Jim's stated aims was to visit all the EU countries where the health system actually worked, meeting experts and professionals in the field. He hadn't travelled much beyond Ireland before becoming a minister and there were apocryphal stories doing the rounds about his lack of social skills. One of these concerned an Irish politician seated next to a French minister at a dinner in Brussels. The Frenchman picks up his knife and fork, smiles at his neighbour and says *'bon appetit'*, to which the

Irishman responds by introducing himself and holding out his hand. It was an urban legend, of course, but it could easily have been applied to Jim.

He walked into Jack's office, looking pensive. 'How's it going Jack?' he said, settling his large frame into the fake Louis XVI chair that Mrs McDonagh had given her son to impress visiting dignitaries. 'Still working at half six on a Friday? Fancy a pint? I have something I want to run past you.'

'Why not?' Jack said. 'I've pretty much finished up for the week – it's been quiet with you out of the country.'

He gathered his papers into a pile and walked into his secretary's office, dropping them into her inbox. She had left a long time before, he noted, no doubt to pick up her children from school.

As they walked out of the building, Jim stopping every minute to shake some hand or other, enquire after someone's wife, child or grandmother, confident and at ease on his home ground, Jack wondered vaguely what his new idea might be. Since taking on the job, Jim had been determined to make his mark and was always coming up with new schemes to revolutionize the department, the government, the country even. In the main, these schemes were quietly but firmly quashed by senior civil servants.

Jim would often invite his closest aides for a drink and discuss his schemes beforehand. Sometimes he listened to their advice, but even if they had managed to convince him that they weren't workable, he would often go ahead anyway 'just for the craic'. He had been away all week in Geneva at a meeting organized by the World Health Organization, so Jack imagined he had all kinds of new hare-brained new ideas up his sleeve.

They walked around the corner to their local pub, avoided the usual crowd of journalists and party hacks standing at the bar and made their way into the snug. With pints of Guinness in front of them, Jim leaned forward, glancing right and left to check nobody could hear him, and whispered.

'Jack, I met a woman in Geneva.'

Jack froze. This was not at all what he had expected and it made him feel uncomfortable. He knew Jim's wife Caroline well; her sister Deirdre was married to one of Lorna's brothers, a fact that had helped him get the job.

Seeing the look on Jack's face, Jim straightened up and wagged his finger at him, laughing loudly.

'One-track mind, Jack! No, no, it's not what you're thinking at all. I'm not like you! I met a woman that I'd like to have heading my new think tank.'

Jim had been bending ears about this think tank for ages, but nobody really expected it to materialize. In the past there had been lots of committees and working parties working on reform, but governments came and went and their offices were littered with unfinished projects. Jack vaguely remembered a drunken conversation with Jim in which they'd agreed that they really needed to bring in someone from outside, unconnected with the various political mafias.

'So, is she Swiss then?' Jack asked, relieved that he didn't have to listen to details of an extra-marital affair.

Jim sat back and looked at him, scratching his head. 'Do you know, Jack, I'm not really sure – I think she could be

French actually,' he said. 'Or maybe Belgian. Anyway, that's irrelevant. I want you to go over there and convince her to take the job.'

'Me? Why me?'

'Well, for starters you know more about this job than I do – and you speak French well.'

He lifted his drink and grinned as Jack looked at him through narrowed eyes. Jim was up to something – he knew that Jack spoke hardly any French. Although the bullshit about knowing more about the job than he did was probably true.

The door to the snug opened, breaking the silence as the room filled with the sound of clinking glasses and that slightly too-raucous laughter associated with a surfeit of Guinness. A man and a woman walked in.

'Jim, Jack, how are you? Hey Jim, I really need to talk to you.'

It was the party leader, a smallish, thin man with grey hair, bristling with an air of authority which belied his looks. Jack often thought that if he had to pick him out in an identity parade, he'd be the one he wouldn't recognise.

He had his secretary in tow. Jack had seen her a couple of times in the typing pool and she beamed at him as if they were old friends.

'Jack, why don't we leave these two to their chat and go and have a drink outside?'

For once, he was lost for words and rose from his seat to follow her.

'Make sure Dympna gets home safely, Jack,' said Jim, winking at him while the other man tried to look uncon-cerned.

Dympna took Jack's arm as they crossed the bar and whispered, 'Let's go somewhere quieter – I need to run something by you too.' This seemed a little forward, given that he had never met her before, but it was Friday, Lorna had gone off for the weekend with the children and he was feeling reckless.

He only half listened to Dympna. It turned out she wanted to ask his advice about whether or not she should stay as the party leader's secretary or take up some other important job she had been offered. He couldn't remember what advice he gave her, but it must have been good, as several years later she became the Party Leader's wife, having disposed of the previous incumbent with calculating efficiency. What he did remember was that he finished the evening in her very tasteful mews house at the back of Leeson Street, and that she was very good in bed.

The following Monday he was back in the office bright and early. Brenda, his secretary, was in before him. She was an excellent secretary, and extremely efficient when she wasn't leaving early to pick her kids up. He never needed to explain things twice, and it often struck him that she could probably do the job as well as him.

'You're off to Geneva this week.' She smiled and picked up an envelope from her desk. 'I have your tickets here – it's a bit tight, I'm afraid. A very early departure from Dublin and a late-ish return the same evening. It should give you enough time for lunch and an afternoon meeting, though. The woman you're meeting is a Madame De Clercq – here's a note with her contact details. The boss wants you to sound her out, see if she would be willing to take on running the think tank for a minimum of a year.'

'De Clercq,' he mused. 'Is that a French name?'

'Belgian, I think,' said Brenda.

'And the De – doesn't that mean she's some kind of aristocrat?'

'I think that's only if it's 'de' with a small d,' said Brenda.

'You should be working in protocol, you know,' he said and she laughed.

'Be careful what you wish for, Jack.'

He had a speech to write for the boss, so he didn't give much thought to Madame De Clercq or his meeting with her until later that afternoon. He decided to give her a call, but got through to some fierce German-sounding female who was obviously not prepared to get her boss out of a meeting to speak to some underling.

'Madame De Clercq is expecting you tomorrow. You will have lunch,' she said, making it sound like a threat.

When he arrived home that evening, there were clothes and toys strewn all over the hall and Fiona, his eldest daughter, was sitting on the stairs, frowning. He had a special affection for Fiona, perhaps because her personality was the most like his own, even if she had inherited her mother's good looks.

'Where's Mummy?' he asked, picking her up and straightening her school tie.

'Having a rest,' she said, shrugging her shoulders. 'She's been in bed all day.'

He'd been here before, he reflected as he trudged up to the bedroom. Lorna had been having bouts of depression for several years now, and he would regularly come in to find the two children left to their own devices while she lay in bed upstairs. He suspected she might also be drinking, but if she was she took care to hide the evidence. At one point he took on a daily help to make sure the girls had some supervision, but Lorna didn't like having a stranger in the house and got rid of her. Nowadays he usually managed to find someone to come in on an ad hoc basis, but sometimes he had no option but to take the girls to the office with him and Brenda would end up looking after them while he worked. It was not a subject they ever discussed openly, either with Lorna's family or his. In any case, they would never have believed him, as she always managed to behave normally when there were other people around.

Lorna was up when he entered the bedroom, and Isabelle, the youngest, was sitting on the bed in her pyjamas. He wondered vaguely if she had been dressed at all that day.

'I was just about to get dinner,' Lorna said. 'My sister came over earlier and brought a beef casserole.'

'Have you been feeling ill?' he asked.

'Oh, I'm fine,' she said, looking away. 'I just didn't feel like going out today, what with this awful weather.'

'Look, Lorna, I've got to go to Geneva tomorrow, so if you're not feeling well perhaps we ought to call your mother and ask her to come over and stay.'

'No, no,' she said nervously, 'it's OK. Olivia said she could come over anytime I needed her.'

Olivia was Lorna's best, and probably her only real friend. They had been to school together. Olivia was single, from a moneyed background, and only worked when it suited her, in some art gallery or other. She made no secret of her dislike of Jack. He made a mental note to try

116

yet again to find a more permanent back-up arrangement for days like these.

The girls played up during dinner and it was late when he and Lorna finally sat down together. He tried to tell Lorna about his day at the office and to elicit some information from her in return, but her answers were monosyllabic and she displayed no interest in his trip to Geneva. When he attempted to find out what her plans were for the rest of the week, she replied evasively and finally said she was tired and went to bed. It had become a pattern. Conversations were confined to school runs, family gatherings and basically anything except their relationship. He had long ago given up trying to broach the subject of her going back to work.

Lorna had studied medicine too – they'd been in the same class and she was usually first in the exams. Learning by rote was her forte and she could reproduce with astonishing accuracy pages and pages of technical text. She could have had a great career as a specialist in something like ophthalmology, but she gave up work a short time after their marriage to devote herself to rearing the children. There was tacit agreement never to discuss the hysterical scene she'd once made in an operating theatre, and this was never mentioned as a possible reason for her leaving the profession.

There was another subject they never discussed, and that was their wedding night.

At the time, Jack had found it rather quaint and even charming when she refused to have sex before marriage. However, after a disappointing wedding night, which he put down to fatigue and stress, the even worse honeymoon and six subsequent weeks of failed attempts to consummate the marriage, she finally agreed to see a doctor. He never asked what exactly happened in the doctor's office that day, but after that they were at least physically able to make love – although the act never matched his expectations and she never seemed to be particularly interested.

Shortly after their wedding, his sister Sarah announced her engagement to Lorna's brother James. He knew then that his fate was well and truly sealed, that his life was mapped out for him and that any thoughts he might have of breaking loose were unrealistic. Ireland was an incestuous place at the best of times.

Chapter Thirteen

JACK SLEPT MOST OF the way from London to Geneva after getting up at dawn to catch the connecting flight. In the taxi, he realized that he hadn't read any of the briefing notes that Brenda had prepared. He began to rummage in his briefcase when the car came to a stop in front of a large building with lots of flags flying outside. He hadn't realized the trip from the airport would be so short, and stepped out feeling uncharacteristically nervous, fuming about having been landed with this ridiculous task.

The formalities at the entrance were minimal, and five minutes later he was seated in the Sturmfuhrer's office, waiting to be ushered into the inner sanctum. He looked around, taking in the expensive furnishings. This Madame De Clercq obviously had an important position, as her secretary's office was better than his own, but then he supposed that these international organizations had money to splash about. It had often occurred to him that he should try to get a job in the UN or the EU, thinking it might be just what Lorna needed – to get away from the family and give her some kind of challenge.

His musings were interrupted as Mrs Sturmfuhrer's telephone rang. Five lights lit up and he wondered who all these people were, calling this woman. She spoke in rapid French for a few moments and then switched to English.

'Madame De Clercq will see you now, Mr McDonagh.'

There was nobody in the office when he went in, and he hesitated to sit down. It was a spacious room, with floor-to-ceiling windows looking out over the lake. Back home in Dublin, the number of office windows was in direct proportion to the level of importance in the hierarchy, and he imagined it was the same here. There was a large desk with two heaps of files and an expensive-looking red leather-bound notebook lying open, a fountain pen beside it. The furniture was modern and sleek. By the window there was a small black leather couch and a chrome and glass coffee table. The whole setup had what some of his colleagues would call a zen-like atmosphere, although he noticed the shelves behind the desk were quite cluttered with papers and books. There was a large black handbag on the floor, with a brightly-coloured silk scarf attached to the strap. It was an Hermès scarf – Jack knew that because Lorna always dropped heavy hints about how her brother always brought one back for his wife whenever he went to Paris.

A dark green coat was hanging on the coat stand by the door and something jogged his memory. He was just leaning forward to have a closer look when the door opened quietly and a woman walked in.

Her hair was different; shorter, with one of those fashionable geometric cuts, and the colour – what he remembered as fair – had been enhanced with some subtle blonde streaks. But there was no mistaking those cool grey-blue eyes, the amused look.

He tried to remember how long it had been since they had seen each other.

'Sinéad...Sinéad Murray.'

'Well, well, if it isn't Jack McDonagh the poker player. I had a feeling it might be you, but I wasn't sure. You haven't changed – except for the clothes of course.' That smile again.

'Speaking of which...' Recovering his composure, he pointed at the green raincoat hanging by the door. 'I seem to remember you wearing that in Killarney. Don't they pay you properly in the WHO?'

She shook her head and laughed. 'I'm very attached to that coat.' She waved airily at the sofa by the window, and he sat down, still disconcerted, as she relaxed into the chair next to him.

'So, Jim sent you to headhunt me after all?'

'He said you were French or Belgian or something.'

She raised an eyebrow quizzically. 'Is that relevant? I thought the whole idea was to get someone in from outside.'

'Of course not, but you know what I mean.'

She had him in a corner and she was obviously enjoying it. He cursed Jim mentally for setting him up and wondered just how much he knew.

She smiled, enjoying his confusion, then stood up, walked over to the desk and picked up a file. 'I only said I thought I might have known someone with that name, if it's his loyalty that you're worried about. Not that that matters anyway. So let's talk about this think tank then, shall we?'

Sinéad had clearly done her homework on the project, and fired questions at him on the timescale, the budget, her exact role and who the other members would be. While waiting outside her office, Jack had managed to flick though the briefing note Brenda had prepared for him so he was able to answer most of her questions and just winged it for the others. Throughout the discussion she scribbled notes in the bright red notebook, barely looking at him. It was quite disconcerting – a bit like a job interview or a visit to the doctor.

Finally, she laid her pen down and looked at him. 'And where do you fit in to all this, Jack?'

'What do you mean?' he asked.

'Will you be a member of the think tank or its support staff – and would I report to you or to the Minister?'

'I'll be working liaison with the Minister's office, so I'll take part in the work and you'd report directly to the Minister,' he said. This seemed to please her.

After they'd spent another half hour looking at the proposed terms of reference for the think tank, Sinéad looked at her watch and asked him what time his flight back was. He was due to leave on the 6 pm flight to London so they decided they could continue the discussion over lunch. She called out to the Sturmfuhrer and asked her to check if there was a table free in the dining room. They were in luck, apparently, and she stood up, smoothed down her dress and picked up her bag.

'*Allons-y,*' she said, smiling.

To get to the dining room they had to walk through the cafeteria, and Jack was impressed by the ease with which she exchanged banter in French and German with all kinds of people, from the security guard to the dinner ladies. When they reached the dining room, four men who were already well into their meal stood up from their table as they walked past. One kissed her on both cheeks and the others shook her hand. She introduced Jack briefly and they all shook hands. He had the impression that he was being scrutinized.

A waiter rushed over and seated them at a table by the window.

The meal was excellent, and they washed it down with an Austrian wine. Jack made a mental note of the name to tell his brother, who fancied himself as a bit of a wine buff.

After firing a few more questions at him about the think tank, she relaxed a little and told him how she had left Ireland almost immediately after graduating and had been in Geneva ever since.

'I love it here, and the job is great, but I've been thinking about going back for a while now, so the meeting with Dempsey really came at a good time.'

'It's probably none of my business, but why would you want to go back?' Jack asked, looking around the dining room. 'I'm sure you have a much better lifestyle here.'

She toyed with her dessert fork and looked out at the lake. 'I have some unfinished business in Ireland,' she said. Her expression and tone didn't invite questions, so he changed the subject and they asked each other the usual stuff about where they lived and what they did in their spare time. He told her he was married with two children and, trying to sound as offhand as he could manage, asked her if she was also married.

'I was, briefly,' she said, smiling again. 'That was my ex-husband you met just now.'

'So that's Mr De Clercq? The one who kissed you on the cheek? You seem on very good terms.'

'We're very good friends, actually.' She shrugged her shoulders. 'The divorce was amicable.'

'How very civilized and continental.' Jack laid his knife and fork down on the table. 'You do know we still don't have divorce in Ireland, don't you?'

'Of course. I'm not completely out of touch. I go back to see my parents, although to be honest, they prefer coming over here to see me – especially at Christmas.'

She looked out across the lake and smiled. Then she turned back to him, her expression changed again. 'So, what do people do when their marriages break down?' she asked.

'Oh, we have our ways of dealing with it,' he said.

She raised her eyebrows. 'We?' That mocking tone again. She hadn't changed that much, he thought, and chose to ignore the question.

'Some people live separate lives, others have affairs, but it's all very discreet. A few get a legal separation, but that's difficult. And I won't even mention annulment, although some people go down that route. Or they go to England to get a divorce, which then of course isn't recognized in Ireland. It's complicated.'

'I'm sure it is. And when people split up or have affairs, nobody ever talks about it, am I right? There was a girl in my school whose parents had separated and she was treated like a pariah. So, tell me, if I went back to live there would I be a sort of latter-day Ellen Olenska?' She saw his blank look and laughed. 'Sorry, I've just read *The Age of Innocence,* but it's maybe not your sort of book,' she said. Jack shook his head. 'Edith Wharton. New York society in the late nine-teenth century. Sounds like Dublin in the twentieth century is pretty similar.'

The waiter re-appeared and asked them if they would like coffee. Sinéad looked quickly at her watch. 'Look at the time! We'd better get a move on if you're to catch your plane. Why don't we have coffee in my office and we can tidy up any loose ends there?'

As they walked out of the dining room, a young woman came up to her and spoke rapidly in French. Sinéad stopped and frowned, then looked back at Jack.

'Myriam has just told me there could be a problem with your flight. Apparently, Heathrow is closed because of fog and there are no flights to London leaving from Geneva this evening. I'll ask her to check to see if you can go back through Paris or somewhere. Don't worry, our travel divi-sion will do their best to sort it out.'

As soon as they got back to her office, Sinéad's secretary appeared with a tray with two coffees on it and placed it on the low table by the window. Sinéad waved at Jack to sit down, then picked up a file and followed the secretary into her office. He could hear her dictating something and some laughter. Then she reappeared, smiling. 'I've just dashed off a quick note to Jim,' she said. 'I can give it to you to take back with you – save the taxpayer the stamp.'

She still had the think tank file in her hand and she opened it again, turning the pages rapidly. 'There are just a few more questions I have for you, Jack.' She was back in business mode, and the intimacy he thought had begun to develop over lunch seemed to have evaporated.

It must have been a half an hour later when her secretary knocked on the door and came back in.

'Oh no,' Sinéad said and sighed after a quick exchange. 'Bad news. They can't get you on any flight out of here this evening – the weather is terrible all over Europe and the few flights that are operating are full. She's managed to get you on a flight to Paris in the morning but we're going to have to find you a hotel for tonight. Do you have somewhere you like to stay?'

'I've never been to Geneva before, so no, I don't. Anywhere will do, I'm not fussy.'

After the secretary had left, Sinéad turned to Jack. 'What are we going to do with you this evening then?'

He couldn't resist it. 'Hmm…well, I suppose you could take me for a walk around the lake?'

She laughed. 'This lake's a bit bigger than the last one, but I see working in the civil service hasn't cost you your sense of humour. Seriously though, Jack, I'm really sorry, but I have a dinner tonight that's been planned for ages and it would be really bad form for me to miss it. Otherwise I could have shown you a bit of the city and we could have had a meal. Maybe one of my colleagues…'

'No, no, don't worry about it,' Jack said. 'I had an early start this morning and I could do with a quiet evening in the hotel.'

Still frowning, she went over to her desk and picked up the phone. He only understood a few words but it was obviously a social call and there was lots of laughter. The initial elation he had felt when she told him his plane had been cancelled had vanished and the prospect of an evening watching Swiss TV in some dreary hotel room was becoming more real.

She ended her call and turned back to him. 'OK. Look, I've spoken to my friend who's organizing the dinner and he said it's no problem – you can come along if you like. It's a small group – we're going skiing next week and we were just getting together over a fondue to sort out the last-minute details. There are five of us, but he's got six fondue forks, so it'll be fine!'

'But I don't speak French.'

'That's not a problem. Everybody speaks English here. And don't worry about dress code – it'll be very casual.' She looked pointedly at his suit. 'You'll be fine in a pullover.'

An hour later he was checking into an attractive small hotel in the centre of the city. He phoned home quickly to make sure everything was OK. He had a brief walk outside and was pleasantly surprised at how picturesque the area was. The hotel had given him a wash kit, but he had to buy some underwear and socks. He also bought a new shirt and an outrageously expensive grey cashmere sweater.

He barely had time to shower and shave when the phone rang in his room at precisely seven pm and the receptionist told him in perfect English that Mrs De Clercq was waiting for him in the lobby.

He had to look twice around the lobby before he caught sight of her, now dressed in jeans and a polo neck, with a leather jacket slung casually over her shoulders. Her hair looked softer and she wasn't wearing much make-up.

'Ready?' she smiled broadly. 'I hope you don't feel I forced you into coming along; it would be such a shame to spend your first night in Geneva watching TV in your hotel. Switzerland does most things well, but television is an exception. Nice pullover, by the way,' she added, looking approvingly at his purchase.

Her car was parked just outside and she made a great show of opening the door for him. She took a detour to show him the lake. Even in the dark it was impressive, although the famous water jet wasn't working.

'They turn it off in the early afternoon at this time of year,' she explained. 'In case it freezes.'

She parked at the back of her friend's apartment block and as they got out of the car another couple pulled up, the woman waving at Sinéad. Sinéad introduced them – Nicole, French, working for the UN, and Stephen, English, working for the WHO and whom he recognized as one of the gang of four in the restaurant at lunchtime. The lift they took to the fourth floor was all mahogany and gleaming brass fittings, like something out of a film.

'Nice building isn't it?' said Stephen. 'Pure Art Deco and very sought-after – but practically impossible for ordinary mortals to buy.'

'You mustn't think we all live like this in Geneva,' said Nicole. 'Thierry was an only child and inherited this from his parents – along with the chalet in the mountains.'

A tall good-looking man in his thirties opened the door to them. He embraced Sinéad and Nicole warmly and shook Stephen's hand. Then, he said in flawless English, 'You must be Jack. Sinéad told me about your visit. What good luck for you that your plane was cancelled – you can taste my world-famous cuisine!'

The apartment's reception hall was large and square, with a marble floor and glass-panelled doors leading into the living room. Everywhere Jack looked there were exquisite paintings and sculptures and oriental carpets that looked as if they should be in a museum. The furniture was mostly antique, pale wood with elegant inlays, and there were a few modern touches like a Corbusier chair and an Eileen Grey table.

Thierry took Sinéad's arm and led the way into the large living room.

'Come and see the view, Jack,' he said, looking over his shoulder at him. 'You can just about see the lake from here.' He opened a French door onto a large balcony and they stepped out.

The doorbell rang and Thierry left them. He returned arm in arm with Inge, the last member of the party. Thierry herded everyone back into the living room and began serving Kir with copious amounts of beautifully-presented hors d'oeuvres, all clearly home-made.

The conversation was all about the next week's skiing. There was much laughter and ribbing as they drew lots for bedrooms in Thierry's chalet and some arguing about which cars they would take and the schedules for household tasks.

'Do you ski, Jack?' Stephen asked.

'I've never set foot on a ski,' he said. 'We rarely get snow in Ireland.'

'Sinéad is better than any of us now,' said Thierry, smiling at her in obvious admiration. Jack wondered if he and she... but then remembered that she had been allocated her own bedroom in the chalet.

'I only do cross-country skiing,' said Inge. 'It's the best way to see the landscape, and it's great exercise.'

'Cross-country skiing is for wimps and Norwegians, and you all look so silly shuffling along in those knickerbockers with your knee-high socks.' Thierry stood up. 'But that's enough ski talk, It's time for the highlight of the evening. Seat yourselves, please.'

He and Inge took the now-empty trays to the kitchen, while the others sat down at the dining table at the far end of the living room. He returned several minutes later with an earthenware pot which he placed ceremoniously on a burner in the middle of the table. The pot contained a thick pale-yellow liquid, and the only other things on the table were a large basket filled with small cubes of bread, a bowl of salad and several bottles of wine. Sinéad, who was sitting beside Jack, must have seen his look.

'Cheese fondue,' she whispered. 'It's great after skiing. Thierry decided to put us in the mood. Here, you just dip the bread in the cheese, like this.'

She spiked a piece of bread with a fondue fork and twirled it in the pot until it was coated with the cheese, let it cool a bit and then popped it into his mouth as if she was feeding a child. Thierry told them he used three types of cheese, and that it was the final splash of Kirsch that gave it its unique flavour.

It's hard to eat fondue without interacting with everyone at the table, so by the end of the meal Jack felt thoroughly at ease and was really enjoying himself. They were an interesting bunch, and he was disappointed when at around ten Sinéad stood up and said that they needed to leave, as Jack had an early plane to catch.

'You should come skiing with us next week, Jack,' Thierry said. 'I'm sure we could find some space for you.'

'Perhaps another time,' he said, shaking his hand warmly.

They took a different, more direct route back to the hotel. They had been driving for about five minutes when Sinéad slowed down and pointed at a small modern block of apartments.

'That's where I live,' she said. 'On the top floor. Nothing like Thierry's place, but still nice.'

'You're not inviting me in for coffee?' he asked.

'No, because if I did I'd have to go out again to drive you back to your hotel. And anyway, my etchings are in storage.' She laughed at his expression and patted him on the arm. When they got to Jack's hotel, she gave her car keys to the doorman and came into the lobby with him. 'If you really fancy a coffee, we can have one here,' she said.

They sat in a corner by the window. Sinéad ordered two espressos and on her recommendation, Jack took a local pear brandy. He sipped it gingerly.

'That was a really nice evening. Thank you for inviting me,' he said.

'They're good friends, we've known each other for years.'

They chatted amiably for a short while and then she looked at her watch. 'You need to get some sleep. We've ordered a taxi for you at 7 am, which should get you to the airport in plenty of time for your flight.'

'I'll call you when I get back to Dublin. We need to discuss the next stage.'

'Yes,' she said. 'I'll need to come over and meet the members of this think tank and figure out how we could make it work.'

As he walked her to the door she turned and kissed him lightly on the cheek. 'Sleep well Jack. It was lovely to see you again after all this time.'

'Ditto,' he said. 'I'm looking forward to working with you.'

As she turned to walk away, he called her back and said, 'I'm really sorry for standing you up in Dublin that night after Killarney.'

She looked puzzled. 'I thought I was the one who did the standing up?'

'What?'

'I sent my friend Karen and she told me you didn't seem too surprised when she turned up in my place. She even told me you tried to chat her up.'

'No, no, that wasn't me. Something came up and I couldn't go, so I sent a friend to meet you.'

She laughed and shook her head in disbelief.

'So that's why she was so dismissive – it wasn't you at all! She told me I was wasting my time and that you were a smart-arse who clearly only liked men but pretended to fancy her. But I saw the engagement notice in the paper a few days later so I reckoned you were taken. No harm done. I wasn't really available either at the time.'

They said goodbye again and he watched her walk out of the lobby and get into her car before turning and walking slowly up the stairs.

Next morning, at Geneva airport with time to spare, he bought some Toblerone for the girls and an expensive watch for Lorna. Christmas was coming up and he never knew what to get her, but Switzerland was famous for its watches and he was pretty sure she would like it.

Chapter Fourteen

By THE TIME JACK arrived back in Dublin it was late afternoon and he went straight to the office. There was a note from Brenda on his desk, asking him to check in with the boss to give him a report on the meeting in Geneva. He looked at his watch – it was already five o'clock, six in Geneva. Maybe she was still in the office. He picked up the phone and asked the operator to put him through to Sinéad, but there was no reply from either her direct line or her secretary.

He fished about in his briefcase to find the letter she had drafted for Jim and went up to the minister's office.

Jim beamed at him as he entered the office. 'I heard about your adventures in Geneva. That was bad luck, but you can never tell what the weather is going to do this time of year. Anyway, you're back now, so tell me all about it.' He took the letter from Jack and looked at him expectantly. 'Did it go well? I hope you persuaded her; we really need to get moving on this.'

'Yeah, I think it went well, and I agree with you that she seems the right person for the job. She also seems ready to move back to Ireland, though God knows why – I'd much rather stay in Geneva if I were her.'

'And why is that?' Jim raised his eyebrows. 'Far away fields are greener, are they?' Without waiting for a reply, he sat up straight, opened the letter and skimmed through it. 'Great stuff. She says she'll give it a go and she's pretty sure the WHO will give her leave of absence. I'll give her boss a call and sort that out, anyway. Get her over here as quickly as you can. She'll need some time to sort things out, but let's try to have her starting after Christmas. I'd like her to pop over before that though so she can get an idea of where she'll be based and meet the other members of the think tank. God, that reminds me, Jack, we still have to appoint them. What about getting her over next week?'

'She's off skiing,' he said, 'but I'll try for the week after that.'

Jim nodded. 'Good – in fact if you leave it two weeks she could be here for the Christmas party. That way she'll get to meet everybody and see what she's letting herself in for! I'll leave that to you, Jack. Just make sure I'm in town when she arrives.'

He stood up and gathered his papers together. 'Sorry Jack, I've got to go to a party function tonight – in Mullingar of all places – and my driver is waiting.'

'Why didn't you tell me she was Irish?' Jack couldn't resist asking.

'I was wondering when you'd ask me that,' he said and laughed. 'Well, when I met her in Geneva, I mentioned your name and she said she thought she remembered someone of that name from way back, so I just thought it would be funny if you did know each other. And as she'd changed her name...' He paused. 'Well, did you know each other?'

'Yes, we met in college briefly, at a poker game. Seems like a long time ago now.'

Jim banged him on the back as he left the room. 'Poker, eh?' he said, laughing. 'I'm sure you'll make a very good team.'

Jack went back to his office. He thought about going home, but sat and opened his diary instead to look at possible dates for Sinéad's trip. Then he went down to Gerry in Personnel and asked how quickly the recruitment process could be set up.

'The boss wants her to start in January, so see if you can meet that timescale.'

'I see her maiden name is Murray,' said Gerry, pursing his lips and looking up at the ceiling as if for inspiration. 'Sinéad Murray. That name rings a bell.'

Jack sat back in his chair, hands behind his head, grinning. 'I'll give you a clue,' he said. 'In fact, I'll give you three clues. Killarney. 1971. Poker.'

Gerry looked at him blankly for a minute or two and then banged the desk.

'You're not serious? Of course. The girl who fleeced Leahy, the one who arrived with Hollis!' He shook his head, smiling. 'It's a small world, Jack!'

By the time he got home, the girls had gone to bed and Lorna had already eaten, so he made himself a sandwich from some leftovers and ate it in front of the television. He told Lorna about his trip and the evening with the cheese fondue.

'I was thinking. We have a fondue set that's never been taken out of its box. Why don't we invite a few people around and put it to use?'

'Oh Jack, do we have to? I've got no idea how to make a fondue, and who would we invite anyway? Who would like that sort of thing?'

'Your brothers, for a start. They'd eat anything,'

She looked dubious,

'I'll organise it,' he said. 'You just invite your brothers and their wives and make the place look nice. I'll take care of the rest. It doesn't have to be perfect, just a relaxed evening.'

The next morning he went to the office early and phoned Sinéad again, this time getting through right away. He phoned her three times over the next two days, each time using the pretext of some minor detail involving her contract. They agreed that she would come over on the 10th for a couple of days – he was relieved that she couldn't make it for the Christmas party which was on the 8th, and to which spouses and partners were invited. He offered to find her a hotel, but she said she would probably stay with her parents in Clontarf.

The following week he was busy in the office, his time mostly taken up with finalising the details of the think tank, or task force as it was now to be officially called. Frank Curzon, a senior consultant in psychiatry, was to be the chair and Sinéad would advise him and be responsible for meetings and the final report. The other members would be chosen by the political parties.

By Thursday Jack had sorted most of the details and had met with Curzon, so he decided to draft a note for Sinéad setting out a blueprint for how he thought the group could work and what resources could be made available to it. He spent hours making sure it was as comprehensive as possible and read well, then Brenda gave it a final tidy up and faxed it across to Geneva so Sinéad would have it when she got back from her skiing holiday.

That weekend they invited two of Lorna's brothers and their wives for dinner. Both were lawyers; James, an up and coming barrister, married to Jack's sister Sarah, and Mark, quieter and less ambitious than his brother, but rising steadily in the ranks at the Department of Justice. His wife Deirdre was a GP. She was warm, thoughtful and funny, with none of the airs and graces his sister had assumed. Sarah, though not that bright in the academic sense, had a kind of innate cleverness that was enhanced by an excellent education. Since she had married, she'd devoted herself to her new role as the wife of a leading Dublin barrister. She did everything just right – entertained a lot, went to every charity event in town, sent her children to the right schools and generally raised them to be part of the next generation of leaders. As he took his sister's coat, he reflected on how different they were, and how he never felt her equal.

The ever-resourceful Brenda had found a recipe for cheese fondue and it seemed quite simple, although he spent some time tracking down the right cheeses and finding a suitable wine and a bottle of Kirsch. For the starters and dessert, he used the local delicatessen, so all Lorna had to do was make a salad and set the table.

To say the evening was not a success would be an understatement.

It all started with the fondue. When he carried it to the table Sarah looked at it in mock horror. 'Is that what you call a fondue?' she said, looking around the table for support. 'It looks like melted cheese!'

'It *is* melted cheese,' he replied, 'That's what people have when they come in from skiing.'

'No wonder we never eat it here then,' she said and laughed. 'Looks a bit heavy to me. Is this what you're supposed to do?' She skewered a piece of bread and dipped it gingerly into the cheese. 'Interesting,' she said, 'I'm not sure I'd want to eat it every day though.'

'I think it's a lovely idea, Jack,' said Deirdre, smiling at him.

'We're going skiing next year with the Johnstons, so I suppose I'd better get used to it,' Sarah chipped in.

Deirdre steered the conversation back to Jack. 'I hear you're just back from Geneva, Jack. How was your trip?'

He told them about the meeting and the plans for the task force.

'Good idea,' said James. 'This country needs shaking up, and the health sector is a real mess. Curzon is a good choice, too. And this woman who's coming over to work with him – what's her name?'

'Sinéad Murray,' he said. 'De Clercq, I should say. She studied medicine briefly at UCD and then did a business administration degree in Trinity.'

'Trinity?' Sarah echoed. 'Is she a Protestant?'

Jack ignored the comment. Deirdre frowned. 'There was a Sinéad Murray in my class when I was in UCD. I wonder if it's the same person. If it is, she was really bright but something happened I think, and she left. Mind you, a lot of people drop out of medicine after the first year.'

'It's a very common name anyway. What school did she go to?' asked Sarah.

'I really don't know,' Jack said. 'Somewhere on the northside probably – she's from Clontarf.'

'We played hockey against a northside school once – somewhere near Howth. Or Sutton, maybe,' said Sarah, helping herself to more bread cubes.

'Did you win?' asked Deirdre innocently.

'What?'

'The hockey match. Did you win it?'

'I can't remember – probably. They don't really have a hockey culture over there. More camogie and that sort of thing. Mind you, at least they had tennis courts.'

Deirdre caught Jack's eye and smiled.

'Well, she appears to have done very well for herself – big job in Geneva, headhunted by Jim Dempsey. That'll put a few noses out of joint,' said Mark.

'Lovely place, Geneva,' said James, reaching for the wine bottle. 'I've been there for a conference. Beautiful lake.'

'Yes, it's lovely. I didn't see much of it but it made me wonder what it would be like to work there. You know, in one of the big international organizations.'

There was a short silence and Lorna looked at her husband in amazement. 'You're not serious, Jack?'

'Why on earth would you want to live over there?' asked Sarah. 'And what about the children and schools and the language?'

'They have international schools there. Children adapt easily anyway. It's more difficult for us adults,' said Deirdre.

'Great salaries, and good perks too,' added Mark.

'Anyway,' Jack said, standing up and starting to tidy away the dishes, 'it was just a thought I had on the plane coming back.'

'A crazy one, if you ask me,' said Sarah. 'Did you even think of what it would be like for poor Lorna, with none of her family around.'

'Well, I'm not asking you, Sarah,' he snapped, 'and anyway it might do us all a lot of good to get away from our families from time to time.'

'That's typical of you, Jack – you're so selfish and ungrateful for the life you have here.' Sarah wiped her mouth with her napkin.

Lorna looked as if she was about to cry.

Deirdre stood up and began to clear the table as James deftly steered the discussion to plans for Christmas. Jack joined her in the kitchen, carrying the fondue set and all the associated paraphernalia.

'Don't mind Sarah,' she said, patting him on the shoulder. 'Too much Riesling. And if it's any help, I think it would do you and Lorna a lot of good to get away from here for a while. It can get a bit claustrophobic from time to time.'

When they went back in, James was in full flow about some big court case he had just won and they tucked into the dessert, listening as he re-lived his triumph.

After everyone had left, Lorna and Jack went to the kitchen and he began tidying up.

Lorna sat down at the table, her head in her hands. 'Why do you always have to put me down in front of my family, Jack?'

'I didn't put you down.'

'Yes, you did. You talked about moving abroad as if it would do me good.'

'Well, it might.'

'As if I was sick.'

'Aren't you bored here, Lorna? Don't you ever wish for something else in your life? Jesus, all those years in college and you just sit at home all day doing nothing. You could do so much better.'

'I don't do nothing. I look after the children and the house, and...'

'Except when I have to take them to the office,' he muttered under his breath, bending over the dishwasher.

'What did you say?'

'Nothing.'

He handed her a tea towel. 'I'll wash, you dry. These glasses need hand washing.'

'I'm going to bed. I told you Mrs Foley will do this in the morning.'

'Why can't we ever talk about anything without you going off in a huff?'

'Because it's always about what you want. You don't care about what I want. You don't listen.'

'Don't listen? You never tell me anything. You never tell me how you feel, what you want. All you care about is your family and what other people think.'

She stood up and threw the tea towel down on the sink.

'See? You've just proved my point,' he shouted after her as she stormed up the stairs to bed.

Once everything was clean and tidy, he sat down with a Scotch to decompress and when he finally went upstairs Lorna was already asleep.

Chapter Fifteen

December 10th

IT WAS COLD WHEN Jack left the house to go to work. It was one of those rare December days in Dublin where the sun is shining, the sky is clear and blue and the air is crisp. He never normally noticed much around him on his way into the city, but that morning the light was astonishing. On impulse, instead of driving straight in to the city, he drove through Ballsbridge and headed for Sandymount strand. The tide was so far out it that was difficult to see where the sea began and the sky ended, and even though it was a weekday there were lots of people walking their dogs or simply sitting looking at the view. He pulled into the car park and got out of the car, watching a plane in the distance making its final approach to Dublin airport. On a day like this, the view from the plane would be spectacular as it descended over Howth Head, with Portmarnock beach to the right and the broad sweep of Dublin Bay to the left.

Sinéad was due in around midday and he crossed his fingers the weather would last until then. He took a few deep breaths, filling his lungs with the tangy sea air and thought about going for a run, but he wasn't dressed for it and it was already half past eight. He had a lot to do that morning and Jim had planned a lunch in the Dáil with the members of the task force. He had a quick cigarette instead and got back into the car for the short drive into the city.

As he walked into the building, he wondered what Sinéad would think about her new place of work. Hawkins House had to be one of the ugliest buildings in Dublin. It was built in the sixties and looked as if it had been transplanted from an Eastern bloc country. Its only redeeming feature was the amazing view from the ninth floor, where he had his office. As he walked in, he noticed that the windows needed cleaning and made a mental note to get on to the Office of Public Works.

Brenda came in as soon as he sat down and handed him a file. 'Morning Jack. Here's the final list of task force members with some notes on their background,' she said.

His coffee was waiting for him on the desk, together with his schedule for the day. He glanced though the file Brenda had given him, and he had to admit that Jim had chosen his people well. There was perfect balance in the choice of the three politicians – one liberal, one conservative and one who could conceivably be described as radical – and between them they represented the main currents of thought of the time. There were only two women – one of the politicians and the patients' representative, and they all had plenty of technical expertise. He began to think this might actually be an interesting exercise.

Sinéad phoned in response to the note he'd sent her as soon as she got back from skiing. She sounded a little surprised – even impressed, which was of course the point. Over the course of the week that followed they had phoned each other a lot and he often put off calling her until the end of the day so he could spend as much time as he liked on the phone with less risk of interruptions.

Just after midday Robert Fitzgibbon, another adviser, popped his head around the door. 'The boss is waiting for you downstairs,' he said. 'You'd want to get a move on.'

The ministerial car was waiting outside the front door and Jim was standing beside it chatting genially to random passers-by.

All the members of the group were already waiting in the grand entrance hall and they just had time to greet them when Sinéad arrived with Eoghan Coughlan, a young official who had been assigned to the task force as general dogsbody, following a short distance behind. He was carrying a small suitcase and Jack wondered if he'd been sent to the airport to meet her, vaguely annoyed with himself that he hadn't thought to go himself.

Coughlan said to nobody in particular, 'The taxi was just stopping outside the gate as I came in so I sorted out the security for Mrs De Clercq.'

Jim was in great form and Sinéad seemed to be engaging well with Frank Curzon. Jim outlined his plan for the group and everyone seemed to agree on the timetable and budget. Jack noted with satisfaction that Sinéad had acknowledged his input. A date was set for the first meeting and at precisely two pm Jim stood up and said, 'Well, ladies and gentlemen, I'm afraid Sinéad and Jack here have some things to sort out in Hawkins House and I have to get back to running the country, so I'm going to leave you to it. Good luck with the work and don't forget my door is always open.'

'I thought that went well,' Jim said as he jumped in the front seat. 'Mind you, we did choose them carefully, didn't we Jack?' he said, winking at him.

Each time the car turned a corner Jack was aware of Sinéad's discreet perfume and the pressure of her thigh against his, although she was wearing a heavy coat so he presumed that she was probably completely unaware of the effect she was having on him.

He showed Sinéad the office they had set aside for her, not far from his. 'Not as nice as Geneva I'm afraid,' he said, but she didn't seem to think it was important. The issue of a secretary hadn't been sorted out, so they went down to personnel to see Gerry Mulcahy.

Gerry was obviously delighted to meet her again, and they spent half an hour reminiscing about student days and who was doing what now. He told Sinéad that with all the budget cuts, they were having a problem finding a secretary to assign to her. He looked at Jack and asked him if he thought it might be possible to share with someone.

'You mean Brenda?'

'Do you think that could work, Jack?'

'Look,' said Sinéad. 'I like to type most of my own work on the word processor so I really don't need a secretary full time, just somebody to take messages and knock my documents into shape.'

They agreed to discuss it further later.

They finally took their leave of Mulcahy and strolled back down the corridor to the lift. As he pressed the button, he became aware of a notice board covered with photos of the recent Christmas party. Before he could distract her, Sinéad was peering at them.

'Jim looks a bit worse for wear here! Must have been a good party.' She looked more closely. 'And there's Gerry. Oh and you. You scrub up well, Jack.'

He had to admit that to any outsider looking at those photos, there was no hint of any cracks in the McDonagh facade. Lorna was extremely photogenic and was smiling broadly. She was even holding his hand. He was beaming at the camera too, but then that's the nature of party photographs, he thought. People smiling and trying to present their best profile, so that when you leaf through the family albums you get the impression that all memories are happy ones.

It was half past four when they got back to his office; he asked Sinéad if she had plans for the weekend.

'Not really, I'm staying with my parents, so nothing very exciting,' she said. 'Seeing some cousins, catching up a bit, a walk along the cliffs in Howth, that's about it. I'm flying back on Sunday afternoon.'

'It would have been nice to have dinner,' he said, 'and a decent talk about the work ahead. It was all a bit rushed at the lunch.'

'Yes, it would,' she said, looking at him. 'Never mind, I'll be back in January and we can sit down and have a proper chat then.'

He offered to drive her to Clontarf. 'It's no trouble,' he said when she protested. 'There's a new toll bridge across the Liffey and apparently it makes the journey much quicker. I've been wanting to try it for ages.'

They were very quickly in Fairview and it was dark as they drove out towards Dollymount; you could see the lights twinkling on Howth Head. There were already some early Christmas trees in the windows of some of the houses along the coast road.

'I love Christmas in Dublin,' she said and sighed. 'But my parents always want to come out to Geneva. They're like kids really. They love the snow and the Christmas markets and all the kitsch. Mind you, so do I.'

When they reached Vernon Avenue, she told him to turn left and guided him in through a series of small roads, finally arriving in a quiet cul-de-sac in front of a modest red brick semi-detached house. As he took her case out of the boot, the front door opened and a woman waved to them. She came to the gate and Sinéad hugged her warmly.

'This is Jack, one of my new colleagues. He very kindly offered to drive me home.'

'Lovely to meet you, Jack,' she said. 'Do come in and meet Sinéad's father. He's trying to put up the Christmas decorations, God knows why, as we're not even going to be here, but he wanted it to look nice for Sinéad.' She smiled, looking at her daughter with obvious pride.

The house was quite small but nicely decorated and had a warm feel to it. Mr Murray was standing on a ladder in the living room, trying to attach a gold star to the top of a smallish tree as classical music played quite loudly in the background. He clambered down off the ladder with some difficulty and held out his hand.

'Pleased to meet you, Jack – we've heard a lot about you.'

He looked at Sinéad, wondering what she had told them, but she just smiled.

'Turn that music down, Noel,' said his wife, and turning to Jack added, 'you can't hear yourself think in this house. We keep telling Noel he should open a record shop. Come and take your coat off and sit down, Jack. Sinéad tells me you have to get back to Mount Merrion. That's a long way – why don't you have a cup of tea before you set off?'

She rushed off to the kitchen and returned a few minutes later with a tray. Before he knew it he was sitting on the sofa drinking tea and eating a perfectly cooked mince pie.

Sinéad's parents were unassuming, interesting people, obviously well-educated. But what struck him most was the warmth and respect they shared, which was quite unlike his own family.

He stayed there for over an hour and it was Sinéad who finally interrupted her father in full flow, reminding him that Jack had to get back home. He left reluctantly; it had been a long time since he had felt so much at ease anywhere. They wished each other a happy Christmas as Sinéad accompanied him to the door. They stood there for a moment while Jack fumbled in his pocket for his car keys.

'Thanks for driving me back,' said Sinéad.

'It was no problem,' he said. 'It was really nice to meet your parents. They're lovely.'

'My dad tends to go on a bit,' she said, laughing. 'I hope you weren't too bored.'

'Not at all,' he protested. 'I really liked him. He's a mine of information.' He jingled his keys and leaned forward to kiss her on the cheek. They both laughed as they bumped noses.

'I'll give you a call next week and we can talk some more.'

'Drive carefully,' she said and waved as he walked to the car.

Chapter Sixteen

CHRISTMAS CAME AND WENT in a haze for Jack. It was the same old rituals year after year, down to the tiniest detail. The last-minute rush for presents in Grafton Street, the round of family parties, Christmas Eve at his parents' and Christmas Day at Lorna's. On Saint Stephen's Day they hosted drinks at their house for family and friends and on the 27th they all went down to Kilkenny for New Year. James had quite a large house there but it was nowhere near big enough for the entire extended family, so he and Lorna rented a smaller one close by.

He gave Lorna her watch on Christmas morning as the girls unwrapped their presents. She seemed quite pleased and even smiled at the irony as she handed him his present – which was also a watch. It was a Baume and Mercier, elegant and understated, and as he put it on, feigning de-lighted surprise, he noticed it had *Genève* written on the face. He wondered what the Murray family were giving each other and how they were getting on in Geneva.

Usually he enjoyed the Christmas break as it meant he could relax and not feel he was walking on eggshells with Lorna, and of course the children loved it, but this year he found it tedious and couldn't wait to get back to the office.

When he got back to work in early January things moved very fast. Mulcahy, with his legendary efficiency, had sorted out all the administrative details and Sinéad was due to start on the 15th. To his surprise, Brenda agreed to work for both of them, backed up by a typist from the pool, and she seemed very happy with the arrangement.

As soon as Sinéad arrived, work started in earnest. In the first few weeks they had already held two full meetings of the task force and their plan for the next six months was approved by the Minister. Most of the meetings would involve hearing submissions from experts and interested parties, but on Jack's not entirely disinterested suggestion, a few trips to other countries were pencilled in so that the group could see at first-hand how the health system operated elsewhere and talk directly to their foreign counterparts.

With Brenda's help, Sinéad found a small apartment on Merrion Square that was being sublet by a female colleague in Foreign Affairs who had been seconded to Brussels for a year. She was delighted as it meant she didn't have to think about furniture and it was a pleasant enough walk to Hawkins House – when it wasn't raining, that is – and it was very close to the Dáil.

Looking back, Jack could honestly say that their working relationship was probably the best he'd ever had with anyone before or since. They were both very good at what they did (and he would say this with no false modesty) and although they didn't always agree on strategy, or perhaps because of that, their discussions were always positive and energetic.

But perhaps more importantly, they shared the same sense of humour. During meetings, Jack would try to sit out of sight at the back of the room and would occasionally pass her notes – some serious, with advice for the chairperson, some silly, poking fun at a member who had made what he thought was a stupid suggestion. He liked to imagine he could see the twinkle in her eye when she read them – but to the rest of the group she was a model of decorum. They spent a lot of time in each other's offices tossing ideas around and comparing notes, and they had lunch together almost daily in the canteen, sometimes with colleagues, sometimes just the two of them. He looked forward to these moments, and on the odd day when she wasn't there, he felt a strange void. He had noticed his colleagues' glances as they walked into the canteen or left the building together, and he put it down to envy. Occasionally, they would work late and he would drop her off at her flat, always hoping she would invite him in, but always afraid to suggest it for fear of breaking the spell.

If anyone had asked him when he first began to realize he was in love with her, he would have to say that it was during the trip to Washington in March. It was a longstanding tradition that each year the Americans invited an Irish government representative to the St Patrick's Day celebrations in Washington. There was always fierce competition among the ministers for what was considered to be a prize junket, and this year it was Jim's turn. He bounded into Jack's office a couple of weeks before the event and told him he had had a brilliant idea. This consisted of Jack accompanying him on the trip, with Curzon and Sinéad as well, so they could talk to their opposite numbers in the States about the American health system.

That year, St Patrick's Day fell on a Sunday and the US President would be out of the country, so the ceremony at the White House was held on the Friday before, the 15th. Jack carefully scheduled the meeting with the Health people for the following Monday so that they had the weekend free. He justified this to himself and everyone else as they already had another meeting set up on the 13th March in Brussels anyway, making it impossible to schedule anything before. So the plan was for Curzon, Sinéad and himself to fly from Brussels to the States on the 14th, travelling back to Dublin on the evening of the 18th.

They flew out to Brussels on the Wednesday morning and went straight to the meeting, which finished in the late afternoon. Sinéad and Jack had already decided to have dinner in the hotel as they had an early start the next morning, Jim was being taken care of by the Permanent Representation, and Curzon was meeting an old friend who was a professor of psychiatry in one of the universities.

As they checked in at the hotel, reserving a table for dinner at the same time, the receptionist looked at Jack's passport, studied it for a second, then smiled broadly and said, 'Happy Birthday Mr McDonagh. Would you like me to ask the chef to make a special dessert?'

Sinéad looked at him in surprise. 'It's your birthday today? Why didn't you tell me?'

'I didn't want any fuss,' he said, a little irritated. He turned back to the receptionist and said. 'Please, no cake, no candles. I'm allergic to them.'

'I've never heard of anyone being allergic to candles,' Sinéad said, and the receptionist laughed.

'No problem, Mr McDonagh, but if you change your mind just ask the waiter and we'll be happy to oblige.'

The luggage was whisked away and they both went to their rooms to freshen up quickly before meeting again in the lobby a few minutes later and heading for the dining room. The waiter found them a quiet corner and they settled in to peruse the menu. He asked if they would like an aperitif and Sinéad looked up, delighted.

'Why not? Champagne, Jack? Since it's your birthday.'

He shrugged his shoulders. Why not indeed?

Sinéad began trawling through the menu. 'Hmm – mouse of lamb – my favourite. I love how these fancy restaurants can pay a fortune for the décor but can't be bothered paying a proper translator for the most important thing – the food.' He shook his head, wondering what she was talking about when she pointed at the menu. '*Souris d'agneau.*' Sinéad raised her glass. 'Happy birthday, Jack,' she said and they sipped the champagne quietly.

He could have left it at that, but something made him say

'About this birthday business, there's something you should know about me, Sinéad.' She looked surprised, but said nothing and waited for him to continue. 'I've never really celebrated my birthday. At least, my parents never celebrated it. They adopted me when I was only a few weeks old and they always considered that my real birthday was the day I arrived in their house, rather than the day I was born.' He was looking down, fiddling with the cutlery as he spoke, and when he looked up again, she had gone very pale and appeared ill-at-ease. There was a silence.

'You're adopted? Do you...have you any idea who your real, I mean your birth parents are?' she asked finally.

'No,' he said, a bit taken aback by the question. It wasn't the reaction he had expected. The few people he had told had either changed the subject or expressed sympathy. There was another long pause.

'Have you ever tried to find out?'

'Absolutely not,' he said, not liking the way the conversation was going. He had expected her to feel sorry for him, not ask awkward questions.

But she wouldn't let it go. 'Why not?'

'To be perfectly frank, I have no interest in them. My parents told me that the mother and baby home I was adopted from mainly took in prostitutes. So my mother is probably a whore and my father's a sailor she met on the docks.'

She looked shocked. 'That's a bit harsh, don't you think?'

Jack cursed himself for having brought it up. Damn that receptionist anyway for noticing his date of birth. He was desperately thinking of how to change the subject.

'And supposing she isn't?' Sinéad said quietly.

'Isn't what?'

'Supposing she isn't a prostitute?'

'Well, why would she have given me up then? She could have got married to my father.'

'Maybe she couldn't,' she said, in an even tone. 'Maybe he was already married. Or maybe she was, but not to him. Or maybe she was raped. Or...I don't know. There can be lots of reasons. Have you ever thought about that?' Her face was reddening and he noticed her hands were shaking. 'And even if she was a prostitute, that doesn't necessarily make her a bad woman. Have you ever thought that somewhere out there could be a deeply unhappy woman, thinking about you today, on your birthday, feeling terrible and wishing she hadn't given you up?'

Despite her apparent agitation, her tone was reasonable and her concern was palpable, but Jack continued.

'Actually no, I haven't really thought about it, and I don't particularly want to. Maybe she should have thought about it too before handing me over to complete strangers. I'm sure my parents are right and it's better this way. Anyway, if she really wanted to find me, I'm damn sure she could have made contact before now. I'm thirty-five years old for God's sake!'

The waiter arrived with the main course. '*Souris d'agneau pour Monsieur,*' he said, putting the plate of lamb down with a flourish. 'We've removed the head and tail sir,' he added, looking at Sinéad. They began eating in silence. Then Sinéad laid down her knife and fork.

'Jack...,' she began

He cut her off. 'Look, Sinéad, I really appreciate your concern, but it's a subject I find very difficult to talk about. In fact, I hardly ever tell people I'm adopted and I don't know why I told you this evening – it just came out. I really don't want to know who my mother is or why she left me. I have a good life – I was adopted by a family who gave me everything I need, including the best education on offer, and that's more than enough for me.'

'Fine, fine, Jack,' she said, but it wasn't. The evening was spoiled, for Jack at any rate, and he was furious with himself, convinced this was going to cast a shadow over the whole trip.

The next morning they all met at breakfast, where Jim made much of the fact that Jack was wearing glasses. He poked fun at him and said he was trying to look like an intellectual. In fact, he normally wore contact lenses but had to take them out on long-haul flights and he worried that Sinéad would think he looked like a nerd. She didn't join in the ribbing, and he found her a little distant and on edge.

On the plane, Sinéad sat beside Curzon and Jack sat in front of them with Jim, who had obviously had a short night in Brussels and fell asleep on a few occasions. From time to time Jack strained to hear snatches of conversation, half wondering if they were talking about him, but it all seemed to be about work, or what concerts or plays they had been to recently. The only time he managed to speak to Sinéad was when they both went to the back of the plane for a cigarette, but even then they got involved in conversation with one of the stewards who after asking them the purpose of the trip, entertained them with a diatribe on the state of the Belgian health system. They made their escape as politely as possible and didn't go back.

When they arrived in Washington, they were whisked off to the VIP lounge to meet the ambassador and wait while their luggage was being collected.

'Jack. Jack McDonagh.' Something about the voice was familiar and when he turned around, he saw Paul Fitzpatrick, somewhat broader in the beam and a lot better-dressed than when he'd last seen him.

'Jack. Great to see you,' he said. 'What are you doing here?' Jack nodded towards Jim. 'I work for the Minister now, we're here for the handing over of the shamrock and so on. You?'

'Oh, I'm working for the EU here in Washington. We have some bigwigs coming in today and I'm here to meet them.'

He clearly knew the Minister already so Jack introduced him to Sinéad and Frank. When Jack said Sinéad's name Paul shook her hand, then glanced quickly back at him and with a wide grin said, 'I see you two finally met up. Let me know where you're staying. We absolutely must catch up.'

'What was all that about?' Sinéad asked Jack, looking after Fitzpatrick with a puzzled expression.

'Never mind, it's a long story. I'll tell you later,' he said.

When they got to the hotel, he and Jim had a quick briefing with the ambassador to finalise the programme for the next day. After the White House and other meetings, there would be an official dinner in Jim's honour at the ambassador's residence in the evening, which Jack was expected to attend. Sinéad and Curzon were basically left to their own devices.

By the time they had finished it was almost five and Jack was beginning to feel the jet lag kicking in, but knew it would be fatal to go to bed early. Once again Jim had his own arrangements made for the evening and didn't need him, and Curzon had disappeared, so he called Sinéad to see what her plans were. The phone in her room was engaged for ages and he wondered who she could be talking to. When he finally got through, she told him that she had been chatting with a former colleague who had worked in Geneva but was now based in Washington, but to his relief she said her friend wasn't available that evening and would be out of town all weekend.

They ended up going to a tiny Italian restaurant close to the hotel near Dupont Circle. No champagne this time, just some sparkling water and a half bottle of not at all bad Valpolicella to accompany a very simple pasta dish.

While they were waiting for the food, there was an awkward silence.

'You asked me about Paul. Fitzer we used to call him.'

She nodded.

'He was in school with me. He's the one I sent that time I was supposed to meet you in Dublin. The one who met your friend instead.'

'Ah, right,' she said, 'that makes sense now.'

He looked around the room, desperately trying to think of something interesting to say.

'It's nice, this place,' said Sinéad, following his gaze.

'Yes, better than last night and the snooty waiter,' he said and immediately regretted it.

Another silence, broken by the arrival of the waiter.

'Everything alright for you guys?' he asked, as he placed the dishes carefully in front of them and opened the bottle of wine. 'Anything you need, just ask.'

Half-way through the dish, Sinéad laid down her fork and pushed her plate away.

'Is everything OK?' Jack asked.

'I'm fine, just not very hungry,' she said, and then took a deep breath.

'Ok, tonight it's my turn. There's something you need to know about me.'

'Don't tell me you're adopted too,' he said, digging into his pasta.

She didn't smile or say anything for what seemed like ages. Just as he began to think she had changed her mind, she began.

'You remember last night you told me you didn't want to search for your mother because you were afraid of what you might find?'

'Well, I didn't put it quite like that, but, yes, why?'

She hesitated again and for a moment he thought she was going to end the conversation, but then she took another deep breath and said, as if reading from a prepared script, 'I fell pregnant in 1970 and I had a little boy in a mother and baby home in Cork. He was adopted and I haven't seen him or had any information about him since he was a week old. I have no idea where he is, or even if he is alive, but I would do anything to find him.' Jack looked at her in disbelief, trying to take it in. 'So you see, your mother might not be a whore down at the docks. She could be someone like me.' Her voice was steady, but he could see her hands were shaking now and he thought he could detect tears in her eyes.

He put his glass down and sat back in his chair. It was beginning to make sense – her leaving college, then leaving the country, and her reaction the previous night when he told her he was adopted. But he still couldn't believe that someone like Sinéad could have had a child in one of those places. From what he'd been told, the girls there were all either poorly educated or prostitutes or both. They weren't anyone he would know.

She told him her story briefly, almost matter-of-factly. He listened in silence, amazed at her self-control.

'Have you finished ma'am?' The waiter was standing at Sinéad's elbow. 'I'm so sorry,' she said, smiling up at him. 'We've been talking too much and we're both a bit jet-lagged.'

He took the plates away and Jack reached across the table and took her hand. 'I'm the one who's sorry,' he said. 'It was so insensitive of me, what I said last night.'

They walked back to the hotel in silence. Jack's head was full of questions, but he had no idea where to start, and Sinéad seemed exhausted, so he was surprised when she suggested they have a nightcap. They ordered at the counter, found a table and the barman brought them a cognac each, with a couple of bowls of nibbles. After he left, Jack leaned forward and took her hand again.

'I'm so sorry if what I said last night hurt you. I had no idea.'

'Nobody does,' she said, smiling wryly. 'Or rather, everybody knows about these things, but nobody talks about them. And I'm sorry for talking so much. I haven't talked about it to anyone for years.'

'So, when we met that time in Killarney, it was only a couple of months after...'

'Yes, and the reason that Hollis was so protective was because he was one of the very few people who knew. He took his role of knight in shining armour very seriously.'

'And the unfinished business you mentioned in Geneva — was that to do with all this?'

'Yes. I've never given up the idea of trying to trace my son. I actually almost attempted to have the adoption order overturned many years ago. But all the experts told me that taking him away from the only family he knew would cause him a lot of harm, so I made a pact with myself to wait until he was an adult before attempting to contact him.'

It was almost eleven when they seemed to run out of words. 'We both need some sleep,' she said. 'You have a busy day tomorrow and you need to be on the ball for the White House. I think it's time to pack it in.'

She lingered for a moment without speaking and he moved towards her as if to kiss her.

'Well, well, there you are, you two lovebirds! Jim said this was where you're staying!' It was Fitzpatrick, looking a little the worse for wear. 'I was just passing by on my way home and thought I'd leave a note for you, but this is much better.'

Sinéad stood up. 'Sorry Paul, I'm really tired, but why don't you and Jack do some catching up.'

Paul pulled a card out of his wallet and handed it to her. 'Look, here's my address. I'm having a St Patrick's Day party tomorrow at my place. It's not far from here and I'd like you both to come. All the golden boys and girls of Washington will be there. Curzon's coming too and Jim said he might drop in after the embassy dinner.'

'Thanks, Paul, that sounds great. I'd love to come to your party. See you tomorrow then.'

Paul watched her approvingly as she walked towards the lift, then eased himself into her seat and turned to Jack. 'You're a dark horse, McDonagh. What's the story here then?'

'There's no story. Jim hired her to run a task force and we're working together. We're here on a work mission, that's all.'

'Tell that to the Marines. I saw you two talking just now and don't tell me it was about work. Mind you, I don't blame you. If I wasn't the other way inclined, I'd fancy her myself.'

Jack looked at him, puzzled. 'Come on, McDonagh, you must have known. Once you leave our suffocatingly tiny emerald paradise you realize that there are people out there who aren't so uptight about these things.'

He leaned back in his seat, stretching his arms above his head.

'So, tell me, what are your plans for the weekend? A romantic escapade? I can give you some pointers if you like.' He stopped for a second, as if seeking inspiration. 'Actually, I know the perfect place to take her – Monticello, Thomas Jefferson's place in Virginia. You could be there and back in a day or, if you really want romantic you could just do the Skyline drive and stay in a luxury inn. The weather would need to be good though, so maybe that's not a great idea at this time of year. Oh, and if you like music, there's a good concert on here at the Kennedy Center on Sunday night. Schubert – the ultimate romantic. I can get you tickets if you like.' He stood up abruptly. 'Anyway, look, I can see you're tired. Think about what I said and make sure you come to the party – I'll keep an eye on your Sinéad until you get there.'

'She's not mine,' Jack said.

An embassy car with a discreet Irish flag on it was waiting outside the hotel entrance when he left the breakfast room next morning, and he spotted Jim and the ambassador in deep conversation in the lobby. There was no sign of Sinéad or Curzon and he wondered what they would be doing all day. But he had little time to think as Jim hustled him into the car for the short drive.

It was Jack's first time at the White House. The ambassador gave them a quick briefing on the house and its Irishborn architect, James Hoban, although Jack knew most of the building's history already, as he had done some research for Jim's speech and had even managed to weave in some jokes on the subject. Jim clearly hadn't read the speech he had so carefully crafted. He rarely did, but Jack didn't mind.

The ceremony was all very jolly and quite informal. The whole place had been decorated in green, including the drinks and the food. Jack was busy making mental notes of it all, down to the bright emerald green uniforms worn by the girl scouts who presented them with cookies, so that he could tell Sinéad when he got back. Jim made a very good speech, with just the right balance of humour and politics, and the President was in top form. He seemed to get a real tickle from Jim telling him about the importance of the Reagan clan in Cork.

The next stop was Capitol Hill and lunch with the Speaker, followed by a meeting with congressmen and senators and a quick dash back to the hotel before dinner at the ambassador's residence.

Jack's mind was elsewhere a lot of the time and the jet-lag was kicking in again. It helped that he was sitting beside the wife of one of the EU ambassadors, who regaled him with salacious gossip about everyone at the table, despite warning looks from her husband, whose reputation as a philanderer was an open secret.

To his relief they managed to get away relatively early and Jim got the embassy driver to drop them at Fitzpatrick's place.

When they arrived, the party was in full swing. Simon and Garfunkel's *Me and Julio Down by the Schoolyard* was blaring on the stereo and he spotted Sinéad dancing with Fitzpatrick and clearly enjoying herself. He stood and watched as they performed a sort of jive. Fitzer was an excellent dancer, he had to admit, and they looked good together. She was wearing a pleated black skirt that whirled around as they danced and an elegant black top with what looked like tiny green leaves scattered on it. As the song ended, she spotted Jack and waved. Fitzpatrick paused the music and came over to greet them. He winked at Jack, then took Jim by the elbow and steered him towards a group of interns standing awkwardly in the corner of the room.

Someone turned the music back on and it went straight to *Scarborough Fair*. Out of the corner of his eye he saw a guy walking towards Sinéad.

'Sorry, but she promised me this dance,' he said, intercepting him and guiding her firmly back to the dance area, leaving his rival standing open-mouthed.

'That wasn't very nice,' she said.

'Would you prefer to dance with him?'

She shook her head and moved towards him, placing her hands on his shoulders.

Whenever he heard that song afterwards it made him want to curl up and cry, but that night he let it envelop them

166

until all he was aware of was this fragile presence in his arms, the softness of her hair against his cheek and the feeling that he was falling totally and impossibly in love.

They made their escape as quickly as was decently possible and returned to the hotel. He didn't have to ask her; he just followed her to her room. As they stepped inside, he took her in his arms and they moved towards the bed. He laid her down gently and began to undress her. 'I didn't sleep last night, thinking about you,' he said, as they began to make love. There was not a hint of awkwardness, there was passion, yes, but there was also laughter, tenderness and total, blissful harmony. Afterwards, as they lay back on the pillows, he brushed away a tear from her cheek.

'Are you crying?' he asked.

'Not that kind of crying,' she said. 'Happy crying. Release.'

They had their breakfast sent up to the room and ate it sitting cross-legged on the bed, discussing plans for the rest of the weekend. When he mentioned Monticello she laughed, got up and walked across to her bag. She looked smaller and more fragile in the fluffy hotel bathrobe which was at least two sizes too big.

'You've been talking to Paul,' she said, waving a brochure at him. 'He suggested it to me too. I got some tourist stuff from the concierge yesterday. Frank wanted to go to the Smithsonian today and a concert tomorrow night, so I told him we'd touch base today. I'd really like to go the concert if we can get back in time. What do you think?'

'Let Curzon go to the Smithsonian and as many museums as he likes. We're going to Monticello, and if you really insist and we are back in time then the concert is fine too. I'm going to go downstairs right now and hire a car. Get yourself ready, take a small bag in case we stay overnight and I'll meet you in the lobby in half an hour.'

He picked up his clothes, still lying in a heap on the floor from the previous night, and dressed quickly, then kissed the top of her head and slipped away. When he left the room she was already on the phone to Curzon, arranging tickets for the concert.

Within an hour they were on the road. The weather was cold but clear so they decided to take the longer route along the Interstate 66 to Front Royal and then follow the Skyline Drive through the Shenandoah National Park. Sinéad fiddled with the radio while Jack drove and they looked at each other and laughed as the sound of Simon and Garfunkel filled the car.

As they left the city behind and reached the borders of the park, visibility wasn't the best but the views soon became spectacular.

'Stop here!' she said. 'The guidebook says there's a waterfall and it's really close to the road.' Jack pulled into the overlook and they got out of the car. 'Look,' she said and pointed with a smile at the only other car parked there, its licence plate boldly proclaiming, 'Virginia is for Lovers'. They scrambled down to the Dark Hollow Falls, giggling at the warning signs for brown bears and wild turkey, passing some red-faced hikers on their way back up.

The walk back up was more strenuous then they expected, and they were out of breath by the time they reached the car. Sinéad took out some pastries she had saved from breakfast and they munched them, arm in arm.

'Look, it's raining over there, and there's blue sky on the other side.' She pointed out over the treetops.

'Mm,' he mumbled, 'just like Ireland. Can you see the leprechaun?' She laughed and kissed the crumbs away from his mouth.

They drove on to Hogback Overlook, and from the viewpoint they could just see the Shenandoah river cutting through the vast expanse of lush greenery stretching all the way to the distant Blue Ridge Mountains, shrouded in mist. Mountain laurel and the occasional hardy wildflower added the odd splash of colour to the landscape.

'Remember that film, *Shenandoah*? It says in my book that it was filmed on the slopes of those mountains. It must be amazing in the autumn when all this changes colour.'

'We'll come back,' he whispered in her ear, putting his arms around her and burying his face in her hair.

After a quick stop at a lodge for a bite to eat, all log fires in the corners, jigsaw puzzles on the tables and huge picture windows to look at the view, it soon became clear that they wouldn't make it to Monticello before closing time.

'Let's go to Charlottesville and find somewhere to stay the night,' said Jack. As they turned off the Skyline Drive and approached the town, the sky darkened and it began to rain heavily. They could just make out the neon sign of a motel flashing up ahead.

'A long drive and a storm. Now why does that make me think of the Bates Motel?' she said.

'You watch too many Hollywood films,' he said, laughing. 'A luxury inn was more what I had in mind.'

But she was adamant that she wanted to stay in a motel and, in the end, the place was quite acceptable. The bed was a bit lumpy, but the room was clean and spacious, there was no psycho hiding in the shower, and the convenience of being able to park right outside the door was a bonus. They were both exhausted from accumulated jet lag, emotion and the sleepless night before, so they just went to a nearby diner for a quick bite, watched some bad TV in the room like a couple of naughty school kids and fell asleep in each other's arms.

Chapter Seventeen

Monticello

Jack woke early the next morning and watched Sinéad sleeping quietly beside him. He felt none of the irritation or guilt that usually followed his one-night stands, when he wished that he'd slipped away in the middle of the night and when he dreaded the inevitable awkwardness – or worse, tears. And he felt none of the flat sense of resignation he knew only too well when he woke up beside the woman he'd married for all the wrong reasons, realizing that this was as good as it was ever going to get.

He stroked Sinéad's hair gently and brushed aside any thoughts of what might happen next. They would find a solution. They had to. Everything would be fine.

She opened her eyes and drew him towards her. She snuggled up to him and whispered, 'Pancakes with maple syrup.'

'What?'

'A proper American breakfast. Aren't you hungry?'

'Yes, but I don't want to have to go out. I want to stay here in bed with you. I told you we should have stayed at a fancy hotel – we could have had room service.'

'The authentic American experience is much more fun,' she said, pulling back the covers and heading for the bathroom. He followed her into the shower, still grumbling. He tried to stand still as she massaged him with shower gel and shampoo, then he turned her around and began to soap her back.

'Forgive my clumsiness, ma'am,' he said. 'It's my first time.'

'Liar,' she said, taking the shower head from its hook and directing the stream of water at him. It was true, though. He had never taken a shower with a woman, not even his wife, and he thought to himself that it was probably because he had never experienced that degree of easy intimacy with anyone before.

'We'll never get to Monticello at this rate,' he murmured, wrapping his arms around her and burying his face in her damp hair. 'And do I care?'

It was ten o'clock before they left the motel and made their way to the diner, where he watched as Sinéad dug into a pile of blueberry pancakes smothered in maple syrup.

'I got a liking for these when I worked in New Hampshire as a waitress. It was the only decent food they gave us – we had them every morning for breakfast. Here,' she said, spearing a piece and holding it out for him to taste. He tried to hold the fork but she pulled it away, and as he tried to hold on to the pancake the maple syrup ran down his chin. She sat back and laughed.

'I wish I'd brought my camera,' she said.

She leaned across again and wiped his face with her napkin. He took her hand and held it for a moment, kissing the tips of her fingers.

'That's better,' she said. 'Now let's go to Monticello.'

'Wait,' he said. 'Promise me one thing before we leave.'

'That sounds very serious,' she said.

'I am serious, Sinéad. Promise me...' He hesitated. 'Promise me that no matter what happens after this trip, no matter where we are or who we are with, promise me we'll meet up again in Washington on St Patrick's Day.'

'When?'

'Oh, I don't know – how about in 2000?'

'That sounds like it's a century away! I hadn't put you down as a romantic, Jack McDonagh.'

Seeing his expression, she smiled and took his hand, 'OK, OK, don't look so crestfallen. I promise. Happy now?'

★

'If you do go to Monticello, don't mention slavery. It's all about life, liberty and the pursuit of happiness now!' Fitzpatrick had said to him at the party. And he didn't, and nor did anyone else, least of all the two middle-aged American couples from Oregon who smiled benignly at them all the time, probably assuming they were on their honeymoon.

According to their knowledgeable young tour guide, Jefferson had followed Palladio's principles for the layout of the building, making the best parts visible, but the 'less agreeable' sections arranged well out of sight so that they offended the eye as little as possible.

'Which is the best way to do it,' Jack whispered, 'if you have a small army of slaves scuttling about in the kitchens preparing your meals.'

'I was born in the wrong century – I could definitely live here,' said Sinéad, as they trailed the guide, admiring Jefferson's study and the dome room. It was certainly impressive, but there was something else about the place that Jack couldn't quite define, a sense of peace and tranquillity. Once the tour was over, they just sat on a bench in the West garden, soaking up the atmosphere.

'Shame the irises aren't out yet,' said Sinéad. 'I love them. And I would have liked to see those blackberry lilies the guide was talking about. Wouldn't you just know it was an Irishman who gave them to Jefferson?'

'Pity we have to go back,' said Jack, stretching. 'I could live here too.' He stood up and pulled her to her feet. 'I need to get something for my girls – let's have a look in the shop before we go.'

Avoiding the more girly items, Sinéad directed him towards a build-your-own paper model kit of the house and some colouring books. While he paid, she wandered around the shop, picked up a packet of seeds. 'I didn't know you could grow these lilies from seed. One for me, one for you,' she said, handing one to him.

'You don't even have a garden!'

'Not at the moment, but I know somewhere these will be perfect.'

They took the direct route back to Washington, arriving just in time to get ready for the concert. It was only when they met Curzon in the lobby that Jack realized he had no idea what music they were going to hear.

When they arrived at the JFK Center, Curzon led them

out onto the river terrace overlooking the Potomac and began to talk about the programme.

'It's a stroke of luck getting to hear Brendel playing here. And especially Schubert — as far as I'm concerned, nobody can play Schubert better than him. Do you know the last three sonatas, Jack?' he asked. Jack shook his head. Unlike Sinéad's family, his had little or no interest in classical music and he had never really been exposed to music in school. Lorna and he sometimes went to concerts, but these were really occasions to see and be seen, usually organized by Sarah.

'People who are not familiar with them can sometimes find them a little difficult to listen to,' Curzon added — a bit pompously, Jack thought.

It was cold and a plane passed overhead, flying quite low and drowning out the conversation. They hurried back into the grand foyer, where Curzon turned his attention to the architecture of the building, explaining that it had been built as a sort of 'box within a box' mainly to keep out aircraft noise, as they were quite close to the airport.

As they gazed up at the sixteen Swedish chandeliers, Jack stood behind Sinéad and kissed the back of her neck gently, while she pretended not to notice. Then, as they stopped in front of the huge bronze of John F Kennedy, Curzon grabbed one of the staff and handed over his camera, asking him to take a photo of the three of them in front of the statue. Jack still had that picture in his office, tucked away behind some books. Three happy, smiling people having an enjoyable evening with no inkling of the storm clouds that were brewing. Him trying to hold Sinéad's hand without Curzon seeing.

He didn't find the sonatas difficult to listen to at all, and he liked to think that his late-blooming passion for music was sparked by that concert, or perhaps it was the sight of Sinéad leaning forward, transfixed, as Brendel played an absolutely exquisite *Impromptu* as an encore. He thought it was the most beautiful piece of music he had ever heard. Sinéad's hair, that wonderful thick hair he loved to run his fingers through, fell forward over one eye and she flicked it back, then turned to him and pointed to her arm.

'Gooseflesh,' she whispered. He pushed up the cuff of his shirt and pointed at his. 'Snap.'

'I love that *Impromptu*,' she said as they made their way back to the hotel. 'A friend of mine once gave me the sheet music for it and it's always been one of my life's ambitions to be able to play it.'

'You must be good if you want to attempt that,' said Curzon. 'The simpler the piece sounds, the more difficult it is to get right.'

'I took up the piano again when I was in Geneva,' she said, 'and I've been slowly working back up to the level I was at when I stopped at thirteen, but I think it'll be a while before I can tackle any Schubert.'

Curzon, who was a keen amateur violinist – was there no end to the man's talents? Jack thought – offered to introduce her to a good teacher in Dublin, which seemed to delight her.

Jack suggested they have a drink at the bar, but Sinéad shook her head.

'It's late, Jack,' she said, 'I'm exhausted and we have a meeting tomorrow – or had you forgotten? But if you and Frank...'

Frank shook his head and they walked to the lift together. They were all on the same floor. Curzon's room was only a few doors down from Sinéad's, and Jack's was at the end of the corridor, so he said goodnight to both of them and went straight to his room. He waited for a few minutes, wondering if he should phone Sinéad first, but then went out into the corridor, telling himself that if he met Curzon, he would say that he had to pick something up from reception. He knocked lightly on Sinéad's door and she opened it almost immediately, putting her finger to her lips as he stepped in.

'How tired are you?' he said, taking her in his arms. She pulled away from him and sat down on the edge of the bed. 'What's the matter?' he asked.

'Nothing,' she said, 'it's just...well it's been a bit intense, these past couple of days, and I'm not sure where we're going with it. I mean, you're married, you've got kids...'

Jack sighed and sat down beside her. 'Sinéad, I know, and we need to talk about it. But maybe now isn't the best time.'

'You're right,' she said. 'We both need to sleep and clear our heads for tomorrow. Do you mind sleeping in your own room?' She smiled almost apologetically and he hid his disappointment, kissing her lightly on the cheek.

'Of course not.' As he made his way towards the door, he turned and said, 'I'm so glad I met you again, Sinéad.'

'I'm glad too, Jack,' she said and they embraced for a long moment.

★

The next morning, he woke with a growing sense of despair at the thought of going back home. They coasted through their meeting with some well-intentioned American counterparts, and Jack's suspicions that Jim had simply set this up as a way for them to spend a bit more time in Washington were confirmed.

They had to leave mid-afternoon as they were connecting through New York for their flight back to Dublin. Because Curzon was travelling with them, there was no chance to talk privately on either plane, and it began to dawn on him as he tried to sleep that this was how it was going to be in Dublin too, something he had tried to avoid thinking about while they were in the States. So he was not in a good mood when they arrived in Dublin airport, and even less so when they walked out of the baggage hall and he heard a loud shriek.

'Daddy!' He first saw Fiona running towards him before catching a glimpse of Lorna standing well back, holding Isabelle in her arms. Lorna never, ever, came to pick him up at the airport. He didn't dare look at Sinéad. He bent down to scoop up Fiona, who buried her head in his neck, giving him time to gather his thoughts before he walked over to his wife, kissing her dutifully on the cheek and turning to Sinéad and Curzon to introduce them. They all shook hands, Fiona still clinging to her father.

Curzon turned to Jack. 'Jack, I'm sure you will want to take all these young ladies home. Can I give you a lift, Sinéad? I'm off to get a bit of a rest before heading to the office.' She nodded, relieved, and having said their goodbyes they walked off quickly together.

Jack tried to behave as normally as possible, even though his mind was running through all the possible worst-case scenarios, but there was no opportunity for a conversation in the car as the two girls chattered all the way home. Did Lorna suspect something? But how could she? – nothing had happened before Washington. Still, Fitzer had noticed their closeness – maybe other people had too. Maybe someone had said something to her.

As they pulled into the driveway, Lorna spoke.

'Mummy called round yesterday and suggested we go to the airport this morning to give you a big surprise. Fiona had a couple of days off anyway, and she thought it would get us all out of the house.'

He looked at her warily, but couldn't detect any trace of irony in her expression, then turned to his daughters.

'Well, thank you girls, that was a lovely surprise, just what Daddy needed after all that boring work.'

He had barely got into the house when they started pestering him about presents, so he opened his luggage in the hall and took out the model kit he had bought at Monticello. Although they seemed quite pleased and made him promise to help them put it together in the evening, they were far more interested in the two packets of chocolate-covered peanut butter he pulled out of his briefcase.

He gave Lorna a silk scarf he had bought at the hotel shop when Sinéad was not around. 'It's not Hermès, but I think the colours suit you.'

His daughters were preoccupied with their sweets, so he made his way quickly to his bedroom to wash and change. As he stepped out of the shower, he was surprised to see

179

Lorna standing almost shyly by the door, fingering the scarf which she had draped around her shoulders.

'I heard Frank saying he was going to the office. You're not going in too, are you? I missed you when you were away,' she said.

'I'm really sorry, but I have to, Lorna. The boss came back ahead of us yesterday and he'll be wanting reports done and so on. You know what he's like.'

'Why can't someone else do them — that new woman who's working for you, for example? Sarah says she's single and has no children, so she probably has nothing else to do anyway.'

He stopped rubbing himself with the towel and looked at her. 'She doesn't work for me, Lorna — if anything I work for her. And how does Sarah know so much about my colleagues and what they do and don't do?'

She shrugged her shoulders. 'You know Sarah, she likes to know everything that's going on.'

He sighed. 'You shouldn't pay too much attention to what Sarah says. She knows a lot less than she thinks.' He kissed her lightly on the cheek and said, 'I'll try to get back early and play with the girls before they go to bed. Then we can watch a film or go out if you want. You choose.'

She smiled, a bit too brightly he thought, and left the room. He picked up his watch and looked at the time — it was almost two and he really needed to speak to Sinéad.

It was nearly three when he arrived at the office. The lifts in Hawkins House weren't working, so he had to leg it up the nine flights of stairs. Brenda looked up, surprised, as he pushed the door open, trying to catch his breath.

'Jack, I didn't expect you back today. I thought you'd be having a rest after the night flight and the jet lag and so on. Did you have a good trip?'

'Yes, thanks, Brenda. I'll tell you about it later. I really need to speak to Sinéad. Is she in?'

Brenda nodded toward the door of Sinéad's office and said she thought she was busy, but he ignored her and walked in without knocking. Sinéad was sitting with Curzon and they were deep in conversation, clearly surprised to see him.

'Hi, Frank,' he said. 'Sorry to butt in, but I need to talk to Sinéad. About the report,' he added in response to Frank's quizzical look.

Curzon got up and smiled. 'Of course, Jack. I'll leave you to it.' He turned back to Sinéad and said, 'Good luck.'

She raised her eyebrows and grimaced. 'Thanks, Frank. I'll need it. I'll let you know how I get on.'

Jack looked after him as he left the office, closing the door quietly.

'You two seem very pally – what's going on?'

She didn't answer, just shook her head and looked at him with a faintly amused air.

'OK, OK, sorry, none of my business,' he said, raising his hands in the air. 'But I really do need to talk to you.' He paused, took a deep breath, 'Look, Sinéad, what happened in Washington...'

'It's fine, Jack,' she said flatly, her smile gone. 'It was a mistake. I knew from the start that you were married.' She shook her head slowly, looking down at her hands. 'I don't know what I was thinking, even contemplating having an affair with you.'

'Please don't use that word!' he said. 'Look, Sinéad, I came in this afternoon because I wanted to tell you that as far as I'm concerned it wasn't just a one-off – a fling, or whatever you want to call it. And I don't want to have an affair with you – I don't want to have to hide away.' She shook her head again and there was a long silence. He paced around the room and then sat in the chair opposite her. 'I'm going to leave Lorna. I'd been thinking about it for a long time before I met you anyway. It's not going to be easy and I'm going to need some time to sort things out. Do you think you can give me that time?'

She shook her head again. 'You need to think very carefully about this, Jack. I don't want you to leave your wife because of me. If you do leave her it has to be because you want to leave her. Full stop. And you need to keep me out of the equation.' She fiddled with a pen and looked down at the desk. 'What I'm saying is that we need to stop this now – I really think it's better that we don't see each other outside work for a while, until you've cleared things up in your own head and done whatever you need to do.' She sighed. 'Anyway, I've taken a couple of days off as I have some things I need to do myself. I've sorted it with Frank and we've re-scheduled the next task force meeting so that we have time to write up the Brussels and Washington trips before it.' She stood up and began to gather some papers together. 'Let's talk again in a few days.'

There was a knock on the door and Brenda came in. She must have sensed the atmosphere, but she didn't bat an eyelid. 'Sorry to disturb you, Sinéad, but Jim would like to see you for a minute. He's in his office.' Sinéad walked out quickly and after she had left Brenda asked, 'Are you alright Jack?'

'Of course I'm alright,' he snapped. 'Sorry, Brenda. I'm just a bit jetlagged, that's all.'

'It's always worse when you fly eastwards,' she added. 'You know Sinéad's taking a few days off, and I think Jim's going to be away tomorrow, so maybe you should take it easy too. Stay at home with the kids – I can call you if there's anything urgent.'

He hung around the office for a while, but there was no sign of Sinéad. He wondered why she had taken two days off and why she hadn't said anything. He thought of asking Brenda, but was afraid of arousing her suspicions, even though he was pretty sure she wouldn't disapprove.

On his way home from work that evening, he drove by Merrion Square and parked a short distance from the building where Sinéad had her flat. He stayed for half an hour, listening to the car radio and watching as the lights in the offices went out one by one until the whole building was in darkness and all its occupants appeared to have left. Just as he was about to give up, a light came on at the top floor. He wondered how she had got in without him seeing her, and then remembered there was a car park at the back. But she didn't have a car, so someone must have dropped her off. And why at the back? Did it mean she didn't want to be seen? Was there someone with her? And if so, who was it? He briefly thought of going to a phone box and calling her but then told himself to stop being paranoid.

When he got home the girls had the model of Monticello open and the pieces all over the dining room table.

'Mummy said we had to do this with you,' said Fiona, who had already spread out the instructions and was poring over them, even though she couldn't read.

It was quite complicated to build, far too complicated for his daughters, but it took his mind off Sinéad, so he threw himself into it and he had to admit the end result was quite impressive. The girls were oohing and aahing and saying they wanted a house like that too when Lorna came into the room.

'What a beautiful house!' she said.

'Daddy went there when he was in America,' said Fiona, 'and he said he'd take us there one day if we were good.'

Lorna picked up the box and read the back. 'This is in Virginia,' she said. 'I thought you were in Washington.'

'Oh, it's not far. We had some free time at the weekend so we hired a car and took a day trip up there,' he said. 'Let's put it up here on the shelf,' he said, turning to Fiona. She climbed onto a chair and he handed her the model which she placed carefully on the bookshelf beside the fireplace. Then she jumped into his arms and he carried her to the kitchen. 'What would you like for dinner then?'

'Pasta,' she shrieked.

Isabelle, trotting along behind, said, 'I eating pasta too!'

By the time he had made their pasta, given them their bath and put them to bed with a story, it was almost nine o'clock and he sat down with Lorna in front of the television with a snack to watch the news.

'Do you remember Paul Fitzpatrick?' he asked as the news finished.

Lorna frowned and said, 'Wasn't he in school with you? The one you called Fitzer?'

'Yes, well he's in Washington now, we met him at the airport. Got a good job there'

He omitted to mention the party, but told her about the ceremony at the White House. She listened politely, as she always did when he talked about anything outside the family circle.

'Curzon got tickets for a really nice concert,' he continued. 'Schubert. A pianist called Brendel.'

'Oh,' she said. 'German?'

'No, Austrian. You know, I was thinking, maybe we should start the girls on the piano, see if they like it. I might even take it up myself.'

He rang the office early the next day to tell Brenda he had decided to take her advice and spend some time with the girls, and asked her do the necessary to fill in his leave form. Then he went to wake his daughters, and over a lazy breakfast asked them what they would like to do. Fiona brushed her hair out of her eyes with the back of her hand – she could be very theatrical at times, and he often wondered where that came from – licking her jammy fingers thoughtfully before clapping her hands together and doing monkey noises.

Isabelle immediately understood and stood up on her chair jumping and chanting, 'a zoo, a zoo'.

Lorna looked at him – he knew she hated going to the zoo. She wasn't keen on animals of any sort, and she particularly hated the noise and the smells in the indoor enclosures. In the end, she decided to stay at home, as it would be Easter before long and she wanted to spruce up the house in case relatives called. She liked things to be perfect.

They had a great day. Jack had always loved Dublin zoo. Dubliners said it was the best zoo in the world, but he figured it was probably just part of the hype about the country in general – Phoenix Park is the biggest park in Europe, O'Connell Street is the widest thoroughfare in the world, the Irish education system beats all others and so on. He had never been to a zoo anywhere else though, so was happy to believe that particular myth.

They bought bags of peanuts from the sellers outside before making their way to the ticket kiosk. The girls' favourite place was the monkey enclosure, with the lion house a close second, even though the big cats terrified them both. After doing the rounds of the various animals they had a very unhealthy lunch of burgers, sausages and chips smothered in ketchup, and then spent time in Pets' Corner. You had to pay extra for that, which his parents always refused to do when he was taken there as a child, so he made up for it by spoiling his daughters now.

They finished up watching the seals being fed, Isabelle bursting with excitement and shouting, 'I swimming too, Daddy!' with Jack holding her tightly to stop her jumping into the water.

They made their way back to the car as he had promised them a surprise. After a quick drive to Sandymount, he parked the car and they boarded the Dart to Howth. They had never been on a train before – Lorna didn't like public transport, it made her feel nervous, being in close proximity to too many people – and they began jumping up and down with excitement. As they boarded the train, Jack spotted a woman he knew further down the carriage, someone he'd had a brief fling with about a year before. He moved as far away as possible and tried to avoid catching her eye, but she saw them and weaved her way up to where they were sitting.

'Jack! How are you? I haven't seen you for ages! And who are these two lovely young ladies? Can I join you?' she asked, sitting down beside Jack. She chatted away, smiling all the time at the girls, who just looked away and refused to engage with her. To his relief she got off at Pearse station, leaving them to enjoy the rest of the trip in relative peace.

They walked around the harbour in Howth and watched some fisherman unloading their catch before heading back towards the train station and getting an ice-cream cone from the colourful stands outside. He would have loved to go to the summit and walk around the cliffs, just as Sinéad did regularly with her parents, but of course that was out of the question with the two little ones.

When they got back to Sandymount, he spotted a florist and suggested to the girls that they go and buy some flowers for their mother. While they were busy choosing the flowers, he spotted some irises and he asked the assistant if they could deliver a bouquet to a Dublin address that evening.

'Any message?' she asked. He took a card from the rack by the counter and hastily scribbled a note – "S – *Thank you for sharing your story with me. Your son is lucky to have such a wonderful mother and I know that if he knew you, he would be proud of you. J"*

When they got home the house smelled strongly of paint, and Lorna was lying on the sofa reading a book about home decoration. She had enlisted the help of her nephew, Fiachra, and had him repaint the downstairs cloakroom. Jack had to admit they had done a great job – Lorna was good at that kind of thing, very focused and almost obsessive about getting things right.

'I was getting your clothes ready for the cleaners and I found a packet of seeds in your pocket,' she said.

His heart skipped a beat. 'Oh yes, it was just a little something I picked up at the shop in Monticello. Very unusual flowers. I thought they would look nice in the garden. Apparently, it was an Irishman who gave the original seeds to Jefferson.'

'Yes, well I read on the packet that the things that look like blackberries can be poisonous, so I'm going to give them to someone who doesn't have children. If that's alright with you.'

'Who was that lady on the train, Daddy? I didn't like her.' Fiona interrupted his thoughts and Lorna looked at him with raised eyebrows. 'Isabelle didn't like her either, did you Isabelle?' Isabelle shook her head, frowning. She would make a good diplomat, he thought, always agreeing with her sister in public and defying her as soon as her back was turned.

'It was someone I work with. I can't say I like her a lot either.'

Later that evening he mulled over the girls' reaction, wondering if children can sense things like that, and how they might react to Sinéad if he ever introduced them.

Chapter Eighteen

Lombard Street, Dublin, 20th March

THERE WAS ALREADY A queue forming in front of Joyce House in Lombard Street when Sinéad arrived. Margaret beckoned to her and she moved forward, apologizing to the people waiting behind.

'So, this is the big day then, is it?' Sinéad nodded, feeling a rush of emotion and not daring to speak. 'Remember everything I told you the last time,' Margaret said. 'Just be polite, but firm. They can't stop you searching, although they can make it difficult for you. And don't forget the pencil and paper in your pocket.'

Sinéad had met Margaret some weeks before when she went to the General Register Office to ask for a copy of Lorcan's birth certificate. It had all been amazingly easy – she just had to give her name and her son's date of birth and there it was, in black and white, in the register. Lorcan Murray, born 6th October 1970 in Blackrock, Cork. Of course, it was completely useless in terms of finding him, but she needed to see it, to hold it in her hand and convince herself it really happened and that it wasn't all a bad dream. Once she had paid the fee and received the copy, she asked to consult the register of adoptions, but the woman behind the desk told her that there was someone already in the room and that they would probably be there all day. She asked if she could book a time to carry out her research, but the woman shook her head and told her she would just have to turn up and take a chance.

Sinéad turned away, despondent, but as she headed for the exit, a woman she had seen earlier talking to some people in the queue caught her by the sleeve.

'Excuse me.' The woman looked a few years older than her, Sinéad thought, and had a bundle of papers under her arm and was carrying a shopping bag with what looked like more official documents inside. 'I saw you wanted to consult the adoption register. I hope you don't mind me asking, but would you like to talk about it? Maybe I can help.'

Sinéad hesitated and the woman rushed on. 'My name is Margaret Dwyer, and I'm helping some friends doing research.' She handed Sinéad a card with her phone number scribbled on it.

'What kind of research?' Sinéad was intrigued.

'Adoption research. We're all either birth mothers searching for our adopted children, or adoptees looking for their birth parents. Have you time for a coffee? I've been here since early morning and I'm dying for one.'

There was something instantly likeable about the woman, and Sinéad badly needed a coffee too, so she walked up Westland Row with her and stopped at the first café they found. The place was practically empty, and they made their way to a small table in the corner.

'I always like to have my back to the wall,' said Margaret, smiling. 'That way nobody can sneak up behind you and stab you in the back.' Sinéad looked at her, not quite knowing how to take the comment, and Margaret laughed. 'It's a joke – don't worry. I'm probably paranoid, but not clinically speaking! What can I get you?'

Sinéad protested, offering to pay, but Margaret ignored her and walked up to the counter to order. Sinéad looked at her more closely. She was probably in her early forties, and her clothes had a faintly bohemian air about them. If Sinéad had to guess, she'd say Margaret was an artist, or perhaps someone involved in the theatre.

'There you are,' said Margaret, placing a large mug of steaming coffee in front of her. 'Would you like one of these?' she asked, offering a packet of Mikado biscuits she had pulled out of her shopping bag.

Sinéad hesitated, conscious of the woman behind the counter watching them, and wondering why Margaret had brought her own biscuits to a café.

'Oh what the hell, why not?' she said, and took one. 'Happy memories,' she said. 'No, not really. My first memory of Blackrock.'

Margaret looked at her for a moment. 'So? Do you want to talk, or would you prefer me to start?'

'You go first,' mumbled Sinéad, her mouth full of the sweet and sticky pink coconut.

Margaret's story was remarkably similar to her own, except that she was from Wexford and her parents had sent her to a home in Dublin where she stayed for over a year.

'My parents couldn't – or rather wouldn't – pay, so I had to stay on in the home to work off my debt. My daughter was adopted almost immediately after she was born. I was looking for her for years, and then one day last year I was up at the home, banging my head against a brick wall as usual, and I bumped into another girl who had been there around the same time as me. She was searching too, and she'd been in touch with some people in the UK who gave her advice about tracing, so we decided to pool our efforts. So now we have a little group – unofficial and completely amateur, of course – mostly women looking for the babies they gave up and a few younger ones looking for their mothers. Some of the women we help are barely literate, so we do the search for them – that's why you'll often see me hanging around the office. I almost know that book off by heart by now.' She smiled at Sinéad. 'You wouldn't believe some of the stories I hear.'

'And…did you find her? Your daughter?'

'Yes, I did in the end,' she said, almost defiant. 'But it didn't go that well. She didn't really want to know me. She was adopted into a "good" family, and I have a feeling I might cramp her style.'

'But you met her?'

'Yes, briefly, twice. She was very uncomfortable. She's not at all like me – tall, blonde, nicely spoken.' Margaret grimaced.

'Maybe she'll come around. When she has children of her own.'

'Maybe she will,' said Margaret. 'But enough about me. That's not why we're here. Tell me your story and I'll see if we can do anything for you.'

'I don't know where to begin,' said Sinéad. She took a sip of her coffee and tried to summarize what had happened to her.

Margaret listened without interrupting, until she came to the part where she left Ireland.

'Had you given up hope at that stage?' she asked.

'No, I never gave up. In fact, a couple of years on, I even thought about going to court to get him back. There was this case before the Supreme Court...'

'Yes, I remember, it was all over the papers.' Margaret paused and shook her head. 'You could go down that route, but personally I don't think it's a good idea,' she said.

'Oh absolutely, I agree. I've been through all that and decided not to pursue it. In the end, I didn't think it was the right thing for my son.'

Margaret nodded. 'So how far have you got in your search?' she asked.

'Well, all I've done really is to get all the official journals – you know, the government publications that list all the adoption orders – *Iris Oifigiúil* – from around the time he was adopted, and I've trawled through them looking for children called Lorcan. But it's a huge job and I feel I'm not getting anywhere.'

'Have you tried the adoption agency?'

Sinéad raised her eyes to heaven. 'Don't talk to me about them. I've been to see them, and I asked them to put it on record that if my son ever wants to find me, I have no objection to being contacted.'

'And I suppose they said no?'

'They told me there was no provision in the law for that. My strategy at the moment is to just keep going in to show them I'm serious, that I'm not some madwoman who's going to cause trouble. It's so humiliating, though.'

'The law will have to change soon,' Margaret said. 'It's been legal in the UK for quite a while now for adopted people to search for their birth parents.' She shifted in her chair. 'OK, Sinéad, here's what I think you should do. First, forget about *Iris Oifigiúil* for the moment – it's a complete waste of time. In the vast majority of cases, the adoptive parents gave the child a new name. It's about wiping the slate clean, getting rid of any reminders of where they came from.'

'Are you sure? Surely some of them would keep the name, even as a second or third name? I know I would.'

'Don't forget we're talking about the turn of the seventies here, Sinéad. I know things have changed since then, but at that time a lot of people tried to hide the fact that their child was adopted. Usually because of the general perception that the mothers were loose women. And don't forget that for some adoptive parents being childless was often a stigma too, especially in rural areas.' She tapped her fingers on the table. 'I've heard of cases where people even pretended the child was their own and where the birth was declared in their name, so there is no so-called original birth certificate like you got today. You can imagine how difficult that makes any kind of search.' She paused. 'But back to you. The next thing you need to do is what you tried to do today, which will definitely help you narrow down your search. It's tedious and it's time-consuming, but it can work. You go back to Lombard Street and you ask to search the Adoptions register. Convince them you need to have an appointment and don't give up until they say yes. Some of the people in there are very understanding – the woman you saw this morning, for example. She's actually very nice, even if she doesn't give that impression.' Margaret picked up her mug and sipped her coffee. 'Now, there's just one book for the period your child was born in, and it covers something like twenty years. And – this is where it gets tedious – the adoptions are listed alphabetically under the name of the adoptive parents. So, unless you know their name, and of course you don't or you wouldn't be searching, you just have to go through the entire book from cover to cover, noting anyone with the same date of birth as your son. Some of those will be girls, obviously, so you can ignore them straightaway. Oh, and they have a rule in there – you can't make notes, so no pen and paper.'

'But if you can't take notes, how on earth are you supposed to remember the names and addresses, and how long will this take?' asked Sinéad.

'Well, you might be searching for a couple of days, it depends on how fast you read. You hide a pen and paper in your pocket and each time you find a child born on that date you memorize the name as best you can and after a while ask to use the facilities. Then when you're in the loo, just write it down and go back. It wouldn't be considered unusual to go out four or five times in the space of two days.'

'And that will narrow it down to how many, roughly?'

'Again, it depends on how many births on that particular day were illegitimate, and how many went on to be adopted. It's impossible to say. I was lucky – there were only three girls born the same day as my daughter who were adopted.'

'Illegitimate, bastard, unmarried mother... God, I hate those words,' said Sinéad. 'OK, and then what happens? I'll just have his new Christian name and the surname of the adoptive parents, right? No address or anything?'

'Yes, but that's where our friend *Iris Oifigúil* comes in. You already have all the pages, so all you need to do is match the names of those people with the adoption orders made around that time. You know the date you signed the adoption papers, so I would look at all the orders made in the year starting from that date.'

Sinéad took a deep breath and began to smile, but Margaret continued.

'Don't get too excited. Unless you are very, very lucky, you're nowhere near the end of your search. Let's say you have five names and addresses. The address published is the place where the parents lived when they adopted the child. But that's, what, fourteen years ago. They could have moved, God knows how many times. They could have left the country, died, separated – anything is possible.'

Sinéad sat back in her chair, her mind racing. 'Well, if it's patience you need, I've got plenty of it,' she said. 'I've been building up to this for a long time. And anyway, even if I find him fairly quickly, I won't do anything until he's an adult. I've done a lot of reading on the subject and have no intention of rushing in unprepared and causing havoc in his life.'

'That's good,' said Margaret. 'That's the right attitude. I've done a lot of reading too. I even went back to college and trained as a psychologist so that I could help other women.'

'You're a psychologist? If I'd known that, I'd have been

more careful in what I said,' Sinéad said, laughing.

Margaret reached down into her shopping bag and pulled out a book. 'Have you read this?' she asked. 'It's called *The Adoption Triangle*. I found it very useful. It looks at the issue from all sides, not just the birth mother and child, but also the adoptive family. It's really important to understand the effect all this can have on everyone concerned, and a lot of people don't realize what a minefield it can be. You can borrow it if you like, but I should warn you. There's some pretty harrowing stuff in there about reunions. It doesn't always go well, you know.'

Sinéad took it and flicked through it. 'This looks really interesting,' she said, taking out a notebook and writing down the details. 'I don't know how long I'm going to be in Ireland. I'll pop down later to Hodges Figgis' bookshop and see if they have it, and if they don't I'll order it,' she said, handing the book back. 'You keep this for someone else.'

'Have you thought about how you're going to manage this from abroad?'

'Sort of. I'm working here for now anyway, but I suppose I could always get someone to do some searching for me here. I still live in hope that the adoption society will cooperate.'

'I wouldn't count on that. And stay away from private investigators. They'll cost you a fortune and you can probably do most of the work yourself. Anyway, we're always here if you need us.'

After their conversation, Sinéad followed Margaret's advice and went back to Joyce House. She held on until there was nobody in the queue waiting for certificates and, her heart racing, she approached the woman she had seen earlier behind the counter.

'Excuse me, I was here earlier.' She waited for the woman to look up from the papers she was sorting, then, with a broad smile and as much charm as she could muster, 'I'm really sorry to bother you, but I don't live in Ireland – at least not permanently – so I was wondering if it would be possible to book a time to consult the adoption register.' She smiled again, 'I know it's not usual, is there any way you could make an exception? I'd really appreciate it.'

The woman looked at her for a moment, then hesitated and looked around.

'Wait here for a minute. I'll see if it's possible,' she said. She went away for a moment and returned with a diary.

'I would recommend the 20th March,' the woman said, keeping her voice low, 'and I could block off the 21st and 22nd too just in case you needed more time.' Sinéad thought she detected understanding in the woman's eyes, and wondered how many times she had made this gesture.

★

The doors opened and the queue moved forward. Margaret tapped her on the back. 'Good luck – you know where I am if you want to talk at any time, but I'm sure you'll be OK.'

After making herself known to the person at the counter, Sinéad was led into a room which was more like a small covered courtyard surrounded by offices, each one with a window looking into the room. In the middle of the room there was a very large book, a bit like an old-fashioned ledger, set on a table. The only other piece of furniture was a wooden chair.

'You do know you're only allowed to consult the register and that you can't make any notes?' the woman inquired.

'Yes,' said Sinéad, conscious of the tiny pencil and notebook in her trouser pocket. 'Thank you.'

'The toilets are there if you need them.' The woman gestured to a door down the corridor. 'And if you need to leave early, just call at the desk and let us know.'

She left, shutting the door quietly behind her, and Sinéad looked around. There were people in some of the offices, but they all appeared engrossed in their work and nobody was paying any attention to her. She pulled up the chair and sat down, took a deep breath, opened the book and began to scroll down through the dates of birth next to the surnames beginning with A, careful not to touch the pages too often, for fear of damaging them.

Not long into the search she came across a girl born on the 6th October 1970 and almost immediately afterwards a boy, Gerald Barrett. She was beginning to feel lightheaded, and wondered if she should go out now to write down the name, or carry on until she had at least two. She stood up and walked around the room to stretch her legs, and as she did so she noticed a man in one of the offices looking at her. He caught her glance and nodded so slightly that it could have been her imagination.

She sat down again and ploughed on. C, D, E, F... By the time she reached H it was almost lunchtime and she began to wonder if she hadn't missed some names, so she slowed down and went back over some of the pages. There were two more girls whom she discounted. Then she came across a John Hogan with the right date of birth and decided it was time to take a break. The offices closed for lunch anyway so now was a good time. She pulled on her jacket, picked up her bag and made her way to the toilets. Once inside the cubicle, she pulled out her notebook and pencil and wrote quickly, terrified she would forget or make a mistake in the names: *Gerald Barrett, John Hogan.*

She took a deep breath and walked out past the desk, telling them she would be back later.

Sinéad was first in the queue that afternoon, and the woman waved her towards the office. The afternoon was less productive, and she only found one more boy's name before abandoning the search at N. She felt stiff from sitting in the one position for all that time, and her eyes were aching with the strain. She walked slowly back to her flat that evening, wondering if anything would ever come out of this. Perhaps it was a wild goose chase, and she resisted the temptation to start looking for the three names in the papers on the table. She had a light supper and tried to sleep.

The next morning, she began again with renewed energy. Very quickly, she found two under O – normal, she thought, given the number of Irish surnames beginning in O. She made a quick trip to the ladies' to add them to her list and slogged on. The man she thought had nodded at her was still in his office, but didn't appear to be paying her much attention.

Shortly after lunch she found a sixth name, but it took her another two hours to reach the end of the book. There was a sense of anti-climax as she closed the huge tome, stood up, stretched and gathered her things. It was almost five, and most of the people in the offices around her had left.

'Hello.' She turned around. It was the man whose gaze she had crossed the previous day, standing at the door.

'Hello,' she said, smiling, trying to look relaxed.

'I was wondering if you'd mind stepping into my office for a moment.'

Sinéad's heart began to beat faster. What if he asked her to empty her pockets? She had noted the names from yesterday and left them at the flat, but would she remember the three from today if they took the paper away? The office smelled of stale smoke. He motioned her to sit down and offered her a cigarette which she accepted, even though she hardly ever smoked now. He offered her a light and then lit his own cigarette, drew heavily on it and sat back in his chair and smiled.

'I hope you don't mind my asking, and you don't have to tell me if you don't want to, but I just wondered what you were doing in there for the past two days.'

He had a very slight accent – Galway, she thought – and from the way he was dressed and the way he spoke he was clearly not a junior member of staff. Sinéad hesitated – she could lie and make up something about genealogical research, but something about his demeanour inspired confidence.

'I was doing research.'

'Yes, I don't doubt that,' he said. 'Can I ask what kind of research?'

'I had a child in 1970 who was adopted, and I'm trying to trace him.'

He blew smoke towards the ceiling and nodded slowly.

'So you're going through the whole book looking for people who were born on that date and were subsequently adopted?'

'That's right.'

'And did you find any?'

'Six,' she said.

'And what are you going to do now?'

'Crosscheck with the adoption orders in *Iris Oifigiúil*.'

'And after that?'

'Try my best to find out where each of these families are now and do more research.'

'Have you tried going to the adoption agency?'

She shrugged. 'They haven't been very helpful.'

'No, they never are, are they?'

He sat up in his chair and leaned towards her. 'I'm sorry we can't make things easier for you, but we're civil servants here and we have to obey the rules. You know, day after day I see people trying to hide the fact they are making notes, not realizing that everyone here can see them. I imagine that's what you've done?'

Sinéad looked at him, nervously. He seemed nice enough, but was he going to ask her to hand over the paper? How should she react, she wondered? Defiance might not be the best strategy.

Someone knocked on the door and said the offices were closing shortly, and as they both stood up he shook her hand. He didn't mention her notes, he just said, 'Thanks for being so open with me. Most people are very defensive and don't want to talk about it, and I can understand that. I have to say it breaks my heart to see the number of women – it's nearly always women – coming in here day after day, searching for their children. Hopefully the law will change soon – tracing is already legal in the UK and we'll surely follow suit. Good luck with your search.'

'Thank you for being so kind – and for turning a blind eye. I really thought I was in for a telling-off.'

It was dark as Sinéad walked back to her flat that evening, back up Westland Row, past the café where she had coffee with Margaret, walking against a tide of busy commuters rushing towards the station. She resisted the urge to stop in the middle of the crowd and shout, tell the whole world she was about to find her son, but instead she walked on, past the Royal Academy of Music, turning into the relative calm of Merrion Square. When she reached her flat she went into the kitchen, opened the window and took in deep breaths of the cool night air, then poured herself a glass of wine, lit a cigarette, and went back to the pile of documents littering the living room table.

★

Jack went into work on Thursday, but the place seemed empty without Sinéad. He spent most of the day shuffling papers and making unnecessary phone calls, wondering all the time why she had taken the two days off and what she was doing.

On Friday morning he left home early and made a detour on his way to the office to drive past her flat. It was still relatively dark and he could see the light on upstairs. He thought briefly about parking the car and ringing the bell but at that moment, a well-dressed man carrying a briefcase and who looked vaguely familiar opened the hall door with a key and went in. Hers was the only residential flat in the building, and the lower floors were occupied by accountants and lawyers. In fact, most of the street was, and the probability of his knowing some of them, or of their knowing him, was fairly high.

The light upstairs went off and for a moment he imagined her walking down the stairs, jumping into his car and kissing him good morning, but as he saw the front door opening, he drove off quickly. He didn't want her to think he was stalking her, but more than that, he didn't want to be seen. God only knew who was looking out those windows.

Sinéad arrived at the office about a half an hour after him. He was with Brenda in her office going through the diary for the following week when she came in, her face lightly flushed from walking in the cool morning air. She seemed relaxed and greeted them both warmly. Jack followed her into her office, carrying the diary as if he wanted to check dates. He asked her if she'd like to go and have coffee and have a chat, but she said she had a lot of catching up to do and some phone calls to make. Deflated, he began to walk out of the office when she called him back.

'I'm sorry Jack, but I really need to get working on this London meeting. It's in a couple of weeks' time, just after Easter, and I haven't done any proper work over the past week, with the US trip and taking a couple of days off.' She smiled apologetically, then added, 'I've got lots to tell you, let's have lunch instead.'

He saluted in mock respect and backed out the door. She hadn't mentioned the flowers. For the rest of the morning he busied himself with all sorts of things he had been putting off and made a few calls to friends in London to see if there was anything on – a special play, a concert that he could take her to, pushing their recent conversation to the back of his mind.

He was engrossed in his work and was startled when she appeared at the door wearing her coat at precisely half past twelve. 'I thought we could go out,' she said. 'The canteen is probably not the best place for a quiet chat.'

'What about Wynn's Hotel in Abbey Street?' he said. 'It's very old fashioned, I know, and the food isn't great, but it's probably the only place around here that's quiet at this time of the day.'

'Sounds perfect,' she said.

The restaurant was indeed quiet. There were some middle-aged women who, judging by the Clery's and Arnott's bags piled up by their tables, were out on a shopping spree. His mother always said somewhat disdainfully that the only people who went to Wynn's were 'country people' – which was ironic, given that she was from Tipperary.

The waitress gave them a small table in a corner, and they ordered the dish of the day, which arrived almost instantly. It was some sort of beef casserole with carrots, peas, cauliflower and the ubiquitous potato, all boiled to within an inch of their lives.

'The continentals never understand our obsession with having so many vegetables with each dish. But it's comfort food,' she said smiling. 'And it's just what I need'.

He was impatient to hear what she had to tell him, but she was clearly in no hurry, talking mostly about work. It was only when the coffee arrived that she began to open up.

'You're probably wondering why I took some days off?'

He nodded.

'Remember I told you I was doing some research into my son's adoption?' She paused, stirring her coffee. 'Well, I've made quite a bit of progress in the last couple of days.'

He was as astonished as she had been to learn that she could just walk in off the street and get her son's original birth certificate, and that it was all there for anyone to see under her name. He knew from experience that getting a certificate for an adopted person was another matter altogether.

He listened in silence to her account of her meeting with Margaret and her search. She told him about the adoption register and was incredulous when she told him she had found twelve children born on the same day as Lorcan – six girls and six boys.

'I have no idea what percentage that is of all the births in Ireland on that specific day, but it seems a lot to have been adopted.'

She nodded and smiled wryly. 'And the whole thing wasn't as easy as it sounds. The room was in a sort of central area with other offices looking onto it and they told me I wasn't allowed take a pen or paper in with me. I could consult the book, but not make any notes.'

'So, what did you do – you can't have memorized all the names?' he said.

'I memorized them two at a time,' she said, 'and then after a while asked to leave the room to go to the Ladies', where I wrote them down.

She reached into her handbag, took several crumpled pieces of paper out and pushed them across the table towards him.

'One of these is my son,' she said softly. He looked at the names scribbled in pencil: John Hogan, William McNamara, David O'Leary, Ronan O'Donnell, Gerald Barrett and Malcolm Sheehy. He asked her what she was going to do next and she took a deep breath, recovered her composure and relapsed into what he liked to call her executive mode. 'Two things,' she said. 'First, I'll match them with the names in *Iris Oifigiúil* to get the addresses. I started to do that last night, but what with the jet-lag and the stress, I fell asleep on the sofa. Second, I'm going to go back to the adoption agency. I'm going to try to wheedle his new Christian name out of them. That, of course, would make the task a lot easier. But I don't expect them to cooperate – at least, not at first. It was Margaret who gave me that idea – it hadn't even occurred to me to ask.'

'I don't know what to say,' Jack said slowly. 'What are you going to do if you do find his new identity and know where he lives?'

'Nothing,' she said. 'I just want to know he's all right, and after that it'll be up to him. I'm not going to barge in and cause mayhem in his life. He's nearly fifteen now. When he's eighteen – they've just changed the age of majority from twenty-one, which is great – I'll send him a letter or ask the agency to act as a go-between, much as I hate the thought of that.' She looked at her watch. 'Oh my God, look at the time! We'd better get back to the office.'

They walked quickly back across O'Connell Bridge. It had started to drizzle, but the sky was bright and there was a fresh breeze blowing up the Liffey. He wanted to put his arm around her, tell her it would be fine and that he would help her and support her in any way he could, but he knew he couldn't.

When they got back to the office, there was a message from Brenda on his desk asking him to call home. Lorna rarely called the office and when she did it usually meant there was a problem, so he dialled the number quickly, worried that something had happened to Fiona or Isabelle. But there was no reply, so he went into Brenda's office to see if she knew why she had called. She told him Lorna had said they were going to go with her brother to Kilkenny for the weekend and wanted to know if he could follow them down later.

'They're probably already on the road by now,' she said. 'Why don't you leave it a bit and then call them when they get there.'

His mind was racing and he caught Brenda looking at him, making him wonder if she could read his thoughts. He would invent a dinner with some politicians and go down the next day.

At about five he went into Sinéad's office.

'Any plans for the weekend?' he asked, trying to sound casual. She shook her head, saying she was going to carry on with her research.

'I could drop you home if you like,' he said. 'It's raining really heavily now.'

She glanced out of the window and to his surprise, she agreed and they arranged to meet in the lobby at six. By then, most of the staff would have left, he thought.

It was a short drive to Merrion Square. They didn't speak much in the car, just listened to the radio. It was one of those current affairs programmes, a documentary about the Mothers of the *Plaza de Mayo* in Argentina. As they reached their destination, the presenter was talking to a woman who explained how young pregnant women who were opposed to the regime were arrested, and when their babies were delivered they killed the mothers and gave the babies to be raised by supporters of the regime. The woman (who earlier in the programme had been waxing lyrical about God) was very emotional and said that it was unbearably awful and that it would make you sob yourself to sleep just thinking about it.

'Bloody hypocrites,' said Jack. 'The church did much the same in Ireland, except that they didn't actually kill the girls.'

'I wonder which is worse,' said Sinéad, leaning back and closing her eyes. 'Being executed or condemned to a lifetime without their babies.'

He pulled up outside her building and turned off the radio. 'Can I come up?'

She seemed to think for a few seconds. 'Yes,' she said, 'I'd like that. But we really shouldn't go in together. You know what this town is like, someone might see you. Park around the back and I'll let you in.' She got out of the car, walked up to the front door and then quickly turned and came back to the car, laughing. 'I'm losing my mind,' she said. 'I have to go in the back way anyway. They've changed the locks on the front door and I haven't got the new key yet. They sent the new set to the main tenant and all her post is forwarded to Brussels, so...'

The car park at the back was empty, and there were no lights on anywhere in the building. They let themselves in and walked up a short flight of stairs to the main hall. There, lying on the floor beside the front door was the bouquet he had sent to her. He walked quickly towards it and picked it up, handing it to her awkwardly.

'They're for you – look, they're addressed to Sinéad Murray. You clearly have an admirer.'

'Irises,' she said. 'Now who could possibly have sent these?'

She opened the envelope containing the little card he had written and her eyes filled with tears as she read it.

'That's the nicest thing anyone has ever said to me. Thank you, Jack,' she said, and as they walked up the three flights of stairs to the flat, she linked her arm through his.

She held the door open and he stepped into the hall. Because the flat was on the top floor, the ceilings were a lot lower than in the majestic rooms below, but if anything, that only added to its charm. A cosy living/dining room looked out onto the square below. There were beige carpets, a sofa and a few pieces of unfussy antique furniture. There were a few subtle watercolours on the walls, mainly views of Dublin, and a single white orchid in a pot by a window. The whole place exuded calm and tranquillity.

He walked over to the window and looked out onto the trees in Merrion Square. In the dusk he could barely make out their shapes and he imagined they were just beginning to show signs of life.

'It's going to be even more beautiful when the blossom starts coming out,' said Sinéad, reading his thoughts. 'And from the back, you can just about see the Dublin mountains over the rooftops.'

He looked around and saw that the dining table was completely covered in large A3 size pages. She followed his gaze and smiled. 'My research,' she said.

He took off his coat and placed it on the back of one of the chairs, then picked up one of the pages. The heading was:

'IRIS OIFIGIUIL. Notice of Making of Adoption Orders. In pursuance of the powers vested in it by the Adoption Acts, 1952 and 1964, An Bord Uchtala has made Adoption orders, particulars of which are as follows: – '

He skimmed down column after column and he began to feel very uncomfortable. All these familiar names: Andrew, Mark, Sean, Ian, Jacinta, Bridget, Orla, all these babies from so many different backgrounds and now living in Dalkey, Foxrock, Artane, Roscommon and Bally-whatever with their new identities. And for most of them, somewhere in the shadows a mother desperate to find out what had happened to them. He was almost afraid to look any further in case he recognized some of the adopters.

The pages were covered in annotations and some names were highlighted in different colours. Sinéad moved closer to him to see what he was looking at and he put his arm around her.

'You'll notice there's no date of birth, only the date of the adoption order. It would have been too easy otherwise. I started by eliminating all the girls, of course,' she explained. 'Then I highlighted all the Dublin addresses in yellow and the others in blue. That's because the adoption agency told me he wasn't living in Dublin. But then maybe they originally lived in Dublin and then moved. Or maybe the agency was lying. I couldn't be sure. After that I looked at the Christian names and I found four who had Lorcan as the second or third name.' She leafed through the papers, pointing out the four names. 'I marked those in red. I did all that before I went into Lombard Street, and obviously I would have saved myself an awful lot of work if I'd waited until I had identified the six names and checked them against this list. But it was therapeutic I suppose. And I suppose I never really believed they would let me look at the book anyway – it took me a long time to get in there.' She moved away and began gathering up the papers. 'It turns out that of my six names, four have addresses in Dublin and two in Wexford, which I suppose is better than being scattered all over the country. That's the next step – tracking them down.' She placed them on a side table, beside a large box file. 'This?' she answered his gaze. 'It's just general stuff about adoption – you can have a look if you like.' She handed it to him and he began to look through it. There were dozens of newspaper articles and letters, and a brochure with a bright yellow cover from an English charity called Jigsaw entitled *The Other Side of Adoption*. 'You should read that,' she said, pointing at the brochure. 'It has all kinds of advice, especially on tracing. And there are some very moving stories too.'

He flicked through it quickly and went to put it back in the folder when a letter fell out. He bent to pick it up and saw the name of a solicitor he knew emblazoned across the top.

'I was at school with this guy!'

Sinéad took it from him and said, 'That? It's a long story – why don't we have a drink and I'll tell you.'

She picked up the flowers she had put on a side table and went to the kitchen to find a vase. Jack followed her in and looked around as she arranged the flowers. He could see his car through the window, looking very conspicuous in the brightly lit, empty car park.

She placed two wine glasses on the work surface and opened the fridge, apologizing for not having any beer and suggesting they have a Kir instead.

'Remember that dinner in Geneva?' she said, noting his puzzled expression. 'You seemed to enjoy it then.'

'It wasn't just the Kir I liked,' he said, putting his arms around her waist playfully. She laughed, pushing him away, and took a bottle of white wine from the fridge. She handed him the corkscrew and an ice bucket while she walked back into the living room with the glasses and the flowers. He followed her with the wine and some nuts he had found. She placed the ice-bucket on the coffee table and took a bottle of dark purplish looking liquid with a garish label from the butler's tray.

'*Creme de Cassis*,' she said. 'From Dijon.' She told him the drink had been invented by a priest from Burgundy who had been in the resistance during the war.

'Can you imagine a priest inventing something as delicious and decadent as this?'

She put a teaspoon of the liqueur into the glasses, saying it was important not to put too much in or the drink would be too sweet, and then she poured the chilled wine in on top. They clinked glasses and he sat on the sofa; Sinéad kicked off her shoes and curled her feet up under her on an armchair.

'So, tell me about this solicitor's letter,' he said.

She looked at her watch. 'How long have you got?'

'I don't have to go home tonight. They've all gone down to Kilkenny to my brother-in-law's place.'

There was a silence and then she sighed. 'Jack, I thought we'd agreed.'

He looked down at his drink and didn't answer; she took the file and put newspaper cuttings and the solicitor's letter out in front of him on the coffee table before curling up on the armchair again.

'You remember when I told you my story in Washington, and I said that I had dropped the idea of trying to have the adoption order annulled?' He nodded. 'Well, not long after I took up the post in Geneva, I came across an article on the subject. It was from 1976, relating to a case involving a young couple who were trying to have an adoption order overturned. The girl had placed her baby for adoption, but later on they got married and decided they would try to find their child and take him back. They claimed that undue pressure had been put on the mother at the time. Well, they lost their case in the High Court, but went to the Supreme Court, which decided in their favour and made an order to return the child to them. The adoptive parents then tried to get an injunction.' She sipped her Kir. 'I followed the case very closely and I began to think about doing the same thing, as the circumstances were very similar to mine. I kept the file for a long time before finding a solicitor I was told would be sympathetic. I prepared my file meticulously and sent it to the solicitor but – you won't believe this – the next day a postal strike began in Dublin and lasted for eighteen weeks.'

Jack nodded. 'I remember, it was chaos.'

'I suppose, in retrospect, it was a good thing. It gave me time to think. I read and re-read the evidence given by experts and social workers on the effect the order would have on the child as well as the adoptive parents.' Sinéad leaned across and rooted through the newspaper cuttings. 'It's all here, look,' she said, handing him a yellowing paper with a psychiatrist's testimony as reported by the journalist in the *Irish Times*:

The boy was at a critical stage in personality formation. If there was a change of environment now it could lead to confusion in his mind and withdrawal...he said some of the disturbance created by the emotional trauma as a child could lead to doubt about identity, academic and social failure.

Further down, there was a quote from another expert:

I cannot see the adoptive parents ever being able to come to terms with giving up the child they feel to be their own.

'Harrowing reading,' Jack said.

Sinéad put her glass down and ran her hands through her hair. She looked more vulnerable than he'd ever seen her.

'Do you know what the worst thing was in all that?'

He shook his head.

'When I arrived in Geneva, I was working with a woman who was unmarried and had a child, and nobody batted an eyelid. There was a very good creche in the building. I couldn't believe how different attitudes were and it made me feel even more guilty. I never told anyone my story because I thought nobody would understand, that they'd judge me.'

'So what happened with the court case?'

'In the end, having read all the evidence, I realised I might cause irreversible damage to my son and his adoptive parents. It was the second most difficult decision I have ever had to take, but I had to do it. When the postal strike finally ended, I phoned the solicitor and told him I wasn't going to go ahead. Actually, the file never turned up – a lot of post went missing during that period – and I took that as some sort of sign that it just wasn't meant to be.'

Jack glanced at the letter from the solicitor, confirming their conversation and her decision not to proceed.

'The bastard charged you a fortune! He didn't even read the file!' he exclaimed.

Sinéad picked up her glass again, took another sip of her Kir and shrugged her shoulders. 'He spoke to me on the telephone – twice,' she said wryly. 'But there's more. You'll never guess what I discovered recently. Frank Curzon worked on that very court case! He helped draft some of the evidence. We talked about it in Washington – it came up quite by accident in the conversation. Plus, I met one of the barristers involved in the case at a party recently. I didn't tell him why I was interested, of course. Ireland is a village...'

'A party?' Jack couldn't help himself.

'Yes, a party,' she smiled. 'It was just before we went to Washington. I do get invited to things you know. And fun-nily enough it was on the Southside and I actually knew some of the people there.' He held his hands up, feigning surrender, but she carried on. 'There was even a man who came up to me and asked me about my work and said he knew you and told me as if it was a State secret that you were going to Washington for St Patrick's Day. You should have seen the look on his face when I told him – sorry, I just couldn't resist – that actually you worked for me and that I was going too. Bernard something...I think he works in Foreign Affairs.'

'Morris?' he said 'Bernard Morris?'

'Yes, I think that was his name,' she said. 'Funny character – funny ha-ha as opposed to funny bizarre.'

'You don't know the half of it.'

Bernard Morris had been a year ahead of Jack at school. He was a snob even then, always holidaying in places no one had ever heard of. Now he knew him by reputation. He droned on and on about the wines he drank. He would go into wine shops asking for an unusual wine called Savennières just to show off his superior knowledge.

When he told her this she laughed and said that they had actually discussed wine and that yes, he had mentioned Savennières and was very impressed that she'd heard of it. He even invited her to go to a wine tasting with him the following week.

'I hope you didn't accept,' he said, 'You do know he's married.'

'Yes, and he wears his ring with pride, unlike you,' she replied.

Jack put his hands up in the air again. 'OK, OK, touché.'

She drained her glass and stood up. 'I suppose we need to think about eating – that is, unless you have other plans.' He shook his head. 'That lunch we had was quite heavy, so how about something light? I could see what I have in the fridge.'

She bent down and pulled out a carton of eggs and a small lettuce, 'Omelette and salad? How does that sound?'

'Perfect.'

She handed him a bowl and a whisk and began to wash the salad. 'Don't beat the eggs too much, just mix them a bit.'

He watched as she prepared a vinaigrette in the salad bowl before starting to cook the omelette.

'There's some cheese here for afters and you'll find some crackers there.' She pointed to a cupboard. 'And there should be some more wine and glasses over there,' she said.

'Nice,' he said, as he took out a bottle of Bordeaux. 'Nice label, at any rate. I'm no expert. My brother is the wine buff in our family.'

She passed him a corkscrew and as he poured out two glasses it struck him not for the first time how relaxed he felt. Afterwards, as they sat drinking coffee, shoes off and feet on the low table, listening to some jazz on the radio, she began to ask him about his childhood, whether the Mc-Donaghs loved him like their own, what his relationship was with his brother and sister, how his adoption had impacted his life. She seemed to feel the need to be reassured that he hadn't been mistreated or suffered in any way.

'Do you talk about this to anyone? Your brother and sister?'

'God, no. They weren't adopted. Apparently, as soon as I arrived in the house my mother got pregnant with Sarah. And Sarah never lets me forget it.'

'I can help you find your mother, if you want. I can put you in touch with Margaret,' she said. 'Or you could just go into the general register and look for people born the same day as you. It would be much easier as it's pretty much

chronological. If there are a few with no father's name registered, that would be a start.'

He shook his head.

'It's not the same for me, Sinéad. You know who the
father is, and you can be fairly sure that your son is going to
be like you in some way. What's the worst that can happen?
He was badly brought up? He didn't get a good education?
He'll still be your son, with your genes. I, on the other hand,
could find out that I'm the son of a serial killer. I have no
idea whatsoever about my background, apart from all the
disparaging stuff my parents have told me, and I'm just not
ready to start digging with no clear idea of what I'm going
to find. Not at the moment anyway.'

She began to say something, but seemed to change her
mind. They sat in silence for a while, listening to the music. When the programme ended, Sinéad leaned over and
switched off the radio.

'You haven't told me much about your wife, except that
you want to leave her. Tell me more. How long have you
been married? Did you love her when you married her?'

Jack was taken aback and thought for a moment before
answering. 'I don't know how to define love,' he said. 'She
was – is – attractive and bright, and I always admired her and
her family. We practically grew up together. I've always had
this sense of not belonging in my own family and I suppose
I felt flattered at being accepted into hers. But nobody told
me she had a history of depression. They don't talk about
things like that in her family. They have a way of shutting
out the rest of the world and its problems that I find difficult
to understand.'

'Oh, I'm sorry to hear that she's depressed,' Sinéad said. 'That must be hard on her. On you.'

She poured them both some more coffee.

'I think our relationship has always been like brother and sister, if that makes sense. There's no desire, no real sharing of emotions. Never was.'

Sinéad thought for a moment. 'She could be, you know,' she said, slowly.

'She could be what?'

'She could *be* your sister.'

He looked at her, wondering if he had heard her correctly. 'What on earth are you talking about?'

'Well, let's suppose for the sake of argument that your mother-in-law had a child before she married and gave him up for adoption. And supposing that child was you. Then you and Lorna would be brother and sister.'

'That's completely ridiculous!' he exclaimed, wondering if she'd had too much to drink.

'It's highly unlikely, but it's not impossible,' she said.

'Mrs Stewart is not that kind of person. She would never...' he trailed off.

Sinéad looked at him with that annoying quizzical, slightly mocking air. 'Not that kind of person? And what kind of person would that be? Someone like me?'

'OK, OK, hold on,' he said. 'You know that's not what I meant. This conversation is getting a bit bizarre. Let's call a truce and talk about something else.'

But she wouldn't let go. 'I could even be your sister.'

'Oh, stop it,' he said. 'You're going to make me completely paranoid.' There was an awkward silence.

'I'm sorry, Jack, I didn't mean to be flippant. But don't you agree that we need to know our roots? And you studied medicine, you must know how important it is to have information on risks of hereditary diseases and so on.'

'No, it's fine. Don't be sorry. You're right of course. But going back to your story, there's something I've wanted to ask you for a while, something that's been intriguing me.' She looked at him warily. 'It's about your parents,' he said, carefully. 'They seem like really nice people, and they obviously think very highly of you. What do they think about all this? And don't you blame them at all?'

She shook her head. 'We never talk about it,' she said. 'We haven't spoken about it since that day I came up from Cork on the train.'

'Not even when you were in the hospital?'

'No,' she said, pulling at a thread in one of the sofa cushions. 'I know it seems strange, but I don't blame them at all. They really thought they were doing the right thing for me, and in the end they, and everyone else, convinced me that I was too. And I think they feel that if they talked about it, it would open up the wounds and make things more difficult for me. So, in a way they're still trying to protect me.'

'They don't know about your search then?'

'I haven't told them. They'd just worry that it might end badly. When – if – the time comes, I'll tell them, and maybe they'll even get to meet their grandson someday.' She sighed. 'The more I think about it, the more I think how very hard it must have been for my mother to have seen him and then given him away – maybe almost as hard as it was for me. They worry about me, but I also worry about them.'

She stood up and began to clear away the plates.

'And the father?'

'What about him?'

'You never mention him.'

'I think we've done enough talking for tonight. It's a long story. I'll tell you some other time.'

'Leave that until later,' he said, taking the plates from her and pulling her back down on the sofa beside him.

Her bedroom was at the back of the flat, separated from the kitchen by a tiny bathroom. The curtains were fine muslin, just barely filtering and softening the light. She said she liked it that way, waking up with the morning light.

The next morning, when the sun woke him, she was already up. He grabbed a robe from the bathroom and went to find her in the kitchen. Everything had been cleared away and she had a jug of coffee in her hand. He looked at her, standing there in a pair of pyjamas that were slightly too big, her hair ruffled, and he marvelled at how she could look so good after only a few hours' sleep.

'I love you, Sinéad Murray,' he said. 'I've loved you from the moment I set eyes on you in Killarney. I've never felt so close to anyone before.' She started to reply, but he put a finger on her lips. 'Don't say anything. I know what I have to do. We – I – need to sort things out. It may take a while, I don't want to lose my kids, but I'll find a way. Just give me time. Please, Sinéad.'

'I've already told you I don't want to be the one to break up your marriage, but I don't want to be your mistress either.'

He took the coffee pot from her and placed it on the table. Then he took her by the shoulders, shaking her gently. 'Don't ever say that word again. You're not and never will be my mistress – is that clear?'

The doorbell rang, shattering the moment. Sinéad shook herself free and ran to the front window.

'Oh no!' she said. 'I completely forgot. They said they'd try to deliver it this morning. Quick – throw something decent on. They'll probably need help.'

'It' was a piano she had ordered.

'It's one of those new-fangled electronic ones you can play without disturbing the neighbours,' she said, laughing as they both dressed in a hurry.

The two delivery men huffed and puffed as they carried the piano up the three flights of stairs and placed it carefully against the wall between the living room and the kitchen. The younger one offered to demonstrate all the special effects but Sinéad laughed and said she only wanted to use it as a piano, not as an organ or a brass band. They both looked a bit miffed so Jack gave them a generous tip and ushered them to the door.

After they had left, Sinéad looked at her watch and said, 'I can't believe how late it is! I have my first piano lesson in an hour's time. I need to get moving.'

She picked up his coat and handed it to him, telling him he would have to shower at home as she needed to get ready. He offered to drive her, but she refused. There was no point taking unnecessary risks, and anyway he needed to get moving too if he wanted to be in Kilkenny before lunchtime.

Chapter Nineteen

THE WEEKEND IN KILKENNY seemed interminable. James spent a lot of the time locked away in his study, as he was working on a big court case, so Jack was left in the company of Sarah and Lorna, who clearly would have preferred him not to be there. It rained most of Saturday, which meant that the children were cooped up inside and there were lots of arguments. James and Sarah had two boys who were roughly the same ages as Fiona and Isabelle but with such vastly different interests it was impossible to get them to play together.

On the Saturday evening some friends who also had a house in the area called in for drinks and stayed for dinner. It was all very pleasant, although Jack couldn't help wondering what the point was of having a house in Kilkenny and seeing the same people you could have met in Dublin.

He did manage to slip away at one point, ostensibly to buy cigarettes, and tried to call Sinéad from the local phone box, but there was no answer and he remembered she usually went to her parents' house at the weekend. He imagined them out walking on Howth pier, bumping into old acquaintances. He wondered how long it would be before she grew frustrated with their relationship.

The following week was busy at work. Although Jack was attached to the task force, he kept his job as ministerial adviser and still had a lot of things to do for Jim. Easter was around the corner and there were all the usual events taking place to commemorate the 1916 Rising. Jim was full of news about the possible election, and they were sitting in his office discussing the impact that would have on the task force. When they had exhausted all the various scenarios, Sinéad stood up and said she had to make a conference call, and left to go back to her office. Jim stood up and took Jack by the arm, leading him over to the window. He looked uneasy as he surveyed the grey Dublin skyline.

'Look Jack, Caroline met Lorna when we were in the US for St Patrick's Day. She somehow persuaded Lorna that it would be a great idea to invite the main players in the task force for an evening at your place so that we could all meet up with our spouses. She'll probably talk to you about it this evening, so I just wanted to warn you.' Jack looked at him in disbelief. 'I really don't think Caroline meant anything by it,' Jim added. 'You know how she is – she just thought Lorna might be feeling a bit left out of things.'

Jack did know how she was – one of the kindest, nicest women you could meet. If it had been Sarah he'd have suspected an ulterior motive, or simple spite, but Caroline's intentions were always good. 'No problem Jim,' he said, trying to look relaxed despite the knots in his stomach. 'It's actually a nice idea – get everyone talking to each other outside the formal setting, and that's good for the work.'

Jim looked at him keenly. 'Get a caterer in so Lorna doesn't get stressed – I'll foot the bill. Let's do it fairly soon. Talk to Mary to see when I'm available.'

Sure enough, when he went home that evening, Lorna brought up the subject of the evening and suggested a couple of dates. She seemed quite laid-back about it, which surprised him. Usually, unless her own family was involved, she found social occasions stressful.

'It's going to be difficult to get them all together on the same day – they're all very busy, you know,' he said, as casually as he could.

'Well, just pick a day they're all here for one of the meetings and we'll do it then,' she said. There was no arguing with that logic and he began to reflect on how to introduce the subject to Sinéad. On the one hand, it was pretty unimaginable, the thought of Lorna and Sinéad being in the same room for a whole evening and him trying to act normally. But then the more he thought about it, the more he began to think it might be a good idea. It would hopefully allay any suspicions Lorna might have, and although in hindsight he knew it sounded cracked, he wanted Sinéad to see where he lived and meet his children.

'That's crazy, Jack,' she said when he told her. 'I'll just have to find some excuse not to come. I'd feel guilty and it's not fair on any of us – your wife, me, you. You can't expect me to behave normally in a situation like that.'

'But if you don't come, it'll look worse,' he said. 'If anyone has any suspicions that will just confirm what they think.'

He decided to organize it as quickly as possible to get it out of the way.

★

They were twelve in all, not all of the guests having brought partners or spouses. A buffet meal had been arranged. Lorna's mother sent her cleaner over in the morning to help out and the house was looking at its best.

Lorna herself had been to the hairdresser and her hair looked different, lighter. She was wearing a very elegant dark blue dress Jack hadn't seen before and a pair of very high heels that made her look much taller than usual. He had to admit she looked striking – a wife any man should be proud of, his guilty conscience whispered.

Fiona and Isabelle had been on their best behaviour for over half an hour and were about to go to bed when Sinéad arrived with Curzon, the pair of them looking for all the world like a married couple. He was wearing a tweed jacket with beige corduroy trousers and carrying a potted plant, and she was wearing a very simple dark green suit with a demure ivory blouse. Her shoes were sensible and almost flat. Jack tried to say thank you with his eyes, but she avoided his gaze and turned her attention to the two little girls, complimenting them on their princess pyjamas, hunkering down to their level and handing them a small packet each. They thanked her shyly.

Lorna appeared at Jack's side, Curzon handed her the plant and they all shook hands before she whisked the girls off to bed, reappearing only a few minutes later.

'Thank you for the books,' she said to Sinéad. 'That was very thoughtful and it will keep them happy this evening.'

Sinéad and Curzon mingled easily with the others, and Jack began to relax, sensing that the evening was actually a lot less stressful than he had imagined it would be. It was when the coffee was being served that he noticed Sinéad standing on her own close to the fireplace. As he moved over to talk to her he saw that she was looking at the shelves where the model of Monticello was displayed. From nowhere, Lorna appeared at his elbow, placing her hand on his arm, and said to Sinéad.

'Lovely, isn't it? It's Monticello, you know, Jefferson's house. Jack brought it back for the girls. We waited till they went to bed and then we spent the whole evening putting it together. It was such fun, wasn't it, Jack?' she turned to him brightly, linking her arm through his. Jack was stunned at the lie, but Sinéad just smiled politely. 'Yes, it's a very interesting house,' she said. 'Jefferson was way ahead of his time.'

'You were there too, weren't you, Frank?' Lorna asked, as he joined them. Frank glanced at Jack briefly and smiled back at her.

'Oh yes, yes, it's a magical place. I've been there several times. Very interesting.' He peered at the model before turning back to the group. 'Actually Lorna, I was just coming over to say that I have an early flight to Frankfurt in the morning so I'm going to have to leave now.' He looked at Sinéad. 'I'm passing by your flat, Sinéad, and I can drop you off if you like.'

'That'd be lovely, Frank,' said Sinéad, and turned to Lorna. 'I hope you don't mind. It's been a lovely evening –

thank you so much for inviting us. We're all a bit tired after today. We don't all get together very often so we try to get through as much as possible when we do.'

After they made a quick round of the room, saying their goodbyes, Jack accompanied them to the door, but got no chance to talk to Sinéad alone. He stood watching the car reversing down the drive, when Lorna said in his ear, almost playfully, 'They'd make a good couple, wouldn't they? Do you think they're already together? It would be so nice for Frank to meet someone. It's been a while since his wife died and he must be lonely.'

'His wife didn't die,' Jack muttered, barely concealing his irritation. 'She ran off with another man. Nobody ever talks about it, that's all.'

He hustled her back towards the living room, where judging by the sound of the laughter, Jim was holding court. He wanted them all to go, so he could sit down and numb his head with a large Scotch, but the party didn't break up for at least another hour when Jim's chauffeur turned up. As soon as the main man had left, the others all began making excuses and headed off.

After he closed the door on the last guest, Jack headed for the kitchen to start tidying up.

'Leave that, Jack,' said Lorna. 'Mrs Foley is coming in the morning and she'll do all that. Let's go to bed, you must be tired too.'

'You go on up,' he said. 'I'll just put the perishables away – I need to chill for a while anyway.'

After a rudimentary tidy-up he opened a bottle of Macallan that someone had brought and poured himself a large glass. It had gone a lot better than he expected, but the Monticello incident worried him. Why had Lorna felt the need to say that she had helped him build the model when they both knew she hadn't even touched it? And how did that make him look to Sinéad? A liar? He looked at the phone, but decided against trying to call her – it was too dangerous. Lorna could easily listen in on the extension upstairs if she heard the click of the receiver. It would have to wait until the morning.

★

As he expected, Sinéad was furious with him about the Monticello incident.

'You told me you did nothing together, that you practically led separate lives and that you had worked on that model on your own with the children, just the three of you. Why did you have to lie to me? It would have been better if you had said nothing.'

'Lorna was lying. It was bizarre, we didn't make it together. You have to believe me – with Lorna it's all about keeping up appearances. She always puts on a show when strangers – or even her own family – are around.'

But he sensed that the seed of doubt had been planted, and that he would have to regain her trust.

The Tuesday after Easter they were due to fly to London for a meeting. Despite his best efforts he hadn't been able to get tickets for anything he thought she might like, so he hatched another plan.

He knew in advance the London meeting would finish early, so he got Brenda to set up a short meeting in Paris for the Wednesday with his counterpart at the French Ministry for Health, late enough for them not to be able to get back to Dublin that night. With the help of Bernard Morris, he then managed to get the address of a 'delightful' little hotel near Montparnasse.

There was still a certain coolness between them so he was careful to tell her well in advance that they would be going on to Paris from London. She seemed surprised, but she didn't raise any objections, and in fact seemed to adapt to the idea quite easily.

They arrived from London in the late afternoon and dropped their bags at the hotel. Jack had secretly hoped they might have a siesta but Sinéad had already found an art exhibition she wanted to see at the Grand Palais. She refused his suggestion of a taxi, saying that she loved the metro from Montparnasse to Etoile, and then they could walk back down the Champs Elysées. Soon after leaving Montparnasse, the metro emerges from the tunnels and trundles along on stilts. He found himself gazing into the windows of incredibly beautiful apartments, amazed at the furnishings and paintings that were just visible from the train, amazed too that that people who could afford such accommodation would choose to live so close to the metro and submit themselves to such voyeurism. As they approached the Seine, the Eiffel tower came into view, lit up like a giant fairground attraction.

'How do you know Paris so well?' he asked.

'I came here on a school trip with the nuns when I was sixteen,' she said. 'We stayed in a convent in a very chic part of Paris – near the Trocadero. We were here for ten days and we saw absolutely everything. I've been back a few times since but it's always been for work, and I've never had the time to just wander around again.'

The thought of a sixteen-year-old Sinéad being chaperoned around the city of love and romance by nuns amused him.

The exhibition was boring – some obscure (to Jack anyway; Sinéad said he was a philistine) collection from the US that the press was raving about. They had to queue for ages to get in and there were so many people shuffling around that it was impossible to see anything properly. They resorted at one point to looking at the people looking at the paintings and Sinéad entertained him by inventing stories about them.

They were sitting on a bench in the middle of one of the rooms, giggling like schoolkids, when Jack became aware of someone looking at them from the other side of the room. He was about their age, well-dressed in that understated way the French do so well, and he was surrounded by a small group of official-looking people.

He nudged Sinéad. 'Look over there,' he said. 'There's a guy who fancies you.'

Sinéad recomposed her features and looked at the group. Suddenly she stood up and, smiling the broadest smile Jack had ever seen, she moved towards the man, who in turn was beaming and walking towards her.

'Sinéad!' he said. 'I'm so glad you made it! Look at you! You haven't changed a bit!'

They embraced, a quick kiss on each cheek, then Sinéad took him by the arm and led him over to Jack. 'Sam, this is

Jack – a colleague of mine. We work together in Dublin. We're here on a mission to undermine the French health system.'

'Hello Jack, nice to meet you,' Sam said as he shook his hand. He wasn't French at all, probably English, Jack thought, and smiled back at him while wishing he would evaporate. *A colleague*, she said. *We work together.* Why didn't she say they were lovers, or even friends? His anger made him hate himself for being so childish, and hate them for being so bloody sophisticated.

It transpired that Sam had befriended Sinéad when she was in London during her pregnancy. He was in Paris to give a concert the following night and of course he insisted that they come.

'I'll have tickets left for you at the box office,' he said. 'The concert is at the Salle Pleyel. I never go out to eat after a concert, but maybe we could have a drink in the bar afterwards?'

'Great – we'd love to, wouldn't we, Jack?' He smiled and said yes, of course. Just his luck to take the woman of his dreams to Paris and then be upstaged by some fourth-rate pianist...

After Sam was hustled off by his minders, they finished looking around and then went straight to a restaurant recommended by Bernard, where according to him all the big names – Sartre, Hemingway, Fitzgerald and even Beckett – used to hang out. It was a little underwhelming, mostly populated with tourists like themselves, but Sinéad seemed to have relaxed quite a bit.

As they settled into their seats she looked at him with a guilty expression and said, 'I have a confession to make.' Jack

waited, as she chose her words carefully. 'That was no surprise meeting with Sam. I told him I would be in Paris – I
knew he was performing this week and he told me he was
going to that exhibition at the Grand Palais today.'

'You told him? You mean you're still in touch with him?'

'Sporadically, over the years, yes. He sends me newspaper
clippings and the odd Christmas – or rather Hanukkah –
card. I got a card from him recently telling me about this
concert but I had no idea I would be in Paris to see it.
It's only the second time our paths have crossed since…you
know…' she trailed off.

'So how did you know where to contact him?'

'He always puts his hotel details when he sends me information about his concerts, so that if ever I was there, I could
get in touch.'

'And when was the first time?'

'Geneva, about five years ago.'

'So why didn't you tell me all this before?'

'Oh, I don't know. I thought you'd probably be jealous,
get the wrong impression. Although there's nothing to be
jealous of.'

'Of course,' he replied. 'I don't suppose you would have
introduced me to him if there was anything between you.'

'Well obviously,' she said, and he thought he detected sar-
casm in her voice.

As they walked back to the hotel he thought back to the
evening at his place and he felt uncomfortable. What was it
he had said at the time – it's the best way to make people
think there is nothing going on?

After a lazy morning and lunch on a terrace near the Luxembourg gardens, they had a pleasant and surprisingly useful meeting with the tall, thin and improbably-named Monsieur Legros at the Ministry. He was impressed to hear that they were going to the Salle Pleyel later and gave them the name of a good bistro for a pre-concert meal.

They barely had time to freshen up and change before setting off again, getting there early enough to have a look around the area and a quick bite to eat in Monsieur Legros' bistro before heading into the concert venue. They were seated in the front row of the first balcony. Sinéad opened the programme and pointed. 'Look – it's almost all Schubert,' she said, 'just like in Washington. Not the same pieces, and not solo piano, but still...'

Jack looked, but didn't recognize any of the pieces – a Trio for piano, violin and cello followed by an Arpeggione Sonata for cello and piano and a couple of short solo piano pieces by Debussy. Pretty much obligatory for Paris, he thought.

'What's an arpeggione anyway?' he asked Sinéad.

'I've no idea,' she said. Then, translating from the programme, she said '*An arpeggione is a type of instrument which no longer exists. While the piece was written for it, it is now almost always played on the cello or the viola.*'

Sinéad was once again transfixed by the concert, although he wondered at one point if it was the music or the pianist that held her attention. Despite his best attempts not to be impressed, he found the music inspiring, particularly the arpeggione sonata with its haunting, recurrent melody.

After a first encore that was greeted with thunderous applause, the cellist and violinist left the stage and Sam sat back down at the piano. Was it Jack's imagination or did he look up at them before starting to play? The first notes were unmistakable – Schubert, Impromptu, Opus 90 number 3 in G flat major. Jack knew it by heart because it was the one Brendel had played in Washington. After the concert he had made a careful note of it and had even bought a recording of it recently to listen to in his car. He stole a glance at Sinéad and saw she had tears in her eyes. She took his hand and squeezed it.

When Sam finished playing there was a moment of pure silence before the rapturous applause began.

They joined the long queue for the coats, and by the time they made their way to the hall, Sam was waiting for them, looking very relaxed in a black polo neck and jeans. He led the way down a couple of side streets to another small bistro where he said the musicians often went after a performance. It was quiet and cosy, and Jack spotted the cellist and violinist sitting in the corner in a group.

'I think this deserves a celebration, don't you?' said Sam. 'Champagne?' He waved at the barman who rushed over and took his order.

Jack tried hard, but couldn't find anything to dislike about Sam. He was affable and funny, and when the conversation turned to his performance, he was really quite modest. Sinéad pressed him to tell Jack all about New York and his career, but he deftly steered the conversation back to them. Sinéad told him about her progress in her search for her son and Sam glanced at Jack.

'It's OK – Jack knows my story. He's adopted himself.'
Sam looked at him again, taking this in, nodding his head slowly, and it somehow made Jack feel uncomfortable. He gathered that in Sam's life there had been a failed marriage along the way somewhere and that he was single again, although that was only hinted at. He was now back living in London but travelling a lot, performing and giving masterclasses.

'I don't suppose you'd give me one if you ever come to Dublin,' said Sinéad. 'I've just taken up the piano again and it's soul-destroying. I play like an eight-year old. There's no way I'll ever play that Schubert Impromptu.'

Sam smiled. 'Ha! You recognized it. Well, if I ever do come to Dublin, I'd be honoured to give you a lesson, Madame. Do you play too, Jack?' he asked.

Jack shook his head, saying it was too late for him to start learning, but Sam said he knew lots of people who had started late and went on to play quite well.

'My own teacher always said that playing well requires only 10% talent and 90% hard graft. That's certainly true in my case,' he said, laughing. He glanced at his watch and stood up. 'I'm really sorry – I would have loved to spend more time with you, but I have an early flight tomorrow. Vienna, another concert, same programme luckily.' He rummaged in his pocket and took out a card which he gave to Jack.

'Glad to have met you Jack, and as for you, young lady, I promise if I'm ever in Dublin I'll give you that masterclass.' He kissed her lightly on the cheek, lingering just a second too long for Jack's taste, and whispered, 'Take care of yourself.'

They took their time going back to the hotel, walking down Avenue Hoche to the Arc de Triomphe and then strolling along the Champs Elysees before taking a taxi back to Montparnasse. It was a pleasant enough spring evening, not too cold, and there were lots of tourists about. A moped buzzed by as they crossed the road to the taxi rank, the girl driver wearing a white t-shirt with the slogan *Trained to kill sticky boyfriends* in bold black letters emblazoned across the back.

'I love this city.' Sinéad sighed. 'I could so easily live here. You can do everything on foot, everything you'd need is within a short walk – green spaces, shops, theatres, cinemas.'

'Just like Dublin,' Jack said and she laughed before changing her expression.

'What are we going to do, Jack?' she asked. 'Do you really think we'll ever be able to walk around Dublin like this?'

'Of course we will,' he said. 'It's just a matter of time, of getting Lorna used to the idea of a separation.'

'But your family, her family, your friends. You know what it's like back home. You all know each other and you live in each other's pockets. They'll cut you off. Do you think you could live like that? Are you sure that's what you want?'

'We'll manage,' he said, putting his arm around her shoulder and kissing her hair, trying to put aside all thoughts of the future.

Chapter Twenty

THEY MANAGED FOR THE next few months. Despite Sinéad's initial misgivings, she and Jack saw a lot of each other. He would often drop in at her place on his way home from work, feigning an evening meeting with the minister. Sometimes he would pretend he had to be in work early, pick up croissants on his way so that they could have breakfast at the flat. They would eat, talk, make love, listen to music, and occasionally she would make him listen to the piece she was working on with her piano teacher. He began to discover a real passion for music.

There were a few work trips abroad, where they could pretend they were a real couple, but it became more and more difficult for both of them to adjust each time they returned. Jack spent as much time as possible at the flat, but began to feel more and more torn between his desire to stay with Sinéad and his family responsibilities. He was beginning to realise that Curzon and most of the people close to them knew what was going on, but nobody ever said anything, and even seemed to facilitate things, which lulled them into a false sense of security.

August was particularly hard, as Lorna's family continued their tradition of renting neighbouring houses in

Ballybunion, moving down there *en masse* for the whole month, which meant that Jack had to go too. Sinéad spent some time with a lawyer friend who had a holiday home on the Ile de Ré in France. Although they had decided not to attempt any contact, Jack found it hard to resist and called her several times, usually without success. He had to make the calls from a public phone box in the town, as there was no phone in their rented house. He imagined it was easier for Sinéad as she simply couldn't phone him. On the couple of occasions when he did get through to her she sounded relaxed and not at all sad to be apart from him, leading him to spend the rest of the day imagining all kinds of scenarios – al fresco meals on rose-covered terraces, smooth-talking Frenchmen chatting her up, her feisty friend advising her to dump him – which just put him in a bad mood.

One evening after dinner, the holiday almost over, they were all sitting around the kitchen table, Lorna, Sarah, James, Deirdre, Mark and Jack. The children were in bed, exhausted after a long day at the beach.

The conversation ebbed and flowed and finally turned to work. Deirdre complained about Mark being a workaholic and Lorna joined in.

'Jack is always sneaking off to the phone box down the road to call the office. Honestly, you'd think they could switch off for a couple of weeks. They're supposed to be on holiday.'

There was an uncomfortable silence for a few moments and exchanges of what he feared were knowing glances before Mark rescued the situation.

'Well, there might be an election in September,' he said 'and by the looks of things the current lot could be put out of office. I expect Jim is keeping his advisers busy.'

'What will you do if there's a change of government, Jack?' asked Deirdre. 'You'd be out of a job, wouldn't you?'

'Yes, well, I suppose I could just go back to the ranks in the Department,' he said.

'God, you wouldn't want to do that,' said James. 'You'd die of boredom after having been at the coalface for so long.' He lit a cigarette and inhaled slowly. 'Didn't you say once you'd like to go and work in Geneva or somewhere like that? Have you given that any more thought?'

'Actually,' Jack said recklessly, filling up his glass, 'a friend in Foreign Affairs was talking the other day about the Representation in Brussels. It's not a permanent posting, and it allows you to keep one foot in the country, so that might be a possibility. Just a short-term thing...' He avoided Lorna's gaze, not wanting a repeat performance of the last time they talked about moving abroad, but the idea began to germinate.

As soon as he got back to Dublin, he began making enquiries. General election or not, the task force would be winding up soon. The report was almost ready, and it looked as if it would go through smoothly. Once her assignment was finished, Sinéad would have to decide whether to stay on and look for a job in Ireland or go back to Geneva.

What she had said in Paris about being together in Dublin had been worrying him for a while, as had a chance meeting with a former senior colleague, a man in his fifties who had shocked everyone a couple of years previously by leaving his wife and moving in with his secretary. It was a Saturday morning and he was sitting in Bewley's, looking harassed as he tried to drink a coffee, read his newspaper and take care of an exuberant toddler at the same time. He seemed delighted to see Jack.

After a brief exchange of banter, he said, to Jack's astonishment, 'I hear you may be in the same situation as me soon yourself. My wife – soon-to-be-ex if they ever get around to legalizing divorce in this bloody country – tells me you have a fancy woman.'

Jack was furious. 'What does your wife know about my personal life and what's that supposed to mean, anyway – a fancy woman?'

'Ah, true love and all that. It's all bollocks, take it from me, Jack,' his colleague said, leaning towards him with a conspiratorial air. 'It's not worth it. This town is too small for separated people. You lose no matter what you do. Look at me. People don't want to have anything to do with me anymore – you'd think it was catching.' He paused as the waitress arrived with an ice-cream and placed it in front of his son. 'I hardly ever see any of my old friends – my ex has seen to it that my name is mud all over Dublin. And even though I've been living with my partner for a couple of years now, I'm still married on paper, and the ex still insists I go back home for all the big family events to keep up appearances. She even organized my fiftieth birthday by taking me and the whole family off to Scotland.' He sat back and laughed bitterly. 'Can you imagine? Separate rooms and all that, but I can tell you that it went down like a ton of bricks with this one's mother.' He pointed to the toddler devouring his ice-cream, blissfully unaware of his father's existential crisis.

As Jack left, mumbling excuses about having to pick up his own kids, his anger dissipated and left him feeling a little depressed.

When he went back to the office the next Monday, Mulcahy came to see him with the news that there was a real possibility of a posting in Brussels. He asked him to keep it to himself for the moment and as his colleague nodded in an understanding way, Jack wondered if there was anyone left in Dublin apart from Lorna, who didn't know about him and Sinéad.

'I don't know, Jack,' Sinéad said, when he told her of his plan. 'That's a huge step, and you haven't even spoken to Lorna about it yet. Not properly, anyway.'

'It's not that huge. With this job I could work in Brussels Monday to Friday and come back for the weekends. That way I can see the girls regularly and it wouldn't change much for Lorna, just that I wouldn't be there in the evenings. But it would get her used to the idea of living apart. She doesn't like change, or surprises.' He lit a cigarette and inhaled deeply. 'And you could easily get a job in Brussels. The place is full of lobbying firms and so on just crying out for someone like you.'

'Maybe you're right,' she said. 'I could go back to Geneva, I suppose, but I'm not sure I want to do that now.'

'The alternative is to stay here. With all the contacts you've made you could get a job here too.'

'You know that's not an option.'

The election was called a few days later, and Curzon decided to wind up the task force quickly. The report was finalized and presented to Jim formally with only the barest mention in the press. The politicians and the journalists had other things on their minds by that point. Jim's fears were realized and the opposition won, so he was back to being a shadow minister, with their shiny new report firmly locked away in his desk.

Sinéad used the election period to go back to Geneva to tidy up loose ends and start looking for a job in Brussels. It only took her a few weeks to land a post with one of the big PR firms there and she began to make contacts and plan her move.

In the meantime, Jack began talking to Lorna, slowly bringing up the subject of his taking up a job in Brussels, trying to convince her that it would be good for his career.

'It wouldn't change much for us,' he said. 'You could stay in Ireland and I'd commute. It'd be easier on the girls too. They wouldn't have to change schools.'

'But what if something happens when you're away – if I get sick or one of the children...'

'You'll still have all your family around you, and I'd be just an hour and a half away by plane. And I'd be home every weekend.'

The day he received a letter confirming that his application had been successful, he waited until the children had gone to bed before showing it to Lorna.

She sat and looked at it for a long time and then said, 'I thought this was all just in the discussion phase. But here, it says you would start in a month's time and that the posting is for three years. This is beginning to sound like a separation to me.' He didn't reply, surprised by what she had just said, and she turned on him in a fury. 'Is that what you want, Jack? Is that what all this is about?'

'No, of course not,' he said, trying to hold her, but she pulled away. 'Look, Lorna, please don't get upset. Let's give it a go and if it doesn't work out, I'll come back and look for something else here.'

'I want a husband, Jack, a husband that's here for me and the children. Not some part-time arrangement at the weekends. If you want a separation, just be honest for once and say it. But I'll never accept it. We don't divorce or separate in my family; you should know that by now.' She began to sob. 'Why can't you just be like everyone else and be satisfied with what you have? Why do I always get the impression that I'm a disappointment to you? And what will everyone think if you go off and I stay here?'

He tried to calm her, but she pushed him away and threw the letter back at him and ran out of the room.

Jack stayed for some time in the living room trying to gather his thoughts, knowing there was no point in reasoning with her when she was in this state. When he finally went upstairs the bedroom was in darkness. He switched on the light and walked toward the bed, trying to make as little noise as possible, then spotted the box of sleeping tablets lying on its side by the bed.

'Lorna!' he shouted and shook her vigorously. He had been here before, once, and after the ambulance had been called and she'd been whisked off to hospital to have her stomach pumped it transpired that she hadn't taken anything at all. He shook her again and she opened her eyes.

'Have you taken something?' he asked, lowering his voice and trying not to sound angry.

She nodded.

'How many?'

'Just one,' she mumbled.

He checked the box and satisfied himself that she hadn't taken an overdose. He took the pills and placed them in a drawer on his side of the bed, then he slid in beside her just in case.

The atmosphere the following morning was tense, neither of them making any reference to what had happened the night before.

When he came home from work that evening, he sat down at the kitchen table and said, 'Lorna, I'm totally exhausted after all this election stuff and we both need to clear our heads before having any more of these discussions. Would you be OK with me taking a few days off and going somewhere to play some golf?'

This was nothing new – golf had provided a very convenient and believable excuse for disappearing on weekends in the past. Lorna just shrugged and said nothing. In fact, she didn't even ask where he was going, which was a relief as he hadn't thought that far ahead.

He called Sinéad in Brussels and told her he had managed to get a few days away, asking her if there was somewhere special she would like to go.

'How did you manage that?' she asked.

'I'll tell you when I see you.'

She thought for a few moments, asked him if he was sure, and then said, 'What about West Cork?'

'West Cork?' he echoed. He had been prepared for Paris, London, even Venice, but not West Cork.

'My aunt has a lovely cottage near Bantry,' she said, 'and I could see if it's free. It's a bit late in the year and the weather can be unpredictable, but it doesn't really matter, does it? The place is beautiful, it's very cosy and it would be good to get away from the city.'

Two days later, having perfected his golfing story down to the last detail, he packed his gear into the car, drove to the airport and parked in the long-term car park. He then went into the terminal with his bag and waited for Sinéad who was arriving on the late morning flight from Brussels. He sat down opposite the arrivals area and took a piece of white card out of his bag. On it he wrote 'MRS CURRY' in large letters. This was an allusion to a meal they had once in a Chinese restaurant, when the receptionist misunderstood Murray on the phone and insisted on calling Sinéad 'Mrs Curry' all evening, becoming increasingly annoyed at their laughter. When he saw from the board that her plane had landed, he positioned himself with all the taxi drivers, chauffeurs and tour guides, holding the card up and hiding part of his face.

She pretended not to see him at first. She'd had her hair cut quite short, and was wearing the same leather jacket and jeans she had worn that first night in Geneva. She looked great and he felt a surge of quite unjustified pride as she stopped in front of him, not showing a flicker of emotion.

'This way, Madame,' he said and she followed him over to the car hire desk, then put her arms around him and buried her head in his shoulder, shaking with laughter.

The desk clerk looked at them with a benevolent smile and, turning to Jack, asked if he had a reservation. Sinéad pulled herself together, wiped her eyes.

'Actually, the reservation is in my name – Murray – with an M, not a C.' She looked as though she was going to laugh again.

Jack looked at the desk clerk, raising his eyes to heaven, and said, 'It's the lack of oxygen on the plane – she's always like this when she lands.'

Everything was prepared and within minutes they had the keys and set off towards the car park, arm in arm, oblivious to the rest of the world, the desk clerk beaming after them.

They savoured every minute of the drive, feeling that sense of freedom they had only really ever had when abroad. They stopped for lunch in Cashel and afternoon tea in Bandon, a town he had always found dreary but which, in Sinéad's company, suddenly seemed lively and interesting. They were like a couple of tourists, exclaiming at the green fields and the friendly locals.

By the time they arrived in Drimoleague it was almost six and getting dark, so they stopped at a small grocery shop to get some basics to tide them over until the next morning, linking arms like a couple of honeymooners who were dis-covering each other's favourite foods.

A few miles further on, just before Bantry, Sinéad took a sharp left and Jack could just make out a signpost saying Sheep's Head Way.

'It's such a pity it's getting dark,' she said. 'This part of the drive along the south side of the bay is spectacular, and I love the moment when you catch a glimpse of the cottage for the first time. We used to come here a lot when we were young, my cousins and I, and we'd have a competition to see who could spot it first.' They drove on a narrow winding road for about seven miles without meeting any traffic, passing a post office standing in splendid isolation in the middle of nowhere. 'That's the landmark,' she said, pointing at the building. 'Now keep your eyes peeled. It's somewhere along here on the right – just a little track.'

About two hundred yards further on she turned at a barely visible entrance into a lane that wound its way back in the direction they had come from. The car bumped and bounced in the ruts as a farmhouse came into sight. Sinéad stopped outside the gate and just as she opened the door of the car a young woman came rushing out, followed by an excitable collie. Jack could see a man standing in the doorway, but couldn't make out his face. The woman had a set of keys in her hand, and she and Sinéad spoke quickly for a few moments. They both looked back at Jack and the woman waved shyly. Then Sinéad was back in the car and they continued on down the lane until they came to a blue gate. Jack jumped out and pushed the gate open and Sinéad drove in and parked in front of the cottage. Jack went back to close the gate, stumbling a little in the pitch dark, trying to see where he was going with just the rear lights of the car to help. When he got back she had opened the door to the house and switched on the outside lights. He stood back and looked at the façade. It was a very plain traditional

249

whitewashed cottage with dormer windows, and Sinéad was looking out at him over the half-door like someone from a John B Keane play.

'Hurry up,' she said. 'You can see all that tomorrow. It's cold out there.'

He took the bags out of the boot and followed her in to a cosy low-ceilinged living room with wooden beams and unusual dark red painted cupboards. There was a turf fire smouldering in the enormous fireplace and the place felt surprisingly warm.

'Maeve – that's the woman you saw – keeps the keys and airs the place, and always makes up the beds, puts on the storage heating and lights a fire when someone is arriving. But my aunt can't manage to persuade her to leave the outside lights on – she thinks it's a terrible waste of electricity.'

She opened the door to the kitchen and put the bags of groceries down on a large old pine table. On each side of the door from the living room there were more painted cupboards in same style as those in the living room but painted a pale greyish blue.

'The house used to belong to a Norwegian musician who fell in love with an Irishwoman and moved here. He was a student of Grieg's and quite an accomplished painter. He painted all these cupboards in traditional Norwegian style. Come on,' she said. 'I'll show you the rest of the house.'

They crossed the living room, at the far end of which was a door leading into a bedroom. 'This is my aunt's room,' Sinéad said. 'She used to sleep upstairs, but she prefers to be down here now because she's not as mobile as she used to be. She had a small bathroom put in just off the kitchen, so she doesn't have to climb the stairs.' They turned back into the living room where opposite the front door there was a small staircase, only about five steps, leading up into what had clearly been an attic before. The tiny staircase divided in two and there were five more steps to the left and five to the right. 'Watch your head,' Sinéad said, laughing as they went up.

The whole of the upstairs area was carpeted, and to the left of the staircase there was a living area with huge floor cushions scattered around, with another two bedrooms leading off it. To the right there was a long corridor leading to a large bathroom and another bedroom. All the rooms were simply furnished and decorated and built into the eaves, exuding charm and comfort.

'We'll take this room – it has a lovely view in towards Bantry and gets the morning sun. And I see that Maeve has made the bed up here anyway,' she said. 'Why don't you get unpacked and freshen up – we don't have such modern luxuries as showers, but have a bath if you like while I go and get some food ready.'

He'd always preferred showers, but his back was stiff from the long drive down, so he unpacked the few things he had brought and turned on the taps.

He had just removed his clothes and slid into the bath when Sinéad appeared at the door carrying a tray with a bottle of wine in an ice-bucket, two long-stemmed glasses, some olives in a little dish and a candle.

She put the tray down by the bath and then disappeared, returning with a portable CD player. 'What music would you like?' she asked, displaying a collection of discs.

'I think Grieg would be appropriate, don't you?' he said.

'I've got two Grieg CDs here,' she said. 'The piano concerto or the Peer Gynt Suites.'

'The Peer Gynt suites – sounds different – what are they about?' he asked.

'They're based on a play by Ibsen, the story of a selfish peasant who goes off on all kinds of adventures, running away from any kind of commitment, while his love, Solveig, stays at home waiting for him to return.'

'So, no message there, then?'

Sinéad ignored him. 'Solveig's Song is very well known and one of the most moving and beautiful pieces of music I know. Even a philistine like you will probably recognise it when you hear it.'

'Ok then, Peer Gynt and Solveig it is,' he said, closing his eyes and luxuriating in the warm water.

She turned the CD cover over. '*The story of a life based on procrastination and avoidance* – my aunt must have written this. I wonder what she meant?'

Before he could react, she poured out the wine. 'Savennières,' she said grandly, passing him a glass.

'At last!' he said. 'Where did you find that?'

'Brussels airport,' she said. 'I thought it might come in handy.' She turned it around and peered at the label. 'It's harvested by moonlight or something like that.' She then turned off the main light, placed two large towels on the heated towel rail, took off her clothes and slid in at the opposite end of the bath. They lay there facing each other in the flickering candlelight, talking, sipping wine and listening to Solveig pouring her heart out.

When Jack looked back on that four-day trip, it seemed to him that every moment was pure perfection. The cottage, seen in daylight, didn't disappoint. It was a traditional white-washed house with dark blue doors and windows and an old slate roof, modest in appearance but clearly well-cared for. There was a tiny, low-walled garden in front of the main door, where there were banks of lilies, hydrangeas and an exuberant clematis that arched its way around the door. The rest of the land, stretching to almost four acres, was used by Maeve's husband to graze his sheep, and was surrounded by massive fuchsia hedges. The cottage nestled down against a bank, well sheltered from the wind, which could be wild in these parts. Some stone steps led to a path through the upper field that passed a long-abandoned vegetable garden hemmed in by yet more fuchsias, from where you could see the whole of Bantry Bay.

They spent their days exploring the majestic bays and peninsulas of the region, sometimes setting off at dawn, and their evenings in the cottage snuggled on the sofa in front of the turf fire or lounging on the floor cushions upstairs, listening to music, reading or watching something on the tiny black and white television with its two channels.

On one of their forays they went east to Mizen Head and found an idyllic spot high up above the lighthouse to have a picnic. There were no tourists around at that time of year and only the crashing of the waves, the baaing of an occasional sheep and the sound of birds to break the heavenly silence. It was cold but sunny and he could still recall the scent of Sinéad's skin, warmed by the sun as they lay in a grassy hollow, well sheltered from the wind, watching

253

the seagulls wheeling above the cliffs against the bright blue autumn sky.

And then there was the day they visited Gougane Barra with its tiny stone church which appears to stand in the middle of the lake. The place had an other-worldly feel to it; total, almost eerie stillness with the grey sky reflected in the waters of the lake and the forbidding mountains almost black against the sky. He had never known a place to exude such peace; as they sat on a bench taking in the view Sinéad laid her head on his shoulder and said, 'This is my favourite place on earth. I want to be buried here.'

'Like the Tailor and Ansty?'

'You see, you're not such a philistine after all.'

She ruffled his hair and they sat in silence for a while.

On the way back from Gougane Barra they stopped in a small pub in Bantry. There were just a few locals sitting around nursing their pints and they looked at the strangers with mild interest as they walked in. Jack and Sinéad sat up on the bar stools and ordered a pint of Guinness for him and a half pint glass for her.

'Do they still not serve pints to women in this country?' she asked.

'Shh,' he said. 'You're driving back.'

On their last evening they went for a walk along the cliffs next to the cottage and clambered down to the rocky fore-shore to watch the shoals of fish coming in towards Bantry. As the sun began to set, they made their way back up the cliff and stood at the fence bordering the garden, watching the light changing over the bay. It was a clear evening, and they could see right across to Castletownbere, fishing boats bobbing up and down with their lights twinkling in the dusk.

'My aunt is going to sell this place soon,' Sinéad said. 'I'm thinking of buying it. I've got such wonderful memories of here and I'd like my children – if I ever have any more – to know this place.'

'Our children,' he said, taking her by the shoulders. 'Our children, Sinéad. I want to have children with you.'

She smiled at him, putting her finger on his lips. 'One step at a time, Jack. Let's not talk about that right now.'

That evening, they feasted on some fresh fish and mussels they had bought earlier at the pier in Schull and raided Sinéad's aunt's wine store for a bottle of Riesling to accompany the meal. Sinéad made a tarte tatin with some local apples left in the cottage by Maeve and they finished that off by the fire. They spent their last night at the cottage reading old copies of *Private Eye* and listening to sixties' music before going to bed early. As they huddled under the duvet, listening to the silence broken only by the occasional rustling of the leaves outside, he had never felt so happy.

★

The drive back to Dublin seemed much shorter and for Jack the parting at the airport was the most painful yet. He had never been so reluctant to go home and took a roundabout route via Sandymount, stopping there by the beach, remembering the day he had watched the planes coming in to land and looking forward to Sinéad's arrival.

When he finally arrived, he parked the car in the drive-way and was surprised to see that Lorna's car wasn't there, but even more so when he turned the key in the front door and no excited little girls rushed to greet him. He had phoned every evening at seven while he was away, and he'd told Lorna exactly when he was coming back. The place was eerily quiet. He left his golf clubs in the car, put his bag on the floor in the hall and went into the kitchen. It was clean and tidy and smelled of cleaning products, but there was no evidence that anyone had eaten there recent-ly. He went upstairs slowly. The bedrooms were neat and tidy, with all the beds made. The whole house looked as it only ever did when their weekly cleaner had been, but she usually came on a Wednesday and today was Friday. With a growing sense of unease he went back downstairs and walked into the dining room. On the table was a large ma-nila envelope with his name on the front in Lorna's hand-writing.

He looked at it for a while then slowly sat down and opened it. Inside there was a typed document and attached to that was a short, handwritten note. He pulled the note away and began to read.

Dear Jack

I have suspected for some time that you have been having an affair, so I followed you to the airport on Monday and saw you with that woman.

I presume that is why you want to go abroad and work in Brussels. After giving the matter much thought I have decided that if you really want a separation, I will accept under certain

conditions and I would ask you therefore to sign the enclosed
documents.

Lorna

He stayed motionless there for a moment, stunned. This was what he'd wanted, but something wasn't right. It all seemed too easy. And why wasn't she here to say this to him directly anyway?

Just as he was about to start reading the document, he heard the front door opening and Mark and James walked in.

'Hello, Jack,' said Mark, 'We knew you were back when we saw the car in the drive, so we let ourselves in. I hope you don't mind. Lorna gave us the key – she asked us to have a chat with you.'

James stood beside him on the opposite side of the table and pulled out a chair. 'Have you had time to look at the document we prepared, Jack?' he asked, before settling his large frame into the chair. They had always been on very good terms, and he was being perfectly pleasant, but Jack began to feel uneasy.

He shook his head.

'We're not judging you, Jack, we're doing this for Lorna,' said Mark, in a business-like tone. 'If you like, we can run through it together.' He noticed that they each had a copy, with parts highlighted in yellow.

After they'd left, he sat for a while in the dining room, the calm and tidy space contrasting with the chaos in his head. He looked around and it struck him, not for the first time, that the room had no soul and looked as if nobody lived there. The model of Monticello was gone from the bookshelf. He would find it later in the bin, torn into tiny pieces.

He put his head down on the table and banged his fist on the polished surface. Then, just as he was beginning to examine his options – of which there didn't seem to be many – he heard the front door open again. This time it was his mother, followed almost sheepishly by his father. He had forgotten they had a key.

The conversation that followed was extremely one-sided. Lorna had apparently gone straight to them rather than to her own parents, when she got confirmation of the affair – a good strategic move, he thought cynically afterwards.

'How could you do that to Lorna?' his mother asked. 'Such a beautiful girl, and such a lovely family.'

He looked at his father, who said nothing. They had never been close, yet Jack had somehow expected some sort of man-to-man support, or even a little understanding from him. But there was nothing, not a flicker of emotion.

'You're a grown man,' his mother continued, 'And you can do as you please. But let me make this very clear. If you decide to leave Lorna and go off with that woman, we will disinherit you and leave your share directly to the children.' She added, quite unnecessarily in his view, given the conversation he had just had with the brothers, that his reputation in Dublin would be ruined and that if he left his marriage it would be difficult for him to stay in the country.

As she stood to leave, she shook her head. 'We're so disappointed in you, Jack. We've done our best by you. We've given you everything, a decent home, a family, a good education, but...' she paused. 'I suppose there was always bad blood there.'

He said nothing, shocked to the core by what she had just said. Again, he looked at his father, who refused to meet his gaze and stared down at the floor.

After they left, Jack stood up and looked out the window into the back garden. He had to hand it to them all, they had him well and truly screwed. The neighbour's ginger cat – inexplicably called Plato, as he was the stupidest cat he had ever known – strolled nonchalantly across the lawn, setting off the security light, then jumped onto a garden chair and curled up there, looking at him with what seemed like contempt.

He looked at his watch – it was almost seven o'clock. He had no idea what to do and was wondering whether he should phone Sinéad when once again he heard a key in the door and his heart sank, wondering who else was going to turn up. It was Lorna, looking pale but quite composed.

'I'm not staying,' she said. 'I just came over to see if you were alright.'

'Alright? Oh yes, I'm fine. I've just had a very unpleasant conversation with my parents about my origins, and I'm facing financial ruin and disgrace and not being able to see my children when I want, but yes, other than that I'm fine.'

She sat down at the dining room table. 'And why do you think that you don't deserve all of it? All of this? I didn't want to have to do things this way,' she began. 'But really, you left me no choice. You're the one who put yourself in this mess. I won't be humiliated by your affair. I presume it's not the first?' She looked at him for confirmation. He didn't reply and she continued. 'I've been thinking a lot about all this for a while and I'm prepared to make an effort – go for counselling, do whatever is needed for us to make this marriage work. Nobody I know is divorced, let alone separated, and I certainly don't want to start that trend.'

She told him he had the weekend to think about the contents of the agreement on the table, but that she wanted a reply by Sunday evening. The document was non-negotiable – he could take it or leave it.

That was the last visit he had that evening. After Lorna left, he sat for a while, reading and re-reading the document. It was quite short, really, when you cut out all the legal jargon. It basically said that if they separated he would transfer ownership of the house to Lorna, continue to pay the full mortgage as in the past and hand over 60% of any savings and investments, his salary and any other income of any kind to her indefinitely. He could see the children every second weekend, from Friday evening until Sunday evening, in the marital home. Lorna would stay with her family during these visits, which he would enjoy alone. He could take them for the occasional school holiday, but only on condition that he did not expose them to any new partner.

He picked up the phone and called his friend and barrister Tony O'Donnell. Tony's wife answered the phone and said that he was out sailing in Dun Laoghaire and wouldn't be back until late. Jack knew what that meant – he would be in the Yacht Club drinking with his mates – so he got into his car and drove down to the coast.

He caught Tony at the club before he had too much to drink and they went off to a side room, where Jack summarized the situation as best he could. His friend had a quick look at the document, put it down on the table and sighed.

'Jesus, Jack,' he said. 'Could you not have kept it short, quiet and foreign like the rest of us?' He shook his head, sighing again. 'Of course, you can go to court. It's over the top and you could fight it. But you'll probably lose because everybody knows the Stewarts, and everybody will feel sorry for your pretty, fragile, wronged wife. Oh, if she was from some corporation estate on the northside you can be pretty sure the judge would tell her to get on her bike and go back to work to support herself. But here, no, it'll be argued by some bastard senior counsel – someone like me, who will incidentally also cost you an arm and a leg – that she gave up a glittering career to devote herself to rearing your children and that she needs not only to be compensated for the sacrifice but also to be able to keep them in the comfort they're used to. How much does it cost, that fancy school they're at? A fortune, with more to come when they go to university. And then there's all the extra-curricular activities, the piano lessons, the ballet classes, the tennis coach…and don't forget the foreign holidays that are so vital for their life balance these days.' He paused and blew his nose loudly. 'You, my friend, are up shit creek.'

'Look Tony, it's not so much the money I'm worried about,' Jack said. 'It's the access arrangements. I love my kids and I want to see them whenever I like, and certainly more than two weekends a month.'

'That's what you say now. Just wait until the new partner/ wife/whatever starts producing more kids, and you have to pay for their education too.'

'But my future partner has a good job – we would be OK financially.'

'Of course you would, Jack, until she stops working to take care of the new brood, or until you start having arguments because you feel dependent on her, or until she feels hard done by because you're giving the bulk of everything you've got to your old family forever. Jack, believe me, I've seen it all too often. And anyway, be realistic, it wouldn't work. If you stay here the whole establishment will freeze you out, and if you go away you can forget about access.' He looked at him and patted him on the shoulder. 'Come on, come and have dinner with us and then go home and sleep on it.'

★

Jack woke the next morning with a splitting headache and it took him a while to realize where he was and what had happened. He got up and went to the window. The car was in the drive and didn't appear to be damaged, which was a relief as he had no idea how he got home.

He turned on the shower at its highest setting and stepped in, somehow hoping that the events of the previous day might be washed away if he stood there long enough, but it took that, a shave and several strong coffees before he began to remember the conversation he'd had with Tony the previous night and before he felt in any way capable of facing what lay ahead.

The first thing he needed to do was talk to Sinéad. That could be tricky, as she was at her parents' house.

He sat for about an hour beside the phone, trying to imagine the conversation, rehearsing and making notes in case he lost the thread. He was terrified one of her parents would answer but, in the end, it was Sinéad who picked up the phone.

'Jack?' She sounded surprised. They had an agreement that he would never call her at the weekend, and this was the first time he had ever broken it. 'Is there something wrong?'

'You could say that, yes,' he said, hesitantly. 'Can you talk?'

'Just a minute,' she said and he heard her putting the phone down. There were voices in the background, footsteps and then a door banging.

She came back a few moments later. 'It's OK. My parents have just gone out for a walk. I was supposed to go with them but I told them I'd catch up with them later.'

He took a deep breath and started at the beginning, telling her the whole story. The empty house, the document, the visits from the brothers, his parents and Lorna. He omitted the night at the Yacht Club, although he did tell her that he had spoken to a friend who was a barrister.

She didn't interrupt once. At one point he thought the line had gone dead and he stopped and said, 'Are you still there?'

'I'm still here,' she said quietly.

When he got to the end of the story he said, 'So that's the situation. I have to make a decision by tomorrow night.'

'I don't know what to say,' she said, almost whispering. 'We've had this discussion before, Jack, and you know it's not a decision I should help you make. If anything, I really need to stay out of it.' But then she seemed to change her mind and said, 'You do have options though. You could move to Brussels with me and worry about getting a job later. I'll be earning enough to keep us both for a while, pay the rent and so on.'

'But I would still have to pay the mortgage here and the maintenance and child support. I couldn't ask you to do that,' he said, and then proceeded to outline all the arguments so well developed by Tony.

'We'd manage,' she said, 'if you really wanted to.'

'Of course I want to,' he almost shouted. 'But I'm backed into a corner here. I can't abandon my children just like that. Especially...Come on, Sinéad, you of all people, you must understand that.'

There was another silence and he said 'hello' again.

'You've already made up your mind, haven't you?'

Before he could reply she put her hand over the mouthpiece and he heard her speaking to someone. 'It's my parents,' she said. 'They're back. It started to rain and they had no umbrella. I'm going to have to go.'

'You can't. Please, Sinéad,' he said, desperation rising. 'We really need to talk this through. Look, I'll go to the office – there'll be nobody there on a Saturday – and you can call me there on my private line. Or meet me at your flat. Please.'

'I don't know. Yes, maybe. I need to think. I'll try to call you at the office in about two hours.'

As he drove into the city to the office past all his familiar haunts, he thought again of the colleague he had met who had separated from his wife and how he had felt nothing but pity for him. He imagined himself in his position, but in Brussels, starting over, living in a tiny flat on a pittance, dependent on Sinéad. And what if after all that she then left him?

Sinéad was right – he had made up his mind, and he had no idea how to tell her.

He waited in the office for over an hour, pacing up and down, until at last the phone rang. He assumed at the time she was calling from her parents' house, but she told him much later that she had driven over to her flat as she didn't want to be interrupted or for her parents to see her upset. Had he known that on the day, he probably would have gone over to see her in person and perhaps the outcome would have been different. Or perhaps it would have made things worse.

'Start from the beginning,' she said. 'Tell me again what happened. I want to be sure I understand.'

She listened in silence as he tried to summarize the situation.

'I've already asked you this, Jack, but have you already made up your mind? Because if you have, there's no point in carrying on this discussion.'

'They haven't left me any choice,' he whispered.

'So there's no room for discussion or compromise? Is there nothing I can do or say that will make you change your mind?'

'You know there's nothing you can do.'.

'So that's it, is it? It's over – just like that. What happens now – we never see each other again? If that's the case why didn't you say that the first time – why did you want me to call you back?'

Her tone scared him. She sounded cold. He had expected tears, pleading, but not this composure.

'I needed to talk to you,' he said, aware how feeble that sounded.

'I need to go, Jack,' she said. 'Call me if you change your mind.' She hung up. He waited for about ten minutes and then rang her parents' number several times but there was no answer. He waited in the office for another hour, hoping she might call back, but the phone remained silent.

He went home just as it was getting dark and spent the evening slumped in front of the television with a pizza he'd ordered in. The next morning, he phoned Lorna and told her he had made his decision. She came back with the children in the afternoon and they tore up the document together, scattering the pieces in the bin on top of the destroyed model of Monticello.

★

Sinéad stayed in Dublin for a few more weeks before taking up her post in Brussels, but surprisingly for such a small place she never once bumped into Jack. She avoided the office, except when she knew he wouldn't be there. Brenda took care of all the administrative details for her departure, and Jack knew that the two of them were in touch almost daily. He thought about having Brenda transferred to another department, but in the end it was he who left, having been approached by a lobbying firm with an offer he couldn't refuse. He suspected Jim may have had a hand in getting him the job, but he never admitted to it.

A short while later, Lorna surprised him by saying she was considering going back to work and that she had asked her father to make some enquiries for her. She felt it was necessary for her to have independent means. They talked a bit more than they used to, although their conversations were still quite stilted. She even told him how angry she'd been that day at the airport when she saw him going off with Sinéad, and how she had gone over to his car after they'd left and almost gave in to the temptation to smash the windscreen. She never once mentioned the time Sinéad came to the house, or whether she had already suspected something then.

The day after Sinéad left for Brussels, Lorna organized a huge buffet lunch party at their house to which she invited absolutely everybody they knew. Ostensibly it was for Jim and Caroline, to mark the end of the old regime, but they both knew that she was making a very public statement. So many people answered the invitation that they had to have a marquee put up in the garden, linked to the house by a covered walkway in case it rained.

He had to admit that the place looked amazing, and Lorna played the perfect hostess. Most of the time she walked around with her arm linked in his, smiling at everybody. At one point she pulled away from him and he saw her go over to Brenda, who had just arrived with her husband and children. She said something in her ear and then took her by the elbow and walked off down the garden as if they were the best of friends.

'Now wouldn't you like to know what those two are saying to each other?'

Jack turned and found Bernard Morris standing behind him, a smug smile on his face. He resisted the temptation to punch him on his patrician nose but instead smiled back politely. 'Can I get you a glass of something, Bernard? It probably won't be up to your usual standard, but...' He stopped, his colleague's look making him feel uncomfortable.

'I have to hand it to you McDonagh,' Bernard said. 'You're a smooth bastard. All this...' he gestured around the room, with its expensive furniture and the professional caterers rushing about. 'Difficult to give it up, I suppose. Oh well, you'll probably live to regret it. I know I would. Anyway, you didn't deserve her. I hope she finds someone who appreciates her in Brussels. I have no doubt she will.'

Before Jack could answer Bernard had turned away towards the waiter hovering in the background with a tray.

Jack looked around and couldn't see Lorna anywhere. He also noted that although everyone who was anyone in Dublin seemed to be there, a few people were conspicuous by their absence. Frank Curzon for one, and Mulcahy and young Coughlan, who had always been in awe of Sinéad and followed her around like lapdogs.

Then Jim patted him on the shoulder and he was back into host mode, playing his role to perfection and behaving as if nothing had happened.

Chapter Twenty-one

THINGS SETTLED BACK INTO their old routine very quickly. The black sheep was welcomed back into the fold and nobody mentioned the subject again. A couple of weeks after the party, Jack arrived home to find Lorna sitting in the kitchen waiting for him, white-faced and furious, waving a letter in his face. He recognised his own writing immediately and his stomach turned over. It was a letter he had written to Sinéad. After all the drama had subsided, he had written several letters to her and discarded all but one, which he sent to her in Brussels. He knew it off by heart; he had read and re-read it so many times before placing it in the envelope. In it he poured out his feelings for her, describing his hopes that one day they would find each other again, comparing the two of them to a pair of travellers on an odyssey through a labyrinth, stuff about Solveig and Peer Gynt meeting in heaven. Awful stuff. Lorna quoted from this missive contemptuously.

'And don't tell me you wrote this before you split up. Look,' she jabbed at the flimsy paper with her finger, 'you talk here about the Christmas lights going on in Grafton Street, and I know as well as you do that that was last week.'

'Where did you get this letter?' he asked her.

Her lower lip quivered. 'It arrived in the post this morning,' she said, and then burst into tears.

He put his arm around her, murmuring apologies and trying to hide the rage he felt at Sinéad. He couldn't believe she would do such a thing.

About a week later, Sinéad called him at the office. She sounded hesitant, and said she had something she wanted to discuss with him.

'I've got nothing to say to you.' He hung up and didn't answer the phone when it rang again several times.

A few days later, a letter arrived from her via Brenda. He put it unopened in another envelope and sent it back.

A week passed during which there were two more phone calls from Sinéad, which he refused to take. Then he got a phone call from Brenda suggesting they meet, asking him what was going on, but he told her it was none of her business and that she could tell Sinéad to stop trying to contact him.

The following day the door to his office opened abruptly and Sinéad walked in. Shocked at first, he quickly recovered his composure. 'Get out,' he said.

She ignored him and approached the desk, pulling up a chair. 'I'm not leaving this office until you tell me what's going on, Jack. You're behaving as if I've done something to you, but I have no idea what it is.'

'Stop pretending you don't know,' he said.

'Don't know what?' she was starting to get angry.

'The letter. The one you returned to Lorna.'

'What letter?' she said, looking astonished.

'Oh, stop playing games,' he said. 'The letter I sent you about the labyrinth and Solveig and Peer Gynt.'

'Solveig and Peer Gynt? What on earth are you talking about?' she said, gripping the sides of the chair.

'I've got work to do,' he said, 'I really think you ought to leave. Don't you have a plane to catch? How did you get in here anyway?'

She went very pale and he thought for a moment she was going to faint. Then she stood up. 'I told the receptionist I was your cousin. You really need to work on the security here. And yes, I do have a plane to catch, but I can tell you this. I never got any letter from you, and even if I had I wouldn't have been spiteful enough to send it to your wife, despite the way you treated me.' She looked at him with undisguised contempt. 'I can't believe you could think me capable of doing such a thing.'

Either she was a better actress than he thought or there was something strange going on. A sense of gnawing doubt began to grow, but he pushed it aside. 'Don't forget to close the door on your way out.'

For a few seconds she didn't answer. Then she stood, looked at him coldly, turned and left the room.

He sat for a while, his hands shaking and beads of perspiration on his forehead. Her visit had unnerved him. He tossed the conversation around in his head and tried to make sense of it. Then he opened the top right-hand drawer of his desk, and rummaged among the papers. There were a few scribbled drafts of the letter in question and then, as he was about to close the drawer, he spotted something else, an envelope which appeared to be stuck at the back. He pulled it out carefully, and it was the envelope he had addressed to Sinéad. There was even a stamp on it, but no letter inside.

He stared at it for a while trying to work out what could have happened. It gradually came back to him. He had been about to take it out to post it when he was interrupted and had shoved it back into the drawer. And then he was away for a couple of days. But he still couldn't work out how the letter had ended up in his wife's hands – who would have sent it, and how?

He went out to the secretary's office and asked her if anyone had been in his office recently. She shook her head slowly and said she wouldn't let anyone in if he wasn't there.

'Apart from your wife, of course,' she said.

'My wife was in here?' he said, trying to sound casual.

'Yes, she came in the other day with the children to surprise you, but you weren't there, so they sat at your desk and wrote you a note. Did you not get it?'

'Oh yes, that note. Of course,' he smiled. 'I forgot. Thank you, Susan.'

He went home that evening and once the children were in bed, he confronted Lorna. After a feeble attempt at denial, she finally admitted that she had been in his office and found the letter.

'I just opened the drawer to get some paper for the girls to write you a note. Honestly, I wasn't looking for anything. And it was just there. I was so angry. I didn't think things through and pretended I'd got it in the post.'

She wiped her eyes and looked down.

'I'm sorry, Jack. I'm so unhappy. I don't know what I'm doing anymore.'

He felt sorry for her, his pity mixed with guilt for the way he had treated Sinéad. For the first time in a long while, he held her in his arms.

Chapter Twenty-two

London, the following week

THE MEETING HAD BEEN set up to mark the merger of two big PR firms in a very plush building near Whitehall. Jack's firm was expanding its activities and had linked up with a London firm who in turn just happened to be linked to the firm Sinéad was working for in Brussels. He was pretty sure she would be there, but it was not until the reception afterwards that he finally spotted her, on the other side of the room, chatting to a group of men who seemed to be hanging on her every word.

He walked over purposefully and said hello and kissed her on both cheeks. She looked surprised to see him but at the same time seemed perfectly at ease as she introduced him to the group. After some polite conversation, the men slipped away one by one and left them facing each other in the corner.

'I've something to tell you, Sinéad. Have dinner with me, please,' he blurted.

'An apology would be nice. Anyway, I can't,' she said, waving at someone over his shoulder. 'I'm having dinner with my boss.' Then she seemed to hesitate. She looked down at her glass and said, 'All right then – what about lunch tomorrow?'

'That would be perfect – I'm staying over anyway,' he lied. He had planned to take the early morning flight back to Dublin.

The next day they met at a restaurant not far from his firm's office and they talked and talked until one by one the tables emptied and they were the only ones left. He told her the story of the letter first and her expression hardened.

'You must have known it wasn't me,' she said.

'I'm so sorry, Sinéad, I was angry, frustrated, and I've missed you like crazy. These past weeks have been hell. The new job, the atmosphere at home…'

He jabbered on, telling her how he was trying to fill his life with all sorts of activities to fill the void she had left. His new job was challenging and kept him busy, and he had even started taking piano lessons with the girls every Saturday morning.

'The one good thing that's come out of this is that Lorna has found herself a job – or rather, her father found a job for her. It's really well-paid, too. A pharmaceutical company. They even gave her a company car – an Audi no less.'

He leaned across the table and tried to take her hand, but she pulled it away.

'I miss you so much,' he said. 'I've written you lots of letters but never sent them.'

'Probably for the best,' she said. 'You never know where they might end up.'

'Sinéad, please. I said I was sorry.'

'I heard about the party.'

'I'm sorry,' he said again.

'That really was a slap in the face, Jack; you do know that, don't you? How could you? It was cruel.'

He shook his head and mumbled that he was sorry, that it wasn't his idea.

She looked at him with a trace of pity and then her expression hardened.

'Do you know that after our second telephone conversation on the day you told me you'd made your decision I was in my flat in Merrion Square. When I put the phone down, I went straight to the bathroom, and threw up. Then I laid on my bed and cried. I don't think I've cried like that since I gave up my son. When I got up, I ransacked the medicine cupboard, took out every single pill, laid them all out neatly on the bed and made a list, calculated exactly how much it would take to kill someone of my weight.'

He looked at her in horror.

'I decided there was just enough there to do the job if I drank some alcohol with them. But then, something clicked, and I got up and went and looked through all my adoption files. And I put all the pills in a plastic bag and threw them in the bin.'

She picked up her briefcase and signalled to the waiter to bring the bill.

'Anyway, that's all water under the bridge now and I have an appointment at my hotel.'

He walked her back, hoping against hope that her client wouldn't turn up and that she would ask him to come up to her room and that for just an afternoon he could bury himself in the illusion that they were together again. As they walked past the front desk towards the coffee dock, where she was to meet her client, the receptionist called her name and handed her an envelope saying, 'It's a message from a...' he seemed to struggle to read the name. '...a Mr Miguel del Pueblo.'

She smiled enigmatically as she took the message and put it in her pocket.

Jack couldn't resist. 'Miguel del Pueblo? What kind of name is that?'

'It's from Sam actually,' she said.

'Sam?' he echoed. 'Your pianist friend? How does he know you're here?'

'Because I told him, Jack. We're good friends, you know. I can rely on him.'

'Is that who you had dinner with last night?'

'Look, Jack, I told you I had dinner with my boss. And even if you don't believe me, I really don't think it's any of your business who I have dinner with. You made your decision and we both know it's final. At least it is for me.'

'I miss you so much, Sinéad,' he said. 'I hadn't realised how bad it would be without you. I'm trying to hold things together for the sake of my kids, but if you could just give me some more time. Please. I love you.'

She sighed and looked away.

'I don't know what exactly you wrote in that famous letter you never sent me, but what I really wanted to tell you earlier, and since apparently you used those terms, is that I won't play Solveig to your Peer Gynt. This is not us beginning all over again.'

'How can you be so cold?' he asked.

'By being good at burying things,' she said. 'I've had plenty of practice. Don't you have a plane to catch?' she asked archly, turning from him and smiling at her client who had just arrived. 'Oh, and by the way,' she said, as she walked away, 'you got your metaphors mixed up – there are no labyrinths in Norwegian mythology.'

Chapter Twenty-three

JACK RETURNED TO DUBLIN that evening, dejected and angry. Two days later Brenda rang, saying she wanted to see him and that it was urgent, but she refused to tell him what it was about on the phone.

They met in a little café in South Anne Street, close enough to both their offices and just across the road from the offices of one of Dublin's biggest adoption agencies. As he waited for her, he watched a couple arriving and mounting the steps to the Georgian door opposite. For a moment he tried to imagine his mother handing him over in this place, and wondered about his adoptive parents. Were they there too, hiding in some dusty back room? Before he could reflect any further, Brenda arrived. He watched her coming in, looking around carefully to make sure nobody they knew was there.

'Hi, Brenda. You're looking great. How are things?' he said, but she didn't return his smile. She sat down and he ordered coffee for both of them. He began to ask her about her new job, but she cut him short.

'Jack, I shouldn't be here, and I shouldn't be telling you this, but there's something you really ought to know.'

He began to feel uneasy. 'What is it, Brenda?'

'It's Sinéad…' she began.

'Has something happened to her?' he asked, feeling a rising sense of panic.

'You could say that,' she said drily. 'You two saw each other in London, right? And by all accounts she didn't tell you, so I'm taking it on myself to do it. She's pregnant.'

It was the last thing he expected to hear, and it took a few moments for it to sink in. He sat back in his chair, thinking furiously, his foot tapping the ground. He fired questions at Brenda – how was that possible? Had she done it deliberately? How did he know it was his? What did she want him to do about it? She looked at him with distaste and shoved a card across the table.

'Don't shoot the messenger, Jack. Here are her phone numbers – office and home. Sort it out yourselves.'

He was going to a charity event with Lorna that evening, so he waited until the next day to call Sinéad, which also gave him time to think about what he was going to say. He called her office number and was taken aback when she answered the phone immediately.

She sounded surprised.

'This isn't a good time,' she said.

'I spoke to Brenda. She told me.'

'And?'

'Why didn't you tell me in London? Or even when you came to see me in Dublin.'

'Seriously Jack? You accused me of sabotaging your marriage and practically threw me out of your office. It didn't seem like the right moment to me,' she said.

'And how…?'

She cut him off. 'No, I didn't do it deliberately, if that's what you're thinking. I forgot to take my pills with me when we went to Bantry and it would have been such a hassle to find a doctor and get a prescription. And I was at a point in my cycle that made me think it would be fine anyway.'

'We need to talk. What are you going to do?' he asked, trying to sound calm, trying to keep the fear out of his voice. This had the potential to scupper everything he had been re-building. The consequences were unthinkable.

The answer was short, blunt and unexpected. 'I'm going to have an abortion,' she said, and though he was taken off guard he suddenly felt a huge sense of relief.

'If that's what you want…I really think it's the right decision, Sinéad – the only one – in the circumstances, that is,' he said.

'Yes, I thought you'd think that,' she said. A pause. 'It's all set up anyway – I'm going in this weekend – tomorrow actually – to have it done.'

'I wish there was something I could do,' he said, thinking it was probably best not to mention money. He asked her which clinic she was booked into, and although she was reluctant she gave him a name in the end but said it was best if he didn't contact her there.

That weekend he couldn't sit still. He called her home several times but there was no answer. He managed to find the number of the clinic and called on two days in a row but they claimed not to have anyone called De Clercq. Brenda told him later that in Belgian hospitals a woman is registered under her maiden name and that that was probably why he couldn't find her. Or perhaps she had left instructions for her personal information not to be disclosed.

He wrote her a long letter which he was very careful to post immediately, but it came back to his office unopened.

The following Thursday he arrived home earlier than usual, and as he put his briefcase down in the hall he heard Lorna's voice coming from the living room. At first he thought that someone was in the house with her, but then realised she was on the phone. Her voice sounded strained and unnatural and he began to listen.

He could hear some of her words but at first he couldn't make out what she was talking about. He crept a little closer to the door until he could hear her more clearly.

'Adopted? Oh no, that's just something he tells people to make them feel sorry for him. He's not adopted at all.' He drew a deep breath and walked into the living room. Lorna stared at him and said into the mouthpiece. 'Well, I have to go now. Thank you for having this conversation with me. I appreciate it. Goodbye.'

She looked perfectly calm but her hands were shaking as she replaced the receiver.

'Who was that?' he asked.

'Your ex,' she said. 'I rang her. I wanted to explain about the letter and apologise. I know I gave you the impression she sent it to me and it's been bothering me for a while. Whatever I might think of her, she didn't deserve to take the blame for that.'

'What else did you say to her?' he asked.

'I just told her that we were making a fresh start and trying to make our marriage work, and she seemed to understand that.'

'And why did you say that I wasn't adopted?'

'I don't know – it came up somehow and I just said it.'
She held his gaze for a few moments and then he turned on
his heel, walked out of the living room and went upstairs,
where he lay down on the bed and thumped his pillow very
hard.

He heard nothing for over a month. Christmas came and
went. Brenda refused to have any contact with him and he
had given up trying to phone Sinéad. She never answered
her home number and when once, in desperation, he rang
her office he was told she was in a meeting.

Then her letter arrived.

He often wrote her letters when they worked together,
especially after the trip to Washington, slipping them into
her briefcase during meetings or hiding them in her desk.
Usually they were funny, silly, even tender, and she would
reply in the same vein. He still had all of hers, securely
tucked away in his safe. But this letter was different. It was
shorter than usual, written in the same steady hand he had
come to love, but the message it carried was very different:

Dear Jack

*I am writing to you because I have some news, and I
would rather you heard it from me than on the grapevine.
Sam has asked me to marry him and I have accepted. He has
been offered a teaching position in a conservatoire in France,
and we will be moving there shortly.*

*I want you to know that I will always value the moments
we spent together, and that I understand the decision you had
to take, although it was painful and hard for me to accept. It*

*was the right thing to do, and I hope you will find happiness
or at least contentment. Your children, and your wife, deserve
that too.*

*Somehow, I hope that listening to my story has helped you
to come to terms with your adoption and that if one day our
paths should cross again you may even tell me that you have
found your birth mother. I sincerely hope so, for her sake as
well as yours. My search for Lorcan will continue and I have
every hope of finding him now; I am glad that the time spent
in Ireland allowed me to make such great progress.*

Sinéad

He read and re-read the short text with mounting disbelief. It had never occurred to him that she might marry
again; he had hoped against hope that despite all she said she
would wait for him. He felt alone, abandoned and absolutely
furious.

He called Brenda and asked her if she knew anything about
this, and of course she did. He asked her when the wedding
was to take place and where. She admitted cautiously that
yes, she and a few others were going to attend. It was to be a
small affair in London, but she wouldn't give him any details.

'And if I did tell you, Jack, what exactly would you do?'
she asked. 'Turn up at the venue like Dustin Hoffman in *The
Graduate*? Hammer on the door, upset everyone and then go
back home? You've made your choice, and you can't expect
her to turn down a chance to be happy just because it might
hurt you.'

She was right, of course. He had nothing new to offer
and his reaction was totally irrational and selfish.

Chapter Twenty-four

Dublin, 1994

Sinéad was sitting in the ante room at the adoption agency, waiting to be seen by the social worker. It was still the same woman after all these years, Miss Brennan, the one who had refused to meet her gaze when she arrived, terrified, with her parents in 1970. The one who had taken her to sign the papers and then left her to cope alone. The place hadn't changed much since then, she reflected, looking around at the dreary wallpaper, uncomfortable chairs and dog-eared religious magazines that sat in an untidy heap on a wicker table. She tried to remember how many times she had sat in this room, feeling nervous, like a teenager about to sit an exam. She wondered how many women like her had sat here before, how much pain had been absorbed into these walls.

She had lost count of the number of times she had called in. The first few meetings had been stilted, but as time progressed and Miss Brennan began to relax – no doubt seeing for herself that she was faced with someone who was neither mad nor likely to cause trouble – they grew relatively cordial.

'You're married? That's nice,' Miss Brennan had said on one of her previous visits. 'And I see from your letter that you have two little boys. That must be a great consolation to you.'

When Sinéad raised the question of contact with Lorcan, however, her tone changed.

'I'll think about it and talk to his mother,' she said. 'She keeps in touch, sends me a letter every year.'

A few months later Sinéad received a curt letter from Miss Brennan saying that she had discussed it with both the adoptive mother and her son but that while he had shown 'some interest', she didn't think he was mature enough for the moment.

'Just keep going in there. She'll give in eventually,' said Sam, holding her as she wept tears of rage and disappointment.

Over the next few visits she updated Miss Brennan on what was happening in her life, and in return she would receive snippets of information about her son, carefully chosen so as to reveal little or nothing that could identify him or his family.

Sinéad took particular care about how she dressed for these meetings – sensible shoes, muted colours and just a touch of mascara. In their conversations she played down anything that might seem too exotic, too foreign. She needed to blend in, not pose a threat of any kind to this woman who held her hopes in her hands.

'He prefers reading to gardening,' Miss Brennan told her as if imparting a state secret. 'He did well in school.'

The main thing, of course, was that Lorcan was still alive. She lived in dread of finding out one day that he had died and that she would never get to meet him again. As the years passed, she was drip-fed more information – he lived outside Dublin, he went to university.

It was three years now since he graduated. She remembered the conversation vividly.

'I have good news for you,' said Miss Brennan and her heart skipped a beat. Was this it? Had he agreed to make contact?

'Lorcan graduated from college last month. His mother sent me pictures of him. I haven't seen him in a while, and I have to say he looks really well. A lovely young man.'

Sinéad forced a smile, but felt unutterably sad not to be able to share this moment with him, not allowed to see the photographs. She said nothing of this to the implacable woman who never stood up, never shook her hand, and always sat facing her across her desk.

'Miss Brennan will see you now.' A voice broke into her thoughts. Sinéad stood, and the secretary watched her carefully, closing the door behind her as she entered the office. Why did everyone involved in this process seem wary and patronizing?

Miss Brennan was sitting at her desk writing something, and didn't look up for a few moments. 'Sinéad,' she said eventually. 'You're looking well. Do sit down.' Sinéad smiled, stifling her desire to be equally patronizing, and the ritual exchange of banalities began.

When they had exhausted the trivia, Sinéad said, 'I heard talk about setting up a contact register for adoptees and birth parents, so I've contacted the Adoption Board and given them my details in case he ever wants to get in touch.'

Miss Brennan raised her eyebrows. 'I didn't realize you'd been in touch with the Adoption Board. Yes, you're absolutely right. The plan is that provided both parties agree and the child has reached the age of twenty-five, some kind of contact may be initiated.'

'Might Lorcan be interested, do you think?'

'I really couldn't say. Nothing has been decided yet and such meetings would have to be carefully prepared. We would have to be involved.'

'I understand,' Sinéad said, but wondered why she couldn't go through a more objective party, some kind of mediator. 'Have you read *the Adoption Triangle*?', she asked Miss Brennan, who shook her head. Sinéad took a copy from her bag and pushed it across the desk. 'I've done a lot of reading on the subject,' she said. 'And I found this book particularly helpful in understanding the issue from all sides.'

Miss Brennan took the book and glanced through it. 'Interesting. I'll certainly have a look at it.'

'Coming back to a possible contact down the line,' Sinéad tried to sound casual. 'You know I always refer to him as Lorcan? I'm sure his adoptive parents have given him another name, and I wondered, would there be any chance you could let me know his Christian name? You know, so I could get used to it before I meet him.'

Miss Brennan turned her pen in her hands and was silent for a while. 'I'm afraid I can't give you that kind of information.'

'I understand,' Sinéad lied. 'Well, maybe not now – maybe next time I drop in, if the contact register project has advanced and there is a real chance of my meeting him.'

She stood up to leave, thanking Miss Brennan for her time.

As she reached the door, Miss Brennan, who had remained seated at her desk, said 'I can't give you his name, but I can tell you one thing. His parents gave him an Irish name.'

'An Irish name?' Sinéad echoed. 'You mean, like Muiris or Diarmuid?'

Miss Brennan remained impassive. 'Yes'

'That's nice to know. Thank you,' said Sinéad, her tone revealing nothing of her excitement. One of the names on the list was Irish.

Once out in the street she almost ran all the way to Buswell's Hotel, where she had arranged to meet Brenda. Racing through the lobby, she headed straight for the Ladies' and once in the cubicle, jumped up and down, resisting an urge to scream. When she calmed down, she wiped the tears away and washed her hands, becoming once again a model of decorum. The door opened and Brenda walked in.

'I thought I saw you haring through the lobby and thought you must be ill,' Brenda said. They embraced and Sinéad shook her head vigorously, smiling.

'I've never felt better,' she said. 'Come on, let's have a coffee and I'll tell you everything.'

Brenda listened intently as Sinéad recounted the meeting at the agency.

'So, you see, I now know who he is,' said Sinéad. 'There was only one boy on my list with an Irish name – Ronan.'

'Ronan O'Donnell,' she repeated the name. 'It's a bit different to Lorcan Murray. It'll take a while to get used to that, but I suppose I'll get there.'

'What's the next step then?' asked Brenda.

'I'll get the address he lived at, when he was adopted, from the *Iris Oifigiúil* and then I'll try to find out if the family is still there. If they aren't, I suppose I'll have to look at the electoral registers and so on to see if I can find them.'

'But how will you do that if you're out of the country?'

'I'll get a private investigator to do it. I don't like the idea, I don't want them to intrude on the family, but I suppose if I brief them properly...I don't really have any choice.'

Before leaving for the airport she had a quick look through the Yellow Pages and noted the names of a couple of detective agencies. She finally chose the only one with a woman's name, hoping she might be more motivated by the search, she might feel something maternal or some empathy.

Several months later, all the woman had come up with for her large fee was that the people had moved and that she had had no luck in tracking them down. The detective had limited her enquiries to the neighbours and when Sinéad suggested she consult the electoral registers she began looking for more money to take it further. Sinéad was furious. It wasn't rocket science – tedious research perhaps, but it was clear she was being ripped off. She should have listened to Margaret who had warned her not to go down that route.

Sam was away for a few days, so she picked up the phone and called Brenda to let off steam.

'I'm not going to say I told you so,' Brenda said. 'Give me his name again, and the exact date of birth. I'll see what I can do, just don't ask any questions.'

A few days later, Sinéad was at home finishing lunch with

Sam and their two sons, James and Ben, when the phone rang.

'Some woman called Brenda,' said Ben. Sam and Sinéad exchanged glances.

'Take the call,' he said. 'Come on, boys, let's clear up and give your mother some space.'

'Can you talk?' asked Brenda. She sounded excited. 'I have it – I have his address!'

Sinéad pulled up a chair and sat down, her heart racing.

'He's living in Cork – in student accommodation.'

'How did you do that?'

'I said no questions, Sinéad!' Brenda laughed. 'But if you must know, I have friends in Social Welfare, and I asked one of them to run a check to see if there was anyone with that name and date of birth in the system. He must have had a grant or allowance of some sort. If he did, he'd be automatically logged.'

'I'm sorry. You could get into trouble.'

'Not unless *you* tell someone, or do something silly like turning up on his doorstep.'

'You know I wouldn't do that.'

'Of course I know.'

'Oh my God,' breathed Sinéad. 'This is getting real.'

After the boys had gone to bed, she and Sam sat up talking until late. Although it was tempting beyond belief to jump on a plane and turn up in Cork, they both agreed that was out of the question and she decided to give it time before contacting the adoption agency again. She waited a while before making another appointment. This time, she felt that the balance of power had shifted, and she knew she had nothing to lose.

Miss Brennan was her usual reserved self, but Sinéad's attitude had changed and her tone seemed to surprise the social worker.

'I'll get straight to the point,' she said. 'I would like you to pass on a letter to my son.'

Before she could answer, Sinéad continued. 'The new legislation provides that contact can be initiated when the child is twenty-five. He's now twenty-four years and seven months old, so I think you can at least make an effort.'

'As I've said to you before, Sinéad, I'm not sure that's a very good idea. Perhaps you should wait until he is actually twenty-five.'

Sinéad sighed, this time showing her irritation. 'Miss Brennan, I've been coming here for years now, and you know that I'm genuinely interested in my son's welfare, and that I've done a lot of reading on the subject. You know that I would never do anything that might jeopardize his relationship with his adoptive parents – or with me, for that matter.' She paused, then added, 'You also know that I'm a fairly resourceful person and that I have quite a few contacts.'

Miss Brennan nodded, and her eyes narrowed.

'So you know that if I really wanted to track down my son, I could easily do so. In fact, for all you know, I might already know where he is.'

Miss Brennan didn't answer and the atmosphere in the room was electric.

'But because I believe in doing things the right way, I'm asking you if you would agree to pass on a message from me.'

Miss Brennan looked down at the desk and fiddled with her pen. 'All right then.'

Sinéad looked at her, trying to hide her astonishment. She hadn't expected it to be so easy.

'On one condition. Don't put your name, address, phone number or any identifying information in the letter, and put the letter in an unsealed envelope. You don't know how he will react, and it is best if the initial correspondence goes through the agency.'

You want to read the letter, thought Sinéad, *and make sure I don't write anything unflattering about the agency.* 'I don't have a problem with that,' she replied evenly.

'Do you have the letter with you?'

'I haven't written it yet – I suppose I didn't expect you to say yes.'

Miss Brennan allowed herself a faint smile. 'Send it to me by post and I'll pass it on.'

★

It took Sinéad several weeks to write the letter. She began by writing page after page, telling him everything she thought he needed to hear, but tore them up one after the other before finally settling on a short text.

Dear Ronan,

I have been drafting this letter in my head, and sometimes on paper, for the best part of twenty-five years, and although I often managed to say what I really wanted, until now there has never been anywhere to send it.

As you probably know, I resumed contact with the adoption agency some years ago. For many reasons, mainly be-

cause I followed the advice of the 'experts', I waited until you reached eighteen before raising the issue of contact with you.

I am writing to you now because the adoption agency has finally agreed, after much persuasion, to pass on a letter, as the new official policy is that they will only initiate contact when an adoptee reaches the age of twenty-five.

After much reflection I have decided to keep this letter short, as I hope it will be the first of many but also because what I want to say to you at this stage is very simple. I want you to know that if I'd had a free choice, I would never have allowed you to be adopted. It was the most difficult decision I have ever made, and I have had to live with the consequences.

You apparently asked Miss Brennan whether I felt guilty and of course the answer is yes, but things are rarely so simple. I hope you will give me the opportunity to talk to you about all of this.

Over the years I have read many books about adoption in an attempt to come to terms with the situation, and I gave one I found particularly useful to Miss Brennan, to be given to you should you wish to read it. It helped me to understand how you and your adoptive parents may feel about my approach and it could help you to understand how I feel, too.

I also have copies of all the correspondence I have had with the agency and the Adoption Board. It's at your disposal.

I live abroad but return to Ireland regularly. My dearest wish is that on one of my next visits we can sit down and discuss things quietly.

From the snippets of information I have received about you, you seem to have done well in school and college, I hope you are happy – that is the most important thing to me. If I

can now contribute in any way to your life, I hope you will
let me do so.

Sinéad, your birth mother.

★

'There's a letter for you on the table,' Ben shouted as Sinéad walked into the house. Sam was away in Paris giving a lecture and Ben and James were having their afternoon tea with the housekeeper, Nadia.

She placed the supermarket bags on the floor and stared at the envelope. It was a large brown envelope with Irish stamps and she immediately recognized Miss Brennan's handwriting.

'Can you help Nadia put this stuff away please, boys,' she called out. She took the letter and went into her bathroom, turning the key quietly in the lock.

Inside the envelope there was another white envelope. Attached to that was a short note from Miss Brennan telling Sinéad that she had received a call from Ronan and that he had seemed 'quite pleased' to have heard from her and asked her to pass on his reply to her letter.

Sinéad sat down on the edge of the bath and looked at the white envelope. It was open, obviously − they must have checked the contents − and it appeared to contain a lot of paper. Her hands were shaking and she felt a strange sensation in her stomach. She put the letter down, nervous of what it might contain. Miss Brennan said he was 'quite pleased'. What exactly did that mean? Was he interested, but only just, or could it be that he was completely indifferent? She had read about adopted children who were perfectly content with their lives and didn't want someone coming along upsetting everything. And what if he was the way Jack was about his birth mother? What if he'd assumed that she was some sort of fallen woman, interested in hearing about his origins but not wanting any contact?

'Mum!' It was Ben. 'What should we do with the flowers?'

She pushed the letter into a drawer and opened the door, went out and helped her sons find a vase. Later, when they had gone off to the village to play tennis with some friends, she went back to the bathroom, took the letter out of the envelope and began to read. There were pages and pages of foolscap paper, covered in handwriting remarkably similar to her own.

Dear Sinéad, it began. *I am filled with only love, warmth and admiration for you. You have given me a gift greater than any I can ever receive – my life. For at least twenty years I have been conscious of your presence and I am hopeful that with so much red tape behind us, we will appreciate and enjoy the opportunity which is now ours to shape.*

I want to tell you about myself and discuss my hopes and fears about the possibility of contact. Thank you for all the effort from your side; it means a lot to me that someone could go to so much trouble just to know me. I hope that when you get to know me better you will consider it worth the effort. For me, no effort would be too large to gain the opportunity to know you.

She turned the page.

It was eerie to see marks on a page made by fingers that once held me and to know that this person was the first person to know me or hold me. Sometimes, thinking too much about the link between us scares me...

...I have never felt anything negative or had any hang-ups about my origins — if anything I have felt fortunate and special and possibly more independent. Not knowing the inherent talents — and flaws! — passed to me from blood relations leaves my boundaries more open...

Like you, I am looking forward to sitting down with you and talking about everything. This is a good time for me to embark on such an important experience. I'm old enough to be sensible about this, yet young enough to be enthusiastic, with many crucial decisions awaiting me over the next five to ten years. With career, marriage and even children ahead of me I'd like you, more than ever, to be part of my life...

...Knowing that you, under difficult circumstances, sacrificed a lot to give life to me and that I, as a direct result, have enjoyed a full and largely happy life, touching countless other lives, made me think about issues like abortion. I don't know your views, but I can tell you that you made the right decision in allowing me to live. I'm glad that my life was in your hands and I'll always love you for the choice you made...

...I want to make it clear that I think no differently of you because of how I came to exist. In my eyes you are perfect...

...There is so much more to say, but we have a lot of time to say it, despite the twenty-five years that have passed since our first and last contact. I'm looking forward to hearing from

*you again. This was weird, but wonderful, writing to some-
one so important who I have yet to meet. Write soon.*

All my love

Ronan.

Sinéad put the letter aside and slid to the floor, in shock.
No amount of careful reading and research had prepared her
for this. Tears welled up and spilled over. She didn't try to
wipe them away, she just sat there and let the emotion flow.
Twenty-five years of grief and loss carefully concealed and
compartmentalized, suddenly released.

She picked up the letter and began reading it again.

It was so much more than she could ever have expected.
She sat there on the floor reading and re-reading the letter,
for perhaps an hour until she heard Nadia calling her.

'Madame! It's five o'clock!'

Sinéad jumped to her feet, washed her face, slapped on
some foundation to hide the blotches on her face from crying, then folded the letter and placed it with great care in her
bedside table. She shouted to Nadia that she would be back
soon and ran to her car. She was halfway to the village when
she realized she hadn't taken her handbag, turned back and
saw James and Ben walking towards the gates of the house.
She pulled into the drive, skidded on the gravel, parked,
jumped out, ran into the house and grabbed her bag, then
gave them both a hug.

'I'm just off to the station to pick up your father. See you
later!'

They looked at her curiously. 'Are you alright, Mum?'
asked James.

She nodded, not trusting herself to speak, and sped off.

She arrived to see the last passengers from the Paris train leaving the platform. She looked around frantically but couldn't see Sam anywhere. She waited a few moments, then pulled a cigarette out of her bag. A hand appeared in front of her face with a lighter. She turned around and buried her head in Sam's shoulder.

'Whoa there! Smoking again! What's the matter?' His broad smile turned to a look of concern. As the story began to pour out, he relaxed and took her by the arm guiding her to the car. 'Here,' he took the keys from her hand. 'I'll drive – you talk.' When she had told him everything, he said, 'So, the next step will be…?'

Sinéad took a deep breath. 'I think it's probably best to take a softly-softly approach. Maybe we can write to each other for a while and then perhaps talk on the phone before meeting. He seems quite up for meeting, but I think I need to prepare this carefully. I've been thinking I'll have to tell the boys too. Do you think they'll be shocked?'

'If they are then we've done a lousy job of raising them. Tell you what, I'll cook dinner tonight and you sit with them and talk.' He paused and brushed her hair out of her eyes. 'I'm so happy for you, Sinéad. All these years of searching and waiting…' They sat in silence for a while before he turned on the ignition and drove out of the car park.

When they pulled up outside the house, she could see the two boys sitting at the piano in the living room and reflected that actually they hadn't done a bad job in raising them. 'You're the best thing that ever happened to me, Sam,' she said, and leaned across to kiss him gently.

'It took you a while to see that, but I knew you'd come around eventually,' he said, laughing.

'I should have married you when you asked me that time on the boat. But then, maybe that would have spoiled your career and we would have fought and resented each other...' she trailed off.

'None of that matters now,' he said. 'Live in the present. You're going to find your son and he's going to be every bit as wonderful as the two you already have. Come on, I'm starving.'

★

Telling her boys was not as difficult as she imagined. Once Nadia had left, Sam sat them all down at the kitchen table and opened a bottle of champagne.

'Boys, your mother has something to tell you and I want you to listen carefully, right to the end and not interrupt. I'm going to go to the study and leave you to it for a while.' He filled up four glasses, two with champagne and two with fizzy lemonade, raised his glass and said, 'To my three musketeers,' and left the room.

'Are you going to have a baby?' asked James, and Sinéad laughed, the tension broken.

'At my age? No – but you're not far off.' They listened, enthralled, to her story. She tried to keep it simple and place it in context, aware that they could well find it unimaginable that she could give up her son, terrified of being judged. 'So, that letter I got today was a letter from Ronan, or Lorcan, as I told you I had named him. He's delighted we made contact and we're going to work towards a meeting.'

'Wow,' said James, turning to Ben and giving him a high five. 'I don't have to be the big brother anymore!' Then, turning back to Sinéad, 'Does he play tennis? He'll have to if he comes here. And is his adoptive father a pianist too?'

Sam appeared at the door, clapped his hands. 'OK, enough excitement for the moment. I'm hungry and we need to eat.'

Chapter Twenty-five

Dublin, July 1995

IT HAD BEEN TEN years since Jack had last seen Sinéad. During that time he had often dreamt about her. He would be walking into a café and she would be there, wearing that leather jacket, her hair cropped in a bob like it was when they met at the airport and went on that ill-fated trip to Bantry. She would look up and smile and everything would be all right again.

This was nothing like his dream. He had an appointment in the Dáil bar to talk to some senators about a Bill he was trying to influence for his client, a large multinational. As he rushed down the corridor, he spotted Brenda in the lobby, talking to someone. It was Sinéad —older, obviously, but unmistakable.

He stopped dead in his tracks, caught Brenda's eye, then thought the better of it and hurried to his meeting.

When he came out an hour later there was no sign of Sinéad, but Brenda was still there, talking to someone else. He paced up and down, impatient to find out where Sinéad had gone. He finally caught her attention and when she suggested they go for coffee across the road in Buswell's, he readily agreed.

He began by asking about her children, but she just smiled and said, 'I suppose you want to know why Sinéad is here. You know, Jack, I'm tempted to tell you to wait until she decides to tell you herself – that is, if you two ever speak again – but I have to confess that I did ask her and she did say I could tell you.' She stopped, waiting as the waitress placed the cups of coffee on the low table in front of them.

'She found her son and she's on her way to Cork to meet him.'

He sat very still. As if sensing what he was thinking, she added. 'Don't even think about getting involved. This is something she has to do on her own, Jack. Sam didn't come with her because he understands that.'

He picked up a sugar cube and toyed with it, crumbling it into his coffee. He didn't even take sugar nowadays. 'Will she be coming back through Dublin?' he asked, trying to sound casual.

'Yes, but I think she'll be flying in and just changing planes at the airport. Like I said, I don't think you should get involved.'

While this conversation was taking place, Sinéad was on the train to Cork clutching the latest letter from Ronan/Lorcan – she still hadn't quite got used to his name. It was a nice name though, she thought. She liked the fact that it was Irish. She looked around the carriage – clean, modern and quite different to the train she had taken all those years ago, with the screaming baby and the sour-faced social worker.

The station had changed, too. It was very different to the dreary place she'd arrived at in 1970 – and the taxis were much smarter, even if this driver wasn't as friendly. She wondered where 'her' driver was now, if he had adapted to life back home or if, like her, he had found it stifling and left again. She wondered if he knew how much his small act of kindness had touched her and how the memory of it still remained with her after all this time. She guessed he would be happy for her, knowing that she was about to meet her child.

The taxi pulled up outside the Arbutus Lodge, an attractive manor-house hotel set back from the road on a hill just outside the city. She checked in, telling the girl at reception she was expecting her son and asking her to book a table for two in the restaurant for dinner, then made her way to her room. It was how she imagined it would be, and exactly what she needed, a cocoon. She gave Sam a quick call to reassure him she had arrived safely and then turned on the taps to run a bath.

She had allowed herself plenty of time to prepare for the meeting, and spent the best part of an hour luxuriating in the oversized bath, running through every imaginable scenario in her head. She pictured herself walking into the lobby, a tall handsome young man – he had to be handsome – pulling himself out of a chair, moving towards her. And then what? Should she kiss him? That's what anyone in France would do, but this was Ireland and she had no idea if such a greeting would be appropriate. What if she tried to embrace him and he pulled back? His letters were warm and funny, but he might be very different in real life. Maybe just a hug then. Or maybe not. A handshake would be too formal. Or would it?

She slid under the water and held her breath for as long as possible, then resurfaced, got out of the bath and started to get herself ready.

Her hair dried and neatly brushed, she stared at her reflection in the mirror. Make-up or not? 'Just be yourself,' Sam had said. So just some eyeliner and a bit of mascara then – otherwise her eyelashes would be invisible – but not too much. Her hands were shaking, and she had to wipe away the smudges with a tissue.

Then the clothes. She had laid out two outfits on the bed – a neat navy-blue trouser suit with a white t-shirt, or jeans and a leather jacket. Definitely the trouser suit. Boring perhaps, but safe, and above all respectable. That was the word. She had to be respectable.

She was dressed and ready fifteen minutes before the time they had agreed and she was debating whether or not to go down and wait for him in the lobby or the bar – no, the bar wouldn't be right – perhaps just wait in the room for a while longer – when the phone rang and the girl at reception said, 'Mrs Bloom? Your son is here.'

She ran to the bathroom, her heart pounding, looked at herself in the mirror, checked her make-up, brushed her hair again then grabbed her bag and made for the stairs.

She was half-way down when she saw him, and she gripped the banister for support. There was no mistaking the tall young man smiling up at her. She managed the last few steps without falling, he walked towards her and without the slightest trace of awkwardness, they embraced and she whispered, 'You're the image of your father.'

They moved to the bar and sat down. The emotion she felt was overpowering and she could hardly breathe. One of the books she had read had warned about this, describing it as the sensation of falling in love, but at the time she had dismissed the idea, thinking the author was being overly dramatic.

'How was your journey over?'

'Fine, fine. No delays. No strikes in France today.' She smiled at him, trying to reconcile the image she had carried around in her head for so long of that tiny baby she once held with this tall, confident young man. 'And you, how has your day been?'

'Quiet. I don't have much on at the moment actually. I have some papers I'm working on, but I'm pretty free.' He sipped his drink. 'I was a bit nervous, to be honest, so I went for a long run.'

'I was nervous too, but I was afraid I'd get lost if I went out and be late. How silly is that, at my age!'

They both laughed and sat in a comfortable silence for a moment.

'Is there anything special you'd like to do over the next couple of days?' Sinéad asked.

'Nothing really. I'd just like us to get to know each other, I suppose. I could show you around Cork.'

The waiter came over and told them their table was ready and they moved to the dining room.

She watched him as he spoke to the waiter, struggling with the French terms on the menu, and marvelled at him. His height, the wavy brown hair, the dark eyes. He was definitely his father's son.

When the food arrived they barely touched it, so intent were they on each other's stories. There was so much to talk about, so much for both of them to take in.

'This is such a strange experience,' said Ronan. 'I had no idea what to expect. Well, I mean I knew from your letters you weren't going to be...'

'Eccentric?' she smiled. 'Embarrassing?'

'No, of course not.' He laughed. 'It's amazing. You're so easy to talk to. I feel like I've known you all my life.'

The waitress hovered anxiously, concerned that there was something wrong with the food.

'The food was lovely,' said Ronan. 'It's just that we haven't seen each other for twenty-four years so we have a lot to talk about.'

The waitress looked confused as she took the plates away. Later, they saw her talking to an older woman, probably her supervisor, and the woman looked over at their table thoughtfully.

'I've brought you something,' said Sinéad, sliding an envelope across the table. 'It's a hodge-podge of bits and pieces where I wrote down what I was thinking around the time you were born, and afterwards too. I meant to put them in a scrapbook, or some sort of attractive presentation for you, but I kept putting it off over the years. I suppose I never thought I'd actually give them to you.'

He touched the yellowing scraps of paper and smiled. 'I look forward to reading them.'

They were deep in conversation again when out of the blue the older woman appeared at the table. 'You two obviously have something to celebrate,' she said, smiling at them as she placed two glasses of champagne on the table. 'It's on the house.'

By the time he left it was nearly midnight, and he promised to call the next morning with plans for the day. Sinéad had booked to stay for four days – they had agreed to that in their correspondence. It seemed like a good amount of time. Enough to start to get to know each other slowly, but not too much for either of them.

As he left, he began to rummage in his pockets. 'I almost forgot,' he said. 'My mother...my adoptive mother...gave me these. She thought you might like to have some photos.'

He handed her an envelope. Sinéad glanced quickly inside and froze, as she saw a photograph of a beaming woman holding a baby, her baby.

'That was very considerate of her,' she said, recovering her composure. 'I'll look at these later.'

Chapter Twenty-six

'I'M AFRAID WE DIDN'T do justice to the food last night,' Sinéad said as she passed the reception desk the next morning. 'I hope the chef wasn't upset.'

The woman smiled back at her. 'You were both obviously elsewhere,' she said.

'Yes – it was a bit of a special reunion,' Sinéad said and paused. The woman looked at her, as if waiting for her to continue.

'I don't want to intrude, but you said yesterday you were meeting your son?' the woman asked.

'Yes,' said Sinéad, relieved at not having to explain.

'It's just that when Marie said you hadn't seen each other for twenty-four years,' she said, 'I thought to myself that he only looks about twenty-four.' Sinéad hesitated, wondering what was coming next. 'My sister had a child when she was very young, and she was adopted. None of us knew at the time – she only told me after I'd had my first child. She tried to find her years later when she was in her forties, and then found out that her daughter had died when she was seven.'

Sinéad gasped, trying to imagine how she'd feel if that had happened to Ronan. She held out her hand and took the woman's. 'I'm so sorry for your sister. I know I'm one of the lucky ones.'

'Yes, you are. It looks as though it'll go well though. You must have been so nervous last night. I'm glad you chose our hotel for your reunion.' She smiled, squeezed Sinéad's hand and let it go.

Another guest arrived and Sinéad moved away, smiling gratefully at the woman.

She took a taxi to meet Ronan near the University, to save him having to trek up the hill to the hotel. As she stepped out of the car, she saw him sitting on a wall by the entrance and her heart missed a beat as she felt guilt and an immense sadness for the woman whose daughter had died.

'Last night was your treat. This is my day,' he said. They strolled around the quadrangle and he showed her where he had attended lectures, where his graduation ceremony had taken place, where he would go for a drink with his friends. They walked up a leafy road to his student accommodation and she recognised the name of the road from the printout Brenda had sent her. Apologizing for the mess, he invited her in and introduced her to a young man rushing out on his way to a lecture.

'Donal, this is my mother,' he said. Donal looked from one to the other in surprise and, realizing his mistake, Ronan added, 'My other mother.'

When Donal had left, he began to apologize, but she shook her head. 'No, no, I like it. My other mother sounds a lot better than birth mother, which I've always found too clinical.'

Later they went into the city as he needed to buy some

books, and they wandered through Waterstone's comparing notes on various works they had read.

'Here's one you might like,' he said, grinning, picking up a copy of *American Psycho.*

'I don't think so,' she said, flicking through the book. 'I think this is the sort of book that resonates very differently with men and women. Now, here's one that I've read and loved – *Snow Falling on Cedars.* I'll get it for you.'

'*Independence Day?*'

'Loved it.'

'Have you read *The Sportswriter?*'

'No, I'm afraid I'm not big into sports.'

'Aha, I bought it thinking it was about sport, but it's not! I think you'd like it – I'll get that for you.'

Later they sat in a café and looked at the paper to see what was on at the cinema.

'*Bridges of Madison County.* Yuck,' he said.

'Come on,' she said. 'I loved the book. It's such a perfect love story.'

'*Braveheart?*'

'Not my thing.'

'No, I didn't think so. Not mine either.'

'I don't mind what we see, as long as it doesn't make me cry,' she said.

'*Outbreak* it is, then.'

Later, as they waited for a taxi to take her back to the hotel she said, 'Why don't I hire a car tomorrow and we could drive over to that cottage I told you about.'

They met at the car hire office next morning and set off towards Bantry. 'I'd always hoped to buy this cottage, but when my aunt died, she left it to her son in her will. He sold it without telling anyone. I haven't been back for years. Apparently, the new owner has made a lot of changes, so I'm a bit apprehensive. I've probably told you this in my letters, but when Sam and I got married we bought a place near Schull.'

Ronan nodded. He had spent many holidays in the area.

'We wanted the boys to have a place in Ireland and found a lovely house close to a sheltered beach – much more suitable for small children than a cottage on the top of a cliff. We can stop there on the way back if we have time.'

They reached Bantry just before lunch and Sinéad nosed the car gingerly into the small, bumpy lane leading to the cottage. That much hadn't changed, she thought. As she slowed down in front of the first house, Maeve came out, clearly delighted to see her and anxious to catch up on all her news. She smiled and said hello to Ronan, showing no surprise when Sinéad introduced him as her son, asking no questions.

'Do you think there's any chance we could have a quick look at the house?' asked Sinéad.

'Of course you can,' Maeve replied. 'There's nobody there at the moment. It's such a shame – they hardly ever come here now. Too busy up in the big city.'

They left the car and walked down the track, Maeve shouting after them. 'You won't recognise the place!'

It was true that little remained of the cottage. The house had been renovated and large plate-glass windows had been put in to take in the views. She resisted the temptation to look inside and they walked up the steps into the top field.

The hydrangeas were in full bloom and the fuchsia hedges were still in place, although they had been trimmed back severely to make it easier to see the views. The vegetable garden was now being used as a children's playground with all kinds of expensive equipment, clearly unused, lying around.

'It's a beautiful spot,' said Ronan. 'I can see why you would have wanted to buy it.'

'Probably just as well in the end,' she said. She thought of the last time she came here, with Jack.

'They're still here,' she said, almost to herself.

'What?'

'The blackberry lilies. Look.' She pointed at a clump of orange flowers. 'I planted them here about ten years ago. I bought the seeds at Monticello, Thomas Jefferson's house.'

'*The* Thomas Jefferson? Wow. That's cool. They're beautiful. Very unusual.'

'Yes, each flower only lasts a day, then it gets replaced by a new one.'

'They don't look like lilies at all,' he said, peering at them.

'I thought you weren't interested in gardening,' she laughed. 'Come on, let's go over to Schull. We can have lunch there and I'll show you our house.'

She took the road over the mountain into Durrus, stopping at one point where they had spectacular views on the one side over Bantry Bay and on the other, Dunmanus Bay, less wild and rugged but just as beautiful. They wove their way along the narrow roads into Schull, where they parked the car near the harbour and walked up the main street to a small tea shop called Adele's.

'Let's have lunch here and then I'll take you to the house.'

She was amused when he chose the hot chocolate fudge cake for dessert.

'That's your brothers' favourite. I can always get them to behave if I promise them we'll go to Adele's for tea and have her special cake.'

'I'm looking forward to meeting them,' he said.

'And they you. I hope you're ready to take on the role of big brother, because that's how they think of you already.'

They agreed it would be best to take it in stages, meeting Sinéad's mother first and then Sam and the boys later.

'My mother is dying to meet you. She's in France with the boys at the moment and I'll tell her all about it when I get back. You can't imagine what this means to her. It's just so sad that my father isn't around anymore to meet you.' After lunch they walked back to the car and drove a short distance to a tiny cove. 'There's the house,' she said, pointing at a traditional farmhouse set back from the road and sheltered by a small hill and some trees to the west.

As they entered, a neighbour waved at Sinéad and shouted a greeting. 'I like it here,' she said. 'We're surrounded by people who live here all year round, unlike further down the road where it's a cluster of holiday homes and it's deserted in winter.'

She went around the back and found the key under a stone. 'Don't tell anyone,' she said, laughing, as she opened the front door.

He looked around the living room, with its piano, family photos and books, lots and lots of them, trying to imagine them all here together on their holidays, reflecting that for so many years he had stayed not far away with his adoptive parents in a similar house. Maybe they had even been on the same beach at the same time, crossed each other in Skibbereen without knowing. He didn't tell her that, sensing that it might sadden her.

'Would you prefer coffee? I've no milk for the tea I'm afraid.' She was in the kitchen, rummaging in the cupboards.

'I like milk in my coffee too,' he laughed.

'Well, you didn't get that from me – I always drink it black.'

'OK, I'll make an exception this time.'

He sat down at the table and said, 'We never got around to it last night. Maybe you should tell me about my father – maybe that's where I got the milk thing from.'

Sinéad sighed and sat down opposite him.

She knew this conversation was going to be inevitable, but she'd been putting it off since they met. 'To tell the truth, Ronan, I'm worried that either you won't believe me or you'll be shocked.'

'Try me,' he smiled. 'I'm pretty broadminded, and not much shocks me.'

She lifted the mug to her lips and then placed it back on the table.

'Right then. I don't know what the adoption agency told you about your biological father – that he was a medical student in the same class as me, that we had only been going out a short while when I got pregnant. That there was no question of us getting married as we hardly knew each other.' He nodded. 'That's what I thought too. We went to a party, had too much to drink, and woke up in bed the next morning to find the condom on the floor still in its packet.

Classic student party scenario in the sixties. I don't even know where he got the condom. Contraception was illegal and you had to go to the UK to get anything like that. God, this is embarrassing.'

She took another sip of the coffee and put the mug back down.

'It was about six weeks later that I thought I might be pregnant, so I had a test which confirmed it. I calculated from the date of the party that you would be born in early November and never thought anything more about it until I went to the ante-natal clinic in London and someone said casually that I seemed to be a month out in my calculations. I dismissed it as I was certain of my dates. Then, when I went to Blackrock, Sister Gerald said the same thing and I refused to believe her, insisting I knew the date of conception. You were born on October 6th and I was convinced you were premature, again refusing to listen to Sister Gerald who said you were full-term.

For a very long time, I simply blanked out everything that happened that year, so I never thought about it, but when I got pregnant with James I began to wonder and think back to what might have happened.'

The silence in the kitchen was palpable and Sinéad shifted uneasily in her chair.

'Before I started going out with Michael – that was his name – I was on a short hostelling holiday with a friend in Germany and we met a Frenchman who was staying in the same place. An anarchist, expelled from France after the riots, he introduced us to Camus and Sartre. To a naïve eighteen-year-old girl, he was impossibly romantic and exciting. We spent our days lazing about, smoking and talking about life with a capital L, and although I didn't understand much of anything he said, I was in complete awe of him. My friend got fed up with all this and left, and on the final day before I was due to head home the warden at the hostel told us that the place would be closed that night and that we would have to find alternative accommodation.' She stopped. 'Oh God, Ronan. I'm not sure you want to hear all the sordid details.'

'You've got this far, you might as well finish — if you'll excuse the pun,' he said, and they both laughed.

'The worst thing of all — and this is where I sound really stupid — is that he told me he was impotent, and I assumed that meant he couldn't...you know...'

'And did he?'

'Well, no, that's the whole point. He never actually...we never, you know, went the whole way. So as far as I was concerned, nothing had happened.'

She blushed.

'I can't believe what I'm saying. It sounds completely ridiculous. But as the years went by, I began to think that maybe, just maybe, I got pregnant that night. It was the 6th of January, exactly nine months before you were born. I asked my gynaecologist and he said that yes, it was possible, highly unlikely, but possible. So, I decided to wait until I met you.'

'And?'

'And, as you probably noticed, I almost fell down the stairs when I saw you. You're the spitting image of your father, the French anarchist. There's no doubt about it in my

317

mind now. Since we met, I've been wondering how to tell you, whether you would be shocked, think I was a complete idiot, or worse, a liar.'

'I'm not shocked at all,' he said 'It's actually quite a story and I quite like the idea of having some French anarchist blood in me. Do you know where he is? Did you keep in touch with him?'

'We exchanged letters for a while. In fact, I told him that I was pregnant and he didn't react at all, which only confirmed my view that nothing had happened. I have no idea where he is now, but with the Internet and all the new possibilities it offers I'm sure I could track him down if you want to meet him.'

'I would like to meet him – eventually,' he said slowly, 'but for the moment, I think I need to really get to know you and your mother, and of course Sam and my brothers. That could take a while, but when all that has settled down maybe we could think about finding him.'

'I've never mentioned my doubts to anyone. This is the first time I've ever spoken about all this. I'll have to contact Michael now and talk to him about it. He didn't do anything wrong like refuse to marry me – that was a joint decision – and he did try to help as best he could. He never told his parents as they would have reacted very badly and again that was something we agreed. I just hope he's as understanding as you have been.'

'I'd actually quite like to meet him too sometime,' said Ronan. 'But maybe later. After all, he is part of the story. Our story.'

Sinéad locked up the house and they set off back to Cork.

As they drove along, Ronan took a cassette from his pocket and put it in the car stereo.

'It's a compilation I made for you – a completely esoteric collection of things I like that I think you might like too. This song is by my favourite band at the moment – Portishead.'

'What a voice,' said Sinéad.

'Beth Gibbons. She's amazing. Maybe someday we could go and see her together.'

Sinéad nodded, overcome with emotion. 'And what would you think about going up to Blackrock tomorrow? I never thought I would want to set foot in that place again, but why not? Maybe it would be good for you to see where you were born?'

'That's a good idea,' he said, 'I'd love that.'

Sinéad phoned the convent the next morning and asked if it would be possible to visit. The woman at the other end of the phone sounded surprised and said she would have to ask. She could hear whispered conversation in the background and finally she was told that she could come at two pm.

They had to buy a map as neither Ronan nor Sinéad knew how to get there, and she was so nervous she took several wrong turns before finally arriving at the imposing gates leading into the home. As they drove up to the stark grey building, she shivered and wondered if this had been a good idea. They parked and got out of the car.

'Great view,' said Ronan, who was unaware of her mis-givings. The statue of the Sacred Heart was still there, arms outstretched as ever, and Sinéad stood beside it looking down at the city that had seemed so far away then, so un-attainable.

The main door opened and a young woman came out. 'Ms Murray?' she said, smiling. Sinéad couldn't tell if she was a nun or a postulant, or even a lay person. It was hard to know these days as the younger ones no longer wore habits

'Hello, I'm Marie, and I'll show you around if you'd like. Where would you like to start – the grounds?' she asked. 'I'm sorry if it's all a bit disorganized; we're not really set up to receive visitors. Girls don't tend to come back afterwards. In fact, I think you're the first mother and child to visit that I remember.'

Sinéad hardly listened to anything Marie said as they wandered the grounds before finally mounting the steps and entering the building. She was looking around, trying to locate familiar landmarks and finding herself unable to recognize very much. *I must have done a good job blotting out the memories*, she thought.

Once inside, they walked along a corridor with a number of doors. On each door there was a plaque with the name of a nun. Sinéad looked at them. Sister Theresa, Sister Patricia, Sister Francis...

'None of these names are familiar,' said Sinéad. 'There's just one nun I remember – one nun in particular,' she said to Marie. 'The midwife. I was half wondering if she would still be around. She must be pretty old now.'

'Do you remember her name?'

Sinéad's mind went blank. 'I don't. Do you think there's any chance you could look her up? It should be easy to find her – it was in 1970 and she was the only midwife.'

Marie looked dubious. 'We'd have to ask the sister in the records office, but she's not there at the moment. Perhaps you could come back another time?'

Just then Ronan, who had gone on ahead, stopped in front of a door, then turned back. 'Look. There's a Sister Gerald. Didn't you tell me in one of your letters that was her name? That you were going to call me after her?'

'Yes, that's it – Sister Gerald!' Sinéad turned to the young woman. 'Could you see if she's there? I'd love to talk to her.'

Marie hesitated, and then knocked lightly on the door. There was no reply, so she knocked again, this time a bit harder.

'I'm sorry, she doesn't seem to be there. But if you'd wait a minute, I'll go and ask Mother Superior.'

'Well done for remembering her name, Ronan. It's the stress. My mind went completely blank.'

'I hadn't really thought about that. It must be hard for you being here again.'

They waited in the corridor for about five minutes. The whole building seemed different – smaller, somehow, and brighter. The place was deathly silent and Sinéad wondered if there were still babies here and if so, where they were. The familiar smell of furniture polish was beginning to make her feel nauseous.

Then they heard the swish of robes and the clinking of rosary beads. She turned, and there she was, Sister Gerald, much smaller and older looking than she remembered her, walking towards them with a big smile.

As they began to speak, Sinéad realized that the nun had no idea who she was, other than a woman who had come back with her son.

'Don't you remember me?' she said. 'Emily – the medical student.'

'Emily?' said Ronan.

'Yes, we had to take a different name – I'll explain later.'

The nun looked at her, then at Ronan, then back to Sinéad, her smile growing wider. 'Of course, I remember you now,' she said. 'Always getting under my feet, wanting to do things, asking questions all the time. And this is your son – I remember him too. You kept saying he was premature, but he doesn't look premature now!'

They walked along the corridor with her, laughing and talking, with Marie trailing behind. The old nun suddenly stopped at a door and looked at Sinéad intently. 'You probably won't remember this, but it's the old delivery room. It looks completely different now – they've turned it into a living room and it's full of sofas and chairs.' She opened the door and Sinéad shook her head. It bore no relation to the room she remembered.

'Do you have a camera?' the nun asked. 'There, look, that's about where the delivery bed was. Sit there the two of you and I'll take a picture.' She pointed at a wicker chair.

Sinéad sat down on the chair and Ronan balanced precariously on one arm. 'This feels so strange,' she said as Sister Gerald took several pictures.

'You must send me a copy,' she said as she handed the camera back to Sinéad. She looked from one to the other, and Sinéad thought she detected a tear. 'Oh, I'm so pleased you came back. Nobody ever comes back.'

Then she turned to Marie and said briskly, 'Marie, would you go and get us a tray of something like a good girl. Bring it to the parlour.' She took Sinéad's arm and said, 'Now you must come and have a cup of tea and tell me all about yourselves.'

Later, once Sister Gerald had the answers to all her questions, she told them that shortly after Ronan was born she went back to her beloved Africa. 'I got to the point where I couldn't stand it here anymore. What we were doing wasn't Christian in my opinion, and it made me very sad. Each time I saw one of those poor girls parting with their child it was a little bit of me dying too.' She looked at Ronan and smiled. 'It's so good of you to visit. And how lovely to see a grown man with his mother. I'm so happy for you both. I'll pray for you.'

As they left, she called Marie and asked her to take a photo of the three of them in front of the statue in the grounds. She looked small and fragile in her white robes beside the tall young man, but her joy was palpable.

They left, promising to stay in touch, and drove down the hill in silence. Suddenly, Sinéad pulled the car over into a layby and got out, taking deep breaths.

'I think I'm going to be sick,' she said.

'Here, I have something for that,' Ronan fished in his backpack and took out a half-empty bottle of Coca Cola. 'This is Donal's cure for everything. Don't mind if it's flat, it's better for you that way.'

She took a sip from the bottle then breathed in deeply once more and leaned back against the car.

'That was pretty intense, seeing the actual room where I was born. And the midwife too,' he said, 'although I imagine it was a lot more so for you than for me.'

'Let's go back to the hotel and go for a walk up that big hill,' she said. 'I need some air.'

They decided to stay at the hotel to eat, but this time they just had a bar snack instead of a full meal. Sinéad felt drained and torn between going home and leaving Ronan and said so.

'I was thinking,' he said, sipping his coffee. 'You told me about that train journey you had to make with me when I was a baby. Why don't I come to Dublin with you tomorrow? That way it might cancel out the bad memory. I've almost finished my thesis and I still have plenty of time before I have to hand it in, so I'm pretty much free. It's ages since I've been to Dublin, and I can go and see some friends there.'

★

Jack had a lot of work that week and some pretty intense viola practice with his friends in the string quartet. It helped stop him thinking so much about Sinéad and what she might be doing.

On the Friday morning he got a phone call from Brenda.

'I had a message from Sinéad about an hour ago,' she said. 'She's changed her plans and she's taking the train up from Cork. She has to fly to Paris from Dublin this evening, so she won't have any free time.'

'Was she still in Cork when she called you?'

'Yes, I think she must have been at the station, as there was a lot of background noise, but Jack...'

He mumbled something about having to go and shouted out to his secretary to find the arrival times for Cork trains, had a quick look at the paper she handed him, then pulled on his jacket, grabbed his car keys and ran out of the office.

He had calculated that there was only one train she could take in that time frame and he got there in plenty of time, parked his car and positioned himself at the only exit. He had no idea what he was going to say to her or even why he was doing this – he just knew he had to see her one more time. What was it she'd said about closure?

He must have been there for over an hour and smoked countless cigarettes when they finally announced the arrival of the Cork train. Standing by the barrier he watched the train slowly emptying, grandparents struggling with luggage and parents with small children, young couples with ruck-sacks arm in arm and harried businessmen with briefcases rushing off to God knows what meeting.

And then he saw her. She looked radiant and was talking to someone – a tall, good-looking young man who was car-rying a case that was clearly not his own. As they approached the barrier it began to dawn on Jack who this young man might be, and he turned to leave. But it was too late. Sinéad saw him and stopped.

'Jack? What are you doing here?'

'Brenda told me about your change of timetable, and I thought you might need a lift to the airport.' He shrugged, aware of how unlikely that sounded.

She turned to the young man and said, 'Ronan, this is Jack, a former colleague of mine. Jack, this is my son Ron-an. Well, this is a surprise and it's really kind of you, Jack. I don't know what to say – we'd planned to take a taxi, but if you insist...'

He shook hands with Ronan and led them to the car. As he opened the boot to put her case in, she stood back and looked at the car in mock awe and said, 'An Audi Quattro! You must be doing well for yourself, Jack McDonagh!'

He shrugged again and opened the door to let her in, realizing too late that one of Lorna's Hermès scarves was trailing out of the door pocket and her sunglasses were attached to the sun visor. Without a word, Sinéad tucked the scarf back in and settled into her seat.

As they drove off, she turned to Ronan in the back seat. 'Jack is one of the very few people who know my story, Ronan. He was adopted too, you know.'

He could see Ronan looking at him in the rear-view mirror. 'And have you found your birth mother too?' he asked.

'It's a long story, Ronan, but no I haven't – not yet anyway,' he said, and changed the subject back to them. They chatted easily, telling him about their meeting in Cork, laughing about how Sinéad had almost fallen down the stairs, the uneaten dinner, the bemused staff. They told him about the four days they had just spent getting to know each other and, finally, the spur of the moment visit to the mother and baby home.

'You won't believe this, but we met Sister Gerald – the midwife who delivered him,' said Sinéad. 'She went back to Africa afterwards and said she never stopped thinking about all the young women and the babies she delivered in the convent. Apparently, we're the first ones who ever went back, and she was overwhelmed and happy that it had worked out. And the funny thing was she actually remembered me – she said she couldn't forget me because I was constantly harassing her to give me something to do.'

'Sounds familiar,' said Jack, laughing as he pulled up outside the airport and jumped out to open her door.

They stood there a little awkwardly for a moment. 'If you have the time, why don't you come in and have a coffee with us,' she said. 'Ronan is going to stay with me until the flight is called.'

He hesitated. 'I don't want to intrude...'

'No, no, come in. You've driven us all this way, the least we can do is offer you a coffee,' said Ronan.

They sat in the coffee bar watching as Ronan walked to the counter to order. 'Well, this certainly is a surprise, Jack, but I'm glad you came,' she said. 'The whole thing is like a fairytale really and I still can't believe it's all gone so well. I'm completely shattered though.'

'It's gone well because knowing you I'm sure you prepared it well,' he said, 'and he seems to be a very intelligent and mature young man. Perhaps it was better to wait until now. Maybe if you had met him when he was younger, he might not have been ready.'

'Perhaps – maybe you're right,' she mused. 'How are you anyway, and how's your family?'

He rushed into a garbled account of his life, the children's school achievements and Lorna's job, adding, quite unnecessarily, that it even had a company car thrown in.

'Yes, you already told me that in London last time we met,' she said, that mocking look back. 'Two Audis. How many will it take, Jack?'

She looked over his shoulder at Ronan who was making his way back and her expression softened. Jack wanted to take her by the shoulders and make her look at him like that.

Instead, he stood up and shook Ronan's hand, saying he had to get back to the office, and kissed her lightly on the cheek. They thanked him for driving them to the airport and waved as he walked from the terminal.

Chapter Twenty-seven

HE HEARD ABOUT THE accident in 2010. He had just opened the Irish Times and seen the headline – *Well-known Pianist and Son Dead in French Car Crash* – when the phone rang. It was Brenda.

'Jack...'

'I think I know what you're going to tell me,' he said.

She agreed with him that it would be completely inappropriate for him to go to the funeral, so he wrote a letter of sympathy to Sinéad instead, but she didn't reply.

It was another five years before he heard from her again. An email this time, out of the blue.

> *Dear Jack,*
>
> *Someone mentioned your name the other day and I wondered how you were. I still come to Dublin regularly to meet Ronan and I thought it might be nice at some stage to have a coffee and catch up.*
>
> *Sinéad*

He read it over and over, trying to read some kind of meaning into it. Perhaps there wasn't any. Someone had mentioned his name. Who? Why? Had someone told her he was separated? Not that he was, really. His friends referred to him as a semi-detached male. He and Lorna lived apart most of the time and led separate lives, but still maintained a façade, attending family and social events together.

With the girls both married, he felt relieved of his responsibilities towards them and had found himself a penthouse apartment in one of the new blocks that were springing up all over the city, while Lorna continued to live in the family home. He liked to think he was quite a good catch – not bad-looking for his age, well-educated, good company, knowing quite a bit about most things. In his work he met lots of interesting women, and almost all his friends were actively looking to fix him up with someone. The string quartet helped too; women seemed to have a thing for musicians. But he mainly just followed the advice of his good friend Tony O'Donnell and kept his flings short and foreign.

He wrote back to Sinéad straight away, agreeing that it would be good to see her again, and a few weeks later he received another email telling him she would be in Dublin for a few days in April.

He blocked off all appointments for those days and suggested lunch.

★

It had been thirty years since he and Sinéad went their separate ways, and she still made his heart beat faster. She had put on a bit of weight, but the extra pounds softened her, took away the edginess. The eyes were still the same though, even if now circled by tiny lines, and there was no hiding from that cool gaze.

He didn't know what he expected – that she would tell him she had always loved him and that she was here, now, for him, forever. Instead they talked about their lives, their children, some mutual friends, Dublin and house prices, the weather, the presidency of the United States.

'You didn't go to Washington in 2000, did you?' he said.

'No, did you?' she replied, without a pause.

'Stupid question, really.' He paused for a moment and fiddled with the cutlery. 'I was really, really angry with you when you told me you were getting married.'

She looked at him in astonishment. 'I can't believe you just said that. What right did you have to be angry?' She laughed, then sat back in her chair and looked hard at him. 'What did you want, Jack, that I sit at home like your famous Solveig, waiting for you to return? Or, no, better still, maybe you thought we'd meet again in heaven?'

'It's a beautiful song.' He smiled apologetically.

She shook her head. 'Ah yes, *Peer Gynt*: '*a life based on procrastination and avoidance*.'

'That's a bit harsh – it's just a folk tale, and like I said, it's a beautiful song.'

'I didn't coin the phrase – I read it somewhere. In fact, it was in Bantry. Remember? Now I know what my aunt meant when she wrote that. There must have been some secrets in her life, too. My God, Jack, of all the complex, powerful women Ibsen created – it's not for nothing they call him the first male feminist you know —you had to choose Solveig.'

'I was just trying to be romantic at the time. It was a different context.'

'It certainly was.' She looked at her watch. 'This time I really do have a plane to catch,' she said.

'Can we do this again?' he asked. 'I have the impression we've still got a lot to talk about.'

'Yes — that would be nice. I'll be back in a few months. Let's stay in touch.'

Jack kissed Sinéad lightly on the cheek. It was the last time he ever saw her.

Chapter Twenty-eight

France, 2016

AFTER THE CEREMONY EVERYONE was invited back to the house. There were three of them from Dublin – Frank Curzon, who had stayed in touch with Sinéad all this time, Brenda and Jack. Brenda had organized the trip, right down to the last detail of the charming hotel in Saint Emilion and the hire car. Jack offered to drive and, as they walked to the car, she pulled him aside and whispered in his ear.

'Are you sure you want to do this?' she asked.

'Not really,' he said. 'But maybe it'll give me, I don't know, some kind of closure?'

'Maybe,' she said, settling back into the front seat.

It only took them about five minutes to drive there. The house itself was just how he had always imagined it, or rather it looked just like the photos on Google earth that he had pored over time and time again on the computer in his office. It wasn't grand, it was more like a small manor house, probably nineteenth century, built in the beautifully muted yellow stone typical of the region. It was on the outskirts of the village, set well back from the road up a gravelled driveway lined with cypress trees.

He parked with difficulty – it looked as if the whole village had turned up and there were cars everywhere. As they walked towards the house, Ronan came to welcome them, and he was about to introduce him to Brenda, but it was clear that they knew each other already. They followed Ronan through a wide hallway with a tiled floor into a large living room on two levels, a garden and a pool surrounded by lavender. Most of the people he had seen at the church were already out on the terrace, sipping their drinks and being served canapés by a uniformed waiter.

Sinéad's mother, Jane, was sitting in a cane chair by a window. Jack calculated quickly that she must be almost ninety. She spotted him and beckoned, and he walked over to her slowly, marvelling at how well she looked but wondering what on earth he was going to say. She had already seen him at the church and they had shaken hands, but now she gave him a warm smile and took his hand firmly.

'Hello, Jack, how lovely to see you again after all this time. It's so kind of you and your colleagues to have come all this way. I know how much Sinéad would have appreciated it.'

She asked him how he was, and the family, and they chatted until he had to step aside to make way for some neighbours. He walked over to where Frank and Brenda were standing, talking to Sinéad's other son, James, who had played in the church. Frank introduced Jack, and Brenda moved away to talk to some other people. As they spoke, he couldn't shake off the feeling that he had seen James before, that there was something familiar about him. He looked like

Sinéad, obviously, but there was something else about the way he smiled, the way he carried himself.

'James and I were just talking about how much his mother loved music,' said Frank, 'and I was telling him about that wonderful Brendel concert we went to in Washington years ago. Do you remember that concert, Jack?'

'Yes, of course I do. Schubert. I think that's when I really discovered classical music,' he said.

'I hear you've taken it up quite seriously yourself now,' said Frank.

'Really?' said James, looking at Jack with interest. 'What instrument do you play?'

'The viola, actually,' Jack said.

'The viola?' James looked surprised.

Jack laughed. 'I get that reaction a lot. I tried the piano first, but it was my daughters' music teacher who told me I had perfect pitch and that I should try a stringed instrument. She suggested the viola because not so many people play it, so it increases your chances of getting into a string quartet. And it's easier to carry around with you than a piano – better for the social life.'

'Tell me about it,' said James, pointing to the grand piano behind him. 'So, what are you playing at the moment?'

'I've been tinkering with the Schubert Arpeggione sonata – I heard your father playing it in Paris once with a cellist and it's always been one of my favourites. I've only got as far as the first movement though.'

Ronan joined them just then and whispered to James, 'Granny wants you to play something on the piano.'

'Come on,' said James, 'let's play the Arpeggione. Nobody will mind if we make a few mistakes. It was one of my mother's favourite pieces too. I always think it sounds better with a viola and I'm sure there's one around here somewhere.'

He went off into a side room and emerged a few minutes later, triumphantly brandishing a viola. 'It's not completely out of tune. Here.' He handed it to Jack, sat down at the piano, struck some notes and they tuned up quickly. Then he took some sheet music out of the piano stool and placed it where they could both see it.

There was complete silence in the room. Even the people on the terrace had stopped talking and were looking in through the large plate-glass windows. Jack's hands began to shake and he shook his head at James, 'I don't think I can do this.'

'Of course you can,' said James and played the first notes. There was something in his look that spurred Jack on. He lifted the bow, closed his eyes and focussed. He was back in the Salle Pleyel with Sinéad, listening to the haunting notes ring out, as if someone else was playing.

When the last notes died away there was a long silence before everyone began to clap and Jack could see Sinéad's mother wiping away a tear. James stood up and shook his hand.

'We should do this again,' he said. 'You're a lot better than you give yourself credit for. Come on, I need a drink.' He crossed the room to the table where the drinks were set out and poured them both a Scotch.

'I've got to drive,' Jack protested, but James wouldn't be deterred. He poured Jack a small measure and they clinked glasses.

On a table nearby there were family photos and one in particular caught Jack's eye – two young men seated at a grand piano, one clearly James, and the other the image of Sam. James followed his gaze.

'That's my brother, Ben. He was a really good musician. A lot better than me.'

'You look very different,' Jack said.

'Ha, yes, well, that's not surprising really,' he smiled, waving at someone. 'Sorry, I have to go and talk to my godmother, catch you later,' he said as a woman came over, taking his arm and guiding him to a group of people who had just arrived.

The waiters brought food in and everyone went to sit down at the tables set out in an adjoining room. Jack found himself seated beside a cousin of Sam's who had travelled from Israel for the funeral. Sam's cousin complimented him on his playing.

'I just followed James' lead,' said Jack. 'He's obviously inherited his father's musical talent.'

'Oh no, I don't think so, he must have inherited it from somewhere else,' he said, shaking his head.

Jack gave him a questioning look.

'Didn't you know? James wasn't Sam's son, you see. Sam adopted him when he married Sinéad and raised him as his own, but the only child they had together was Ben. Such a tragic accident – so much talent wasted. And poor Sinéad, she'd been ill before the accident, but after it she never really recovered. Sam was her rock. Such a wonderful, wonderful couple.'

'So… what age is James then?' Jack asked, hesitating and half-hoping his table companion didn't know the answer.

'Let's see,' he said, frowning. 'Ben was born two years after James and he was twenty-two when he died, so that would make James twenty-four in 2010. That means he'll be thirty this year.'

Jack looked across to the table where James was sitting between his two grandmothers, Ruth and Jane, who clearly doted on him. Ronan was sitting beside Jane, and they too seemed very close.

'Frank and I were thinking it's about time we left. What do you think, Jack?' Brenda's voice broke in on his reverie. 'I'll drive if you like.'

'Yes, yes, you're right. I suppose we should be going.' Jack mumbled an apology to his neighbour and stood up, robot-like. They said their goodbyes to the family, then walked out to the car accompanied by James and Ronan.

'By the way Jack, I never got a chance to ask you about your birth mother,' Ronan said. 'Did you ever find her?'

Out of the corner of his eye he saw Frank and Brenda exchange glances.

'It's very complicated, Ronan,' he said. 'Maybe someday we can talk about it.'

'Yes, I'd like that. I'm living in Dublin now.' Ronan fished in his pocket and gave him a card. 'Let's meet up sometime.'

'And do come back whenever you're in France,' said James. 'Maybe we can finish off that sonata.'

'I'll have to put in a lot of work if we're to do that, but yes, I'd love to,' Jack said, waving at them both as he walked over to the car and got into the passenger seat.

They drove back to the hotel in silence. Brenda parked the car and they walked slowly to the hotel door. 'One last drink?' she said as they reached reception. Curzon demurred, pleading an early start the next morning, but Jack shrugged.

'Why not?'

As the waiter placed their drinks in front of them, Brenda rummaged in her bag and took out an envelope. Without saying anything, she slid it across the table to Jack, who looked at her quizzically.

'This is for you. It's from Sinéad,' she said. 'She gave it to me some time ago and asked me to give it to you if anything ever happened to her and Sam. I thought it best not to give it to you before the funeral.'

He looked at it for a few minutes and then stuffed it into his pocket.

'I'm pretty sure I know what's in it,' he said. 'I'll read it later – maybe. Or maybe I'll just throw it in the bin.' He began to stand up, but Brenda pulled him back down.

'Jack...'

'You don't need to say anything,' he said. 'Some things are best left unsaid.'

'With all she had been through, she could never have had an abortion. You must have realised that.'

He hadn't. He hadn't even thought about it at the time, but of course it made sense now.

'If she'd told you then that she was going to keep the child you would have felt you had to leave Lorna, and she didn't want to destroy your family. She knew how much your kids meant to you and she genuinely believed that you needed to rebuild your marriage. That you would.'

He sighed. 'Rebuild my marriage? Yes, I made a great job of that.'

'I'm sure if your children knew, they would appreciate what you did.'

'Would they?'

'You know they would.'

He thought of the time he and his daughter Fiona went to see a film – the film of that book Sinéad had been on about – *The Age of Innocence*. He never did get around to reading the book, but he went to see the film to please Fiona. Afterwards, over coffee, she'd raged against what she perceived as Newland Archer's spineless behaviour. He didn't think he was anything like him and knew for a fact that had it been him, he would have moved in with Ellen, or even if he hadn't done that, he would definitely have walked up the stairs to her apartment in Paris.

Perhaps Fiona would understand. Perhaps she and her sister would be happy to know they had a brother. Perhaps…

Jack drained his glass and felt the unread weight of the letter in his pocket. 'I need to go to bed. It's been a long day,' he said.

Acknowledgments

THANK YOU TO EVERYONE who gave me encouragement and advice while writing this book.

My sons, daughters-in-law and stepdaughter; my brother, sister-in-law and all my friends who had to listen to endless ramblings about titles and read constantly revised drafts. Thank you for being honest, even if it was sometimes not what I wanted to hear.

The Irish Writers' Centre in Dublin for putting me in touch with Nuala O'Connor for a mentoring session. Her gentle but firm guidance and great advice kept me on track when I thought I would never see the end of the tunnel.

My proofreader/copyeditor, Perry Iles, for his pertinent comments and painstaking corrections.

Rebecca and Andrew Brown of Ardel Media, for their professionalism, pulling it all together and making it happen.

And finally, my husband, Neil, for his patience, love, support and endless cups of tea, and for keeping me grounded throughout the process.

Made in the USA
Middletown, DE
13 January 2021

31577360R00208